Bolton

SNOW

SNOW

The Double Life of a
World War II Spy

Nigel West and Madoc Roberts

First published in Great Britain in 2011 by
Biteback Publishing Ltd
Westminster Tower
3 Albert Embankment
London
SE1 7SP

Photographs of bank transfer, wireless transmitter, Major Robertson, Captain Liddell, pen and official photo of Snow reproduced by kind permission of the National Archives and Security Services Archives. All others from personal collections. Every reasonable effort has been made to trace copyright holders of material reproduced in this book, but if any have been inadvertently overlooked the publishers would be glad to hear from them.

ISBN 978-1-84954-093-3

10 9 8 7 6 5 4 3 2 1

A CIP catalogue record for this book is available from the British Library.

Printed and bound in Great Britain by
TJ International, Padstow, Cornwall

For Susan

Contents

Acknowledgements

The authors are indebted to the following people who have helped in the production of this work: Susan Roberts, who has been supportive during every stage of both the research and writing. Graham and Norma White for their unfailing generosity and willingness to make Arthur Owens' story public. Without them the later stages of Snow's life would still remain a mystery. We would also like to express our gratitude to Jenny Owens, for sharing her husband's part in the story, and to Adam Nathanson, for being prepared to reveal his mother Patricia Owens' role, adding an extra unexpected element to her glittering career. Thanks are due to Jean Pascoe née Owens for information about her mother Lily. We also thank Rhys Lloyd and Gareth Evans, for their help with the German language documents; Ceri Price, for contributing his knowledge and research of Gwilym Williams; and Diane Kachmar for sharing her knowledge of Patricia Owens. We are also grateful for the assistance of the National Archives staff at Kew.

Abbreviations

BUF	British Union of Fascists
DMI	Director of Military Intelligence
GPO	General Post Office
IRA	Irish Republican Army
MI5	British Security Service
MI6	British Secret Intelligence Service
NID	Naval Intelligence Division
PVDE	Portuguese secret police
RAE	Royal Aircraft Establishment, Farnborough
RSLO	Regional Security Liaison Officer
RSS	Radio Security Service
SOCONAF	Societé de Consignation et Affrètement
VCIGS	Vice Chief of the Imperial General Staff

Dramatis Personae

Bade, Lily	Arthur Owens' 27-year-old mistress
Biscuit	MI5 codename for Sam McCarthy
Borreson, Jurgen	Abwehr detainee in Dartmoor prison
Boyle, Archie	Director of Air Intelligence
Brooman-White, Dick	MI5 officer
Brown, Jack	Alias of Walter Dicketts
Burton, Maurice	Prison officer and amateur radio licence-holder who acted as operator for Snow
Buss, Air Commodore	Director of Air Intelligence
Canaris, Wilhelm	Chief of the Abwehr
Caroli, Gösta	Abwehr agent codenamed Summer by MI5
Celery	MI5 double agent named Walter Dicketts
Charlie	MI5 double agent named Eschborn
Davidson, Gen.	Director of Military Intelligence
Del Pozo, Miguel	Spanish journalist and Abwehr spy, codenamed Pogo by MI5
Dicketts, Kaye	Walter Dicketts' wife
Dicketts, Walter	Ex-RAF officer and convicted criminal, codenamed Celery by MI5 and known to the Abwehr as Captain Jack Brown
Dierks, Hans	Abwehr officer
Eschborn	A Manchester photographer codenamed Charlie by MI5
Ford, Major	MI5's RSLO in Cardiff
Foster, Albert	Special Branch superintendent
Giraffe	MI5 codename for Georges Graf, a French double agent
Graham, Thomas	Alias adopted by Arthur Owens

G.W.	MI5 double agent named Gwilym Williams
Gwyer, John	MI5 officer
Hamilton, Hans	Director of the Owens Battery Company and the Expanded Metal Company
Hansen, Georg	Abwehr sabotage expert
Hill, Dr	Scientific Adviser to the Air Ministry
Hinchley-Cooke, Edward	MI5 officer
Hussein, Obed	Abwehr courier, later arrested in Eire
JOHNNY	Abwehr codename for Arthur Owens, also known as 3504
Krafft, Mathilde	Abwehr paymaster in England
Kryger, Lisa	Abwehr agent who had been active in England before the war
Lahousen, Erwin	Senior Abwehr officer
Langbein, Alfred	An Abwehr spy in Canada thought by MI5 to be a candidate for LLANLOCH
LEOHARDT	Abwehr codename for TATE
Liddell, Guy	MI5 officer
LLANLOCH	Abwehr codename for a spy intended to operate in London
McCarthy, Sam	A petty criminal codenamed BISCUIT by MI5
Marriott, John	MI5 officer
Masterman, John	MI5 officer
Owens, Arthur	Welsh chemist, codenamed SNOW by MI5 and JOHNNY by the Abwehr
Owens, Jean Louise	Daughter of Arthur Owens and Lily Bade
Owens, Jessie	Wife of Arthur Owens
Owens, Patricia	Daughter of Arthur and Jessie Owens
Owens, Robert	Son of Arthur and Jessie Owens
POGO	MI5 codename for Miguel del Pozo
Rantzau, Dr	Alias for Nikolaus Ritter
Reisen, Hans	Abwehr agent
Richardson, Lt	Assistant to the VCIGS
Ritter, Nikolaus	Head of the Hamburg Abwehr
Robertson, Tommy ('Tar')	MI5 officer
Rolph, William	Former MI5 officer and SNOW's business partner. Committed suicide

Schmidt, Wulf	Abwehr parachutist, codenamed TATE by MI5
Stewart, Samuel	Shipowner considered suspect by MI5
Stopford, Richman	MI5 officer
SUMMER	MI5 codename for Gösta Caroli
TATE	MI5 double agent named Wulf Schmidt
Theakston	MI5 handler for SUMMER
TRICYCLE	MI5 codename for Dusko Popov, a Yugoslav double agent
Vesey, John	MI5 interrogator
White, Dick	MI6 officer
White, Graham	Son of Arthur Owens and Hilda White
Whyte, Jock	MI5 officer
Williams, Gwilym	Retired Swansea police inspector codenamed G.W. by MI5
Wilson, Thomas	An alias occasionally adopted by SNOW
W.W.	Welsh-speaking MI5 nominee replaced by G.W.
Yule, Col J. F.	MI5 radio expert

Prologue

'Heil Hitler… you bastard!'

Sam McCarthy spat the words out at the pathetic little Nazi spy lying tied up below deck on the trawler *Barbados*. McCarthy's previous career had been as a small-time crook and conman who dabbled in drugs smuggling, and he was used to meeting some pretty desperate characters, but it seemed to him that he had never met anyone quite so despicable as Arthur Graham Owens, the 41-year-old Welsh battery salesman known to his MI5 handlers as Snow.

It was May 1940 and McCarthy had put his criminal career on hold for the duration of the war, using his skill at hustle and subterfuge on behalf of British intelligence. But the MI5 officers who'd briefed him on 'Operation LAMP' and Snow's treachery had not known the half of it. There wasn't much McCarthy – codename Biscuit - hadn't been prepared to do in his pre-war existence, but befriending this wretched little man had turned his stomach even more than the supposed fishing trip out onto a grey and choppy North Sea.

From the first supposedly chance meeting with Snow in the Marlborough pub in Richmond where, under orders from his masters at MI5, McCarthy had drunkenly allowed himself to be recruited as 'a German spy', the Welshman had been a constant irritant. During the rail journey up to Grimsby from King's Cross, Snow spent most of his time making notes of any airfields, power stations and military installations they passed. And when he wasn't doing that, he was showing McCarthy a list of MI5 officers he was planning to hand over to 'the Doctor'. Among those named was Tommy 'Tar' Robertson, the MI5 officer who was running the operation they were taking part in. 'The Doctor' would be very pleased to have the photographs, Snow confided to McCarthy, because 'when our advance guard get here they will know who to get and where to get them.'

The mysterious 'Doctor' was in fact a Dr Rantzau, the pseudonym of Major Nikolaus Ritter, the German spymaster running agents into Britain. SNOW naively believed that the trip on the *Barbados* was taking him to a mid-sea rendezvous with 'the Doctor' during which he would be able to hand over intelligence in return for large sums of cash. In fact, SNOW was just there as the bait to lure Rantzau into a trap. Another fishing-boat, painted to look exactly like the *Barbados,* manned by armed Royal Navy ratings and equipped with depth-charges, hand grenades and an anti-aircraft gun, was waiting at the real rendezvous with the German spymaster. It was accompanied by a British submarine, HMS *Salmon*, ready to snatch Rantzau and take him back to England for interrogation, where he would be forced to reveal every detail of the German spy networks in Britain. That was the MI5 plan and if the British sailors were unable to capture Rantzau, their orders were simple – 'kill him'.

But it was very soon clear to McCarthy that the MI5 plan – codenamed 'Operation LAMP' – wasn't going to work. The trawler carrying 'the bait' was soon being followed by a German seaplane, presumably with 'the Doctor' on board. The aircraft had RAF markings, but in the wrong place. It was clearly German. The seaplane circled lazily above them, following their nets like a giant seagull, watching their every move. If Rantzau was on board the aircraft, then the navy snatch team must be waiting at the rendezvous for a man who was never going to turn up. What's more SNOW seemed to be expecting the German seaplane, although he had claimed in his conversations with MI5 that he did not know how Rantzau would get to the rendezvous. McCarthy had little choice but to abort 'Operation LAMP' and return to port. He tied SNOW up and locked him in the captain's cabin as a precaution, to stop him signalling to the German seaplane, and they headed for Grimsby. Once they got back to England, SNOW would be arrested and every other German agent he was associated with rounded up. Not before time, in McCarthy's view. His own preference would have been for something much more violent. SNOW had even had the nerve to accuse him of being a German agent. The man was clearly a lunatic, and a dangerous one at that.

In fact, SNOW was a truly complex character. The MI5 officers who were running him could never be entirely sure whether he was working for them or against them. Even his claims to McCarthy that he was working for the Germans rather than MI5 would seem with hindsight to have been more braggadocio than reality and, whatever the truth of his loyalties, it was ultimately the British who got what they wanted from him, not the Germans.

What McCarthy did not know when he tied up Snow and dumped him in the captain's cabin – what he could not know, because even the MI5 officers running the operation didn't then know – was that for all his failings as a secret agent, the recklessly unreliable Snow was to go on to become one of the most important British spies of the Second World War. Arthur Graham Owens, aka Snow, was the first member of what would become one of the most successful British intelligence networks of all time, one that would ultimately play a major part in ensuring the Allied victory over the Germans.

I

Contact

ARTHUR OWENS WAS an entrepreneur, inventor and proprietor of a company manufacturing batteries... and an international spy. As the source of an innovative electric storage cell that he had patented, Owens had plenty of clients, and among them was the German Navy, the *Reichsmarine*.

Under the terms of the 1919 Treaty of Versailles, Germany's navy had been the subject of severe restrictions, and Part V of the agreement imposed a total ban on all German submarines. However, a U-boat construction programme was begun in 1933 and the first vessels were launched in April 1935. This flagrant breach was a matter of great controversy at the Admiralty in London, especially when the naval attaché in Berlin, Gerard Muirhead-Gould, reported that he had been informed that the *Reichsmarine* had started work on twelve U-boats of 250 tons each. Four days later, on 28 April, Prime Minister Ramsay MacDonald made this news known to the House of Commons and he announced that his government would open negotiations to find a permanent formula to regulate the size of what was then the *Reichsmarine*, very soon to be renamed the *Kriegsmarine*.

The Anglo-German Naval Treaty, signed on 17 June 1935 in London by the Foreign Secretary, Sir Sam Hoare, introduced a relaxation of the Versailles terms, allowing the total tonnage of U-boats to reach parity with the Royal Navy. Whereas a ratio of 35:100 was set for the *Reichsmarine*'s overall tonnage, thus allowing the Germans to reach 35 percent of the combined British and Commonwealth fleet, that figure was extended to 45 percent for submarines. Thus the construction project already underway in Kiel was legitimised, albeit retrospectively, with the first German submarine hulls to be launched since 1918 having taken to the water two months earlier, in April.

In these circumstances, and suspicious that Adolf Hitler's regime might breach the terms agreed, the Admiralty in London monitored activity in the Baltic shipyards and collected information about the size and number of new hulls under construction. Analysis undertaken by the Naval Intelligence Division suggested that most of Germany's submarines were small, 250-ton coastal vessels, but verification of compliance was a priority, and Owens' business appeared to be in possession of potentially vital data. He often travelled to Hamburg and Kiel, supplying his advanced batteries which extended the underwater duration of the electric motors that powered the U-boats, and these sales were regarded as an accurate method of gauging German plans to expand the *Reichsmarine*'s strength. Accordingly, Owens had been approached to help the Admiralty, and he had readily agreed to assist by handing over the requested sales figures so they could be examined by naval experts.

The NID's intelligence acquisition project was hardly foolproof, but as part of a much larger jigsaw puzzle, with various different components such as agent reports and visual observations made by naval attachés, it offered an opportunity to develop a reasonably accurate picture of German intentions and, most importantly, distinguish between the development of twenty-two ocean-going U-boats capable of operating in the Atlantic, and the remainder, which were suitable only for deployment in the Baltic. The Admiralty's insight into Germany's strategic planning came chiefly from a highly reliable SIS agent, Dr Otto Kreuger. A marine engineer, originally from Godesberg, Kreuger had been cashiered in November 1914 when he made the mistake of striking a fellow officer who happened to be related to the Kaiser. Soon afterwards he had approached the British legation in The Hague to volunteer his services, and he was enrolled as TR-16, one of the most important and productive spies of the era. Later he would be appointed a director of the Federation of German Industries, which allowed him a unique insight into his country's naval planning during the inter-war years, and his reporting only fuelled fears that Hitler and the *Kriegsmarine* had every intention of repudiating the Anglo-German Naval Treaty and dramatically expanding the U-boat fleet with the objective of having no fewer than 249 operational by 1944, when the intention was to pose a realistic challenge to the Royal Navy's supremacy of the international trade routes.

Under normal circumstances, Owens' contribution to this covert assessment would have gone undisclosed, but the duplicitous Welshman had decided to play a double game by revealing his role for the Admiralty to the very Germans he was engaged in spying on. His offer was accepted with enthusiasm by the Germans who gave him a cover-address in Hamburg so he could mail letters written in a primitive code, intended to convey details of his travel plans and similar information. However, neither he nor his German controllers were aware that the suggested post-box number had been compromised months earlier by another spy, Christopher Draper. A former First World War air-ace who had developed a relationship with the Abwehr with the approval of the Security Service, MI5, Draper had been tempted by a newspaper advertisement to post letters containing supposedly helpful information to Postfach 629, Hamburg. Draper had reported this attempt to MI5 and consequently the details had been placed on a watch-list which meant that the GPO intercepted and copied every item sent to it. One of those examined was Owens' very first letter to Hamburg, apparently arranging to meet a Mr Sanders 'in order to discuss his work'. Instantly this alerted MI5 to the fact that Owens was in direct contact with the Germans, and had failed to declare this link to his handlers in London.

Agents such as Owens, who were in possession of information of potential value to the Admiralty, were routinely run by experienced Secret Intelligence Service personnel who then relayed the agent reports to their NID colleagues. But by failing to mention that he had opened up a channel to the Abwehr, Owens had unwittingly brought himself to the attention of the country's counter-intelligence organisation, MI5.

The moment Owens' correspondence was examined, and revealed an illicit, undeclared relationship with a German contact, he became an espionage suspect. MI5 checked to see if there had been any previous contact with Owens and discovered that he had been stopped by customs once because he had a foreign camera, at which point Owens had claimed that he was employed by the British Secret Service. On 9 January Scotland Yard contacted Naval Intelligence where Owens claimed to be 'on the books'. They confirmed that Owens had been known to Mr Fletcher of D.E.E. Admiralty for some considerable time and had frequently given him German technical information. He had also told Fletcher that he would like to work for the British Government as he frequently visited Germany.

MI5 and the Abwehr shared uncertain histories; neither had performed particularly well during the 1930s and neither had the complete trust of their political masters. MI5 was a small organisation, largely manned by a mix of old army officers and debutantes. It had been involved in a series of bungles during the 1920s and 1930s and would begin the war disastrously, completely unprepared for its vastly increased role. The Abwehr had been set up in 1921, taking its name, which means simply 'defence' in German, as a sop to the stringent restrictions imposed by the Versailles Treaty, which prevented Germany mounting any offensive military activity. By 1936 it was already entangled in a long and ultimately unsuccessful turf war with the Nazi Party's internal intelligence and security service, the Sicherheitsdienst.

So Owens' indiscretions in Germany resulted in a transfer of responsibility for the Welshman from SIS to MI5 in October 1936, and he was placed under surveillance. In charge of his case was Major Edward Hinchley-Cooke, a German-speaking counter-espionage expert who had learned his trade by posing as an enemy prisoner of war in various POW camps, collecting information in the role of a stool-pigeon. In the very early stages of his enquiries, he received a description of Arthur Owens from Colonel Edward Peal, an SIS colleague:

> Very short and slight; thin brown hair; clean-shaven; rather thin bony face; small, almost transparent and ill-shaped ears, disproportionately small for size of man; curious brown eyes set wide apart and slightly oblique, which gives him a somewhat shifty look; wears brown felt hat, pepper and salt overcoat. Usually wears brown shoes or boots. Very small bony hands stained from cigarette smoking; typical Welch 'underfed' Cardiff type. Speaks fairly correct English without pronounced accent; soft-spoken and lacks assurance in manner. Often wears white or light necktie.

During the course of MI5's investigation, the organisation acquired plenty of information about Owens and his background. He was the proprietor of the Electric Battery Department of the Expanded Metal Company, based at Burwood House, Caxton Street, Westminster, a company engaged in the manufacture of batteries. His full name was Arthur Graham Owens and he had been born in Graig Road, Cilybebyll, near Pontardawe in South Wales on 14 April 1899, the son of William Thomas Owens, a master plumber and occasional inventor, and his wife Ada.

According to his Owens' own version, he had served in the Royal Flying Corps and had flown a Sopwith Camel. He also claimed that, with his father and brother Frederick, he had invented a special anti-aircraft artillery shell that had been designed to bring down Zeppelins, but that the British government had ensured that they made no money from it. This perceived slight was to make him very bitter and thereafter he held a grudge against the authorities in London.

MI5 took the decision to extend the mail cover and examine letters sent to the Welshman at his office in an effort to 'ascertain the nature of his activities'. One of the first letters intercepted had been posted in Germany by a 'Mr L. Sanders'. Dated 15 September 1936, it instructed Owens to make his way to the Minerva Hotel in Cologne so a meeting could be held 'in order to discuss the different contemplated matters'. This development prompted a wider surveillance operation, and immigration officers at Dover were requested to 'scrutinize discreetly the passports of all British subjects embarking on the morning boat to Ostend and if they come across the name of Owens to memorise as many particulars of his passport without arousing any suspicion'. Sure enough, Owens was among the cross-Channel travellers, and was carrying a Canadian passport.

Once he had left the country MI5 sent a Special Branch detective to his London home to conduct what were represented as routine enquiries. Owens' wife Jessie was interviewed and declared that her husband was on a visit to West Hartlepool. Her own background was unremarkable, and she had married Owens in Bristol in September 1919 when she was aged twenty. The following year they had moved to Swansea where she had given birth to Graham Robert Owens. At the time, Arthur was combining his skills as a chemist and a salesman to run a confectionery shop in Lime Kiln Road, in the Mumbles district of Swansea.

A year later, on 29 October 1921, the couple and their baby son had joined the Cunard liner *Scythia* in Liverpool, bound for Halifax in Canada, and established themselves in Golden, British Columbia, where in January 1925 Jessie gave birth to a daughter they named Patricia. The family remained in Canada for thirteen years, with Owens working as a teacher and as a public utility engineer before moving to Toronto where, with money inherited from his father, he opened a battery business. Using his skills as a qualified chemist, Owens developed his innovative electric accumulators. Between 1928 and 1929 he registered several patents for dry cell batteries that he had initially intended for use in flashlights; however he soon realised their portability gave them plenty of other applications. Although his invention seemed to offer great potential, Owens came to realise, as his inheritance dwindled, that he would have to return to England to attract interest and begin large-scale manufacturing. Accordingly, on 7 January 1934, Owens boarded the Red Star Line ship *Pennland*. On the passenger list Owens described himself as a research engineer and gives his intended destination as the Grosvenor House Hotel in Park Lane, one of Mayfair's most exclusive addresses. Later he would move his family into a rented flat in Sloane Avenue Mansions.

Once in London, Owens sought the financial backing he needed for his newly-formed Owens Battery Company, and found an investor with Hans Hamilton who headed the Expanded Metal Company, which was in the same field and had acquired the rights to an invention by Herbert Williams which employed expanded sheets of lead in accumulators. Actually, Owens warned against the use of the lead sheets in his batteries but Expanded Metal ignored his advice and sold them to the Royal Navy to power diesel-electric submarine motors. However, just as Owens had predicted, these lead plates proved too weak and the batteries failed, thereby ruining his hopes of future lucrative contracts from the Admiralty.

Owens' growing financial problems may have been at the heart of his decision to develop a clandestine relationship with the Germans, and it is believed that during the summer of 1936, while on a business trip to Belgium, he approached the German embassy and volunteered to provide them with information. The only knowledge that he possessed of value, apart from his technical understanding of the chemistry behind his batteries, was his role as an informant for the Naval Intelligence Division. Having been recruited as a source of reporting about the *Kriegsmarine*'s building programme, picked up regularly while touring the shipyards of Hamburg, Bremerhaven and Kiel, his role, and the detail of his observations, would have been of intense interest to the Abwehr's naval branch. However, the Welshman's entry into the clandestine world had been spotted at the outset by the British.

On 8 October 1936 the Welshman was seen by MI5 watchers to post a letter to someone named L. Sanders at Post-box 629, Hamburg, written on the headed paper of the visitors' writing-room of the Canadian High Commission in Trafalgar Square. The envelope was intercepted and subsequent scrutiny of its content suggested that Owens had adopted an alias, 'G. D. Hunter', and employed a primitive code in an attempt to convey information he was anxious to conceal. 'Tooth Paste, shaving cream, etc. And the prices are very good and I am sure subject to duty being reasonable they should find a ready market in Holland and Germany.'

MI5's postal inspector, who noted 'submarine batteries being Owens particular line of electrical business', ventured that 'Tooth Paste' meant 'torpedoes, and 'Shaving Cream' stood for 'submarines'. In his opinion, Owens was seeking to convey a secret message to his German contacts, so his SIS handler was warned and the decision was taken to confront him. Owens was summoned to a meeting at the St Ermin's Hotel, a large establishment in Caxton Street, conveniently close to Owens' office in the same street, and to SIS's headquarters in nearby Broadway Buildings. The location was much favoured by the British intelligence establishment, and at just after half past twelve on 14 October Edward Peal, a Royal Marines officer seconded to SIS's Naval Section, picked a well-lit table in the centre of the room. While there he was under constant observation by MI5 personnel, and he would later report to Hinchley-Cooke that his 'two blokes were at the next table and I could almost hear them swallowing their drinks.'

At this stage Owens was clearly unaware that his illicit links with the Germans had been discovered, and when he was asked by Peal if he had anything to disclose, the Welshman seized the opportunity to make a sales pitch, asking for help to get in touch with someone at the Home Office to discuss portable searchlights. Far from realising that he was being given the chance to make a declaration of his contacts with Mr Sanders in Germany, his only admission was a passing reference to his intention to travel to Hamburg to meet a business acquaintance. Once again, the officer asked Owens if he had anything he wanted to say, but Owens' answer was a simple 'No, thank you' and the two men went their separate ways. The SIS officer strolled back to his office in Broadway to draft a report of his encounter that would be circulated immediately to his Security Service colleagues. The result, inevitably, was a more intensive surveillance on Owens, and his MI5 file contains the Watcher Service's daily returns, reflecting the increasingly suspicious behaviour of their quarry. Typical were his activities recorded on the morning of Tuesday 27 October:

Leaving home at 9.20 a.m. Owens first called for 15 minutes at Burwood House, then travelled by train to Dollis Hill, where he loitered and after making enquiries entered premises of Williamson Manufacturing Co. Ltd. Aircraft Camera Manufacturing and Engineers, 22, Litchfield Gardens NW10, where he stayed from 11.15 to 11.45 when he left with what appeared to be a catalogue.

On the next day the watchers again trailed him from his home:

At 10.45 a.m. he entered the Admiralty. South Arch Block, where he remained until 11.20 then went to the shop of 'James A. Sinclair & Co.' Opticians and camera dealers... two public houses, where he was seen to be examining a camera catalogue.

Then, on Tuesday 3 November, the MI5 surveillance team was on duty as the target made an unusual purchase.

From 9.35 to 10.10 a.m. Owens visited Caxton Street, then posted a letter and afterwards watched Royal procession to Houses of Parliament. He then loitered in different parts of the West End, then at Victoria Station from Smith and Sons Bookstall, Owens purchased an Aviation paper entitled *Flying* returning home at 2.45.

Owens' purchase for sixpence of a magazine illustrated with pictures of aeroplanes, together with a copy of a War Office pamphlet, *Photographs of Some Military Vehicles and Weapons in Service 1936,* at a cost of one shilling, and his simultaneous acquisition of a camera suggested that he planned to re-photograph both documents and then try to pass the pictures off as his own work. If that was truly his intention, it implies a certain desperation and lack of sophistication, but his intercepted mail confirmed that his financial circumstances were deteriorating. He had apparently abandoned his office without paying for its redecoration, as required by the terms of his lease, and had been sent reminders from the Colebrook Motor Company that his account was 'seriously overdue'. It was at this crucial juncture, in November 1936, that SIS and the Naval Intelligence Division washed their hands of him, and told him bluntly that their relationship was terminated, permanently.

Although SIS was keen to learn more about the German intelligence services, the organisation was anxious not to put itself in the hands of someone beyond its control who had singularly failed to demonstrate candour in his dealings with the Germans. Actually, SIS knew very little about its counterpart in the Reich, known as the Abwehr and thought to be headed by a *Reichsmarine* officer of Greek extraction named Wilhelm Canaris, but the employment of a demonstrably unreliable source such as Owens as a means of learning more would have been sheer folly. Chances were, calculated SIS, the Germans would learn more about SIS and its operations than it would learn about the adversary. Any experienced case officer would have weighed the risks of continuing with Owens against intangible, likely advantages, and with the balance of opinion firmly against him, Owens had been cut loose.

Undeterred by his rejection, Owens was also seen in the company of a certain Erwin Pieper, who turned out to be a German agent to whom he had been introduced by Hans Hamilton. Initially Pieper had claimed to be in possession of valuable information that he wanted to impart to Owens, but although the pair met several times, and the mysterious Pieper reimbursed

Owens for his expenses, nothing transpired, even when Pieper mentioned that in the past he had been engaged in sabotage in Canada. Apparently this was all part of some elaborate test that was intended to ascertain the Welshman's true loyalties, and it was one he must have passed because when he agreed to meet Pieper in Hamburg in December he was instead approached by a Luftwaffe intelligence officer and a man who introduced himself as a member of the *Kriegsmarine*'s intelligence branch.

During the two-hour meeting that followed, the two Germans asked for information and stated that in return they were prepared to pay very well. They offered to cover all of Owens' expenses to and from Germany, his travelling and hotel costs in England, and any money that Owens needed for bribes. He was also provided with travel papers which would allow him to move in and out of Germany freely. Finally, he was handed a questionnaire listing the information required, together with instructions on how it should be communicated.

Having reached agreement with the two German officers, Owens now had a decision to make. Should he cultivate this much-needed source of finance or report this contact to the British?

By the time he returned to London in December 1936 Owens had made his decision and went to see the British Security Services. He was taken to Major Hinchley-Cooke of MI5. Owens told him about the meeting in Hamburg and that he had been given a map of England, and asked to acquire samples of the equipment used by the Royal Air Force. His questionnaire included particulars of the Sperry Auto-Pilot system, how it was used, and details of the RAF's organisation, weapons and equipment, and the deployment of individual squadrons. The Germans were also keen to know about the location of fuel and ammunition storage depots and they wanted drawings of natural caves in the south-west of England where supplies were to be stored. Of special interest were any pictures of an electronic height-finder in use by the RAF.

The nature of the items listed in the questionnaire gave a good indication of what the Germans already knew on certain subjects, and suggested they already possessed a good deal of sensitive information concerning the RAF. Indeed, Owens told Hinchley-Cooke that Pieper had claimed to be already in receipt of information from 'English people' working in aircraft factories and that photographs were being taken by 'people in authority' in England. His role, he alleged, was to keep the information up to date and to act as the central link between Hamburg, Berlin and London.

At the time Owens made his offer, it might superficially have seemed quite attractive, in intelligence terms, for MI5 had only recently encountered a fully-fledged German agent based in Broadstairs who had been engaged in conducting a survey of RAF airfields in the south of England. Dr Herman Goertz had been arrested in November 1935 and had remained in custody until March the following year when he was convicted at a trial held at the Old Bailey in London and imprisoned. MI5's review of the evidence, and the interrogation of Goertz, who was a lawyer who had flown a fighter in the First World War, proved that the Germans had taken the very closest of interest in the RAF. If Owens was telling the truth, it seemed that Goertz's prison sentence had not acted as a deterrent. Indeed, the suggestion that others had been recruited in aircraft establishments to take photographs was especially alarming because MI5 had monitored a series of newspaper advertisements that had offered employment to men with service or business backgrounds and undefined technical skills who were invited to write to a post-box in Hamburg. Some thirty people had responded, including Christopher Draper, and no less than twenty-six had reported their correspondence to MI5. The Security Service had been unimpressed by this rather clumsy attempt to recruit agents, but had thought the amateurish operation had been quashed. Owens was now asserting that the Germans had been much more successful than MI5 had believed, but could he be trusted?

During the course of the interview, Owens let slip that he had been in touch with Pieper since September 1935, prompting the MI5 officer to suspect that the admission had been made deliberately, perhaps because he now realised that he had been placed under surveillance, or even because he had detected that his mail had been intercepted. Hinchley-Cooke supposed that, having failed to mention Pieper previously, Owens was now seeking to give the impression that he was now being entirely candid. It was a strategy that was bound to have the very opposite effect.

On 9 December, soon after the meeting with Hinchley-Cooke, Owens received a letter from Hamburg which he delivered straight to MI5, observing innocently that for some mysterious reason all his mail was arriving late. The content showed that 'Mr Sanders' was dissatisfied with Owens' efforts and suspected he was peddling recycled information and pictures that were readily available in newspapers and magazines.

The newspapers of your country as well as ours are much quicker than your letters. Since a number of years I am also in possession of the magazine pictures you sent me and you will understand that all this is rather disappointing; I don't own a museum, you know. Kindly take notice therefore, that henceforth your letters will have to be a little more up to date.

Having made a gesture of goodwill by submitting the original of a letter he must have been certain had already been intercepted and copied by MI5, Owens now made the bold offer to continue the illicit liaison and collect information about German troop movements. However, the problem was that, just like the material rejected by Sanders, the British were unimpressed. However, the appearance of a new correspondent, a certain Dr Rantzau who expressed an interest in scientific matters, seems to have persuaded MI5 to encourage the relationship, entering him in the Security Service files under the codename SNOW, a partial anagram of his surname.

The growing tensions in Europe caused by the rise to power of the Nazis resulted in large numbers of people having to flee Hitler's Germany. Although they were badly undermanned and lacking in resources, MI5's role as the primary counter-intelligence organisation meant that it would be their responsibility to sort through these refugees. The worry was that among their number might be German spies hoping to infiltrate the U.K and establish a network that could inform the Abwehr about Britain's defenses. MI5 needed to know how the German Security Services operated and the number of agents they had in Britain. Arthur Owens offered MI5 a short-cut through this arduous task and a way of getting their hands on this information. Through Dr Rantzau, MI5 hoped he had gained a direct link to the upper eschelons of the Abwehr, so for all their concerns about Owens this was an opportunity which MI5 were keen to exploit.

During 1937 Owens exchanged several letters with Dr Rantzau, signing them JOHNNY, a codename that he had been given by his German contacts. All were intercepted by MI5, and some referred to 'tests' and 'samples', and at times to 'batteries', and on 23 August he reported: 'I am unable at present to let you know when I will be able to assemble the Type FY 12 Volt 3 plate, battery with ebonite and wood [sic] as this type is continually changing however I will do my best.'

This letter was interpreted by MI5 as a coded message about aircraft, where the letters 'FY' referred to the Fairey Aviation company. A further letter, dated 21 August, mentioned a 'SB 16 Volt 3 plate' which was taken to mean Short Brothers, the arms manufacturers based in Belfast. These were potentially sensitive topics, so SNOW was called in for a discussion with MI5, and serious consideration was given to mounting a criminal prosecution under the Official Secrets Act. However, as Hinchley-Cooke was absent from the meeting, this proposal was put on hold until he could be consulted, but before any decision was taken Owens requested a further meeting which was arranged for the afternoon of Thursday 23 September.

At this gathering, attended by officers from both SIS and MI5, Owens was asked why he wanted to see them, given that as far back as November 1936 he had been told that SIS no longer wished to employ him on any kind of intelligence work because his information was of no value. Owens replied that he had made a good contact in Germany and entered into discussions about batteries, but Hinchley-Cooke reminded him that he had told them already that he was in touch with the German Secret Service, and that this was an additional reason why SIS did not want to work with him, as there could be no question of his 'running with the hares and hunting with the hounds'. Owens was informed that the British had no further use for him, and he was asked to sign a document in acknowledgment. Owens queried the need to do this, but it was pointed out to him that if he chose to have dealings with the Germans and got into difficulties, a record on his file was required, so that his dependants could not claim compensation. Apparently mollified, Owens then signed the document, acknowledging 'I fully realise that I am not employed and have not been employed since November 1936 by any British Intelligence Service.'

There was a certain finality about this humiliating rejection, but the ever-resourceful Owens seemed unconcerned and posted a letter to Rantzau in which he referred to various tests and technical matters, and then made a bold suggestion.

> My wife and youngster are completely fed up here in England and I am think-ing of sending the girl to school in Germany and the wife to live over there most of the time, I am quite sure they will be happy there, let me know what you think.

Far from being discouraged, Owens pursued his cultivation of Rantzau, and his next letters reverted to being concerned with tests and batteries. The content appeared harmless and the tone was friendly, occasionally raising the prospect of a visit to Dr Rantzau, sometimes suggesting he would be accompanied by his wife, but also mentioning the possibility of other lady friends too.

By now, at the end of 1937, Owens' shortage of money was escalating into a crisis, and he was served with a court summons by Central & District Properties Ltd. But he remained determined to be in the intelligence business and, once again, in early 1938 approached the Security Service with a series of photographs that he claimed showed German warships moored in Hamburg.

Unwittingly, Owens had demonstrated remarkable timing, for in January 1938 MI5 intervened to close down the network that had been built on the newspaper advertisements that had attracted Draper – by arresting one of the three women implicated. One, Mrs Brandy, was traced to Dublin; Mrs Duncombe disappeared from her London address, and Jessie Jordan, a hairdresser of German parentage in Aberdeen, was taken into custody successfully.

Altogether MI5 had identified no fewer than thirty individuals to whom the Germans had made a pitch. Twenty-one were British, and most of them had made no attempt to collect intelligence of value to the Germans, but simply passed on items of little significance in a bid to get maximum reward for minimum effort. They had received no training at all, and the Abwehr's methodology had appeared inept. Half of the cases involved individuals who were never in a position to procure intelligence of any value, but among them were four ex-officers, four businessmen and four members of the armed forces. Almost all had reported the approach to the authorities immediately.

The Germans had managed their recruitment campaign by responding to ads in the classified columns of the newspapers inserted by men seeking jobs. The Germans also placed advertisements themselves in British papers offering jobs for commercial and technical experts. Eleven of the thirty approached told MI5 about the German offer; nine were exposed by mail intercepts, five were denounced by private individuals whose suspicions had been aroused, one was reported by an immigration officer, and one was denounced by an anonymous informant; the other two were uncovered by accident. Of the eleven agents who reported they had been recruited by the Germans (who would probably have escaped detection), half had been recruited through an intermediary.

Three Post Office boxes, registered in the names of different women, yielded a great deal of information. Mrs Duncombe in London received intelligence collected in France, while Mrs Jessie Jordan was used as a mail-drop in the United States for another spy, Sergeant Guenther Rumrich. When Rumrich's brother was arrested in Prague he was found to be in possession of the address of a Mrs Brandy in Dublin, and this was the third mail-drop. Clandestine examination of her correspondence showed that she was receiving accurate and therefore dangerous intelligence messages from a French merchant navy officer named Aubert who was arrested at the end of 1938 and shot.

Once Owens' photos had been studied by experts, he was called to a meeting at the Naval Intelligence Division's suite of offices in the Admiralty on 7 April 1938, attended by Hinchley-Cooke and other MI5 officers, but the photographs were returned to him and he was required to sign a receipt for them. He was then reminded that he had been warned that the British intelligence services did not wish to have any dealings with him, and was escorted out of the building with a warning not to return.

While the Admiralty remained keen to learn more about the *Kriegsmarine's* U-boats, there was rather less interest in the remainder of the German fleet, as all the evidence available confirmed that Germany had stuck rigidly to the terms of the Anglo-German Naval Treaty, and possessed just two old battleships, two battle-cruisers, two pocket-battleships, eight cruisers and twenty-two destroyers. Their movements were easy to monitor and there was nothing to suggest that Hitler's rearmament plans for the Wehrmacht and the Luftwaffe had been extended to the *Kriegsmarine*. Whatever Owens' photos purported to show, it could not have been news to the NID analysts.

Owens' next move was to contact the British Union of Fascists and in July 1938 he told the organisation that he had returned to Britain in 1934 to do unspecified technical work for the government, after which he joined the intelligence service and was engaged in espionage in Germany. To prove his bona fides, Owens alluded to various companies that he claimed were fronts for the Security Service, such as Indexes Ltd, Kell Products Ltd, and the St Ermin's Hotel, as well as the names of certain officers. He also insisted that his work had revealed to him serious corruption in the British intelligence service and that it was run by Jews. He claimed to be well posted with regard to current international affairs and said that the Jewry was preparing an attack on Germany, and that England would find an excuse, probably via Russia, to declare war on Germany.

Obviously unaware that the BUF had been heavily penetrated by informants working for MI5, Owens asserted that the best way to stop this war was through propaganda broadcast from secret radio stations, adding that he wanted to find six men 'who could be trusted to do what they were told', and asked whether the BUF could supply them. He offered them money from Germany to fund the scheme and added that it might be necessary to employ measures more drastic than propaganda: if the BUF had a reliable following who would 'stick at nothing' to show the government how much they were in favour of Germany and detested the Jews, he could arrange for a cargo of arms for use in an attempt to seize power.

He also mentioned that he was keen to get details of naval bases, numbers of anti-aircraft guns, and in particular information about aerodromes in Kent and Essex, including Biggin Hill and Manningtree. He went on to claim to be 'a direct personal agent of Hitler'. Perhaps suspecting him to be an *agent provocateur*, the BUF's leadership ignored Owens, but the approach, monitored by MI5, prompted a secret and urgent memorandum dated 8 July 1938 addressed to Hinchley-Cooke:

> Owens is on the warpath again... Owens is pressing in a good many directions and in a very clumsy manner for photographs and information which are quite clearly intended for his German masters. It would seem that some definite action is required to clip his wings and in this connexion I am not quite sure whether you already have enough evidence on record to prosecute him under the Official Secrets Act.

Apparently irrepressible, Owens had ventured into dangerous territory, for the BUF was widely regarded as a potential Fifth Column, a pool of political activists, some of them well-connected, who were not only sympathetic to the Nazis, but included Blackshirts thought to be subversive. Led by a former Labour Member of Parliament, Sir Oswald Mosley, the movement espoused patriotism, but within Whitehall contingency plans had been drawn up to apprehend the most dangerous fascists and place them in emergency detention in the event of war. MI5's role was to identify the ringleaders, so Home Office warrants had been issued to monitor the telephone lines into the BUF's headquarters in London, and intercept the organisation's mail. The correspondence from SNOW was found among the intercepted letters.

Before any decision was made about prosecuting him, Owens made his way to Germany, accompanied by his wife Jessie so that she might have a holiday. Their departure and return were observed by MI5 and the monitoring of Owen's mail revealed that he had begun communicating with a Dr Wilhelm Wertzel of Hamburg, to whom he sent reports on troop movements and even some political commentaries which included references to the Foreign Secretary, Anthony Eden, and his reaction to the German seizure of the Sudetenland: 'Spent afternoon with War Office officials. Informed that

Eden is taking an active part in Czechoslovakia. One official said, "we have been too damned easy with Germany, now we are ready."'

In another message he wrote: 'Feeling against the Jews in military and army circles getting very strong, heard several rumours of desertion.' And in a further letter he informed Wertzel that: 'Chamberlain leaving for Germany sometime today. This move is a stall.'

The correspondence suggested that, operating independently, Owens had developed his relationship with the Germans and had become quite close to Dr Rantzau, having spent time with the doctor's family and introduced him to Jessie. As a result, he had been well paid and had earned the Germans' trust. This collaboration had left him in possession of yet more sensitive material, and on 24 September 1938, at the height of the Munich crisis when war with the Nazis looked imminent, Owens once again visited Scotland House with what he believed was knowledge so important that the Security Service would have to take notice. The interview with Hinchley-Cooke, accompanied by a police inspector, was recorded, and the resulting transcript showed that Owens had tried to tempt Hinchley-Cooke with what was purported to be vital information, but the MI5 officer had opened the conversation by reminding Owens of their previous meetings when he had been told that the authorities wanted no further dealings with him.

'Well, look here, Mr Owens, before we start, I want to make the position quite clear. Do you remember when I saw you on 23 September, 1937?'
'Yes.'
'When you signed a statement which reads: "I fully realise that I am not, and have not been employed since November 1936 by any British intelligence service?"'
'Yes.'
'You acknowledge that as your signature?'
'Yes.'
'You will also remember that some months ago I saw you?'
'Yes.'
'In the room of the Assistant Director of Naval Intelligence?'
'Yes.'
'And told you then, so far as the Naval, Army and Air Force intelligence services were concerned, what our view was?'
'Exactly.'
'Therefore, before I talk to you, it is my duty as a duly authorised person to caution you that whatever you say will be taken down and may be used in evidence. You quite understand that?'

'I quite understand that. I will do the best I can.'

'It is important that I caution you that whatever you say, you say voluntarily.'

'I think I have done my duty.'

'Do you understand the caution – that whatever you say now may, if necessary, be used in evidence at a later stage?'

'Quite.'

Having forced Owens to acknowledge the gravity of his situation, Hinchley-Cooke confronted him.

'You have been in touch with the German Secret Service.'

'Yes, I have. At least, they have been in touch with me.'

'Were you a paid agent?'

'Yes, I was.'

'And how much money did you receive a month?'

'Well, it varied really...'

'Well, how much?'

'Thirty to forty pounds a month.'

'A month? Regularly?'

'Not regularly. It varied.'

'But ever since I saw you last?'

'Oh no. Not since then. I only had that during the last three or four months. Because they treated me with suspicion until then.'

'They treated you with suspicion?'

'Definitely.'

'Why?'

'I didn't know their method of working.'

'There was then a gap from the time I saw you. Until the last three or four months you haven't been in touch with them at all?'

'Yes, I was in touch with them occasionally. I can't exactly tell you how, but at different times – only when I got a letter from them.'

'With whom were you in touch?'

'Five or six different people.'

'What were their names?'

'Let us get away from this. I have done everything I can. I have brought you information here now – which is the most vital information – where you can obtain the German Secret Service codes.'

'Do you suggest that you, as a self-admitted Secret Service agent, just came to see me...'

'I have seen right from the beginning exactly what has been in the wind and I have known there has been danger. I have tried to tell you. I have phoned you several times because I have known the danger.'

'Yes. The point you don't seem quite to realise is that you seem to have been working for us against our instructions. We told you quite definitely that we did not want anything more to do with you.'

'It is most difficult when anything like that starts.'

'You need not have seen them.'

'They would probably come to me here.'

'Who are the people with whom you are in touch?'

'At least seven or eight different names.'

'Do you mean just one person with six or seven different names?'

'Oh no, quite different people.'

'Do you remember their names? Have you seen them?'

'Yes.'

'Don't answer unless you want to...' cautioned Hinchley-Cooke, obviously aware of the impact Owen's incriminating admissions would have at any future criminal trial.

'I am quite prepared to do everything,' said Owens. 'I want you to know that I knew the danger. I want to give help, but I won't take chances unless I am prepared. I am only trying to explain to you that I have always done everything I could for this country. Probably my system is different from yours but I have always had one object in view and that was to help the country when I could. I can now. I risked my life to get it for you, at least I deserve a little thanks. I am prepared to go on and I will take further chances if you wish it, but I will do no more – it isn't worth it.'

'You wish to go on and you know our view?'

'Of course, and I know what the view on the other side was and I know the danger there was. My duty at that time was to get all I could and be in a position to help this country. And I have taken that risk.'

Later in the interview the police inspector referred to a written report and started to read from it, quoting Owens:

'I will start from where you stated you were appointed chief operator. "I have been appointed chief operator in England with authority to travel to America with a special German Secret Service code and I am to receive here in England a special secret transmitting set which will enable me to be in direct touch with secret German headquarters in the Rhine district."'

'Now, who appointed you actually?'

'The heads from Hamburg. I am going to give you them.'

'Well, why not give them now so that I can get the story in correct sequence?'

'I will give you them in time.'

'Why not now?'

'I would like to see the end of these questions... My duties will consist of receiving, coding and sending to Germany, information supplied to me and information which I may obtain in connection with general war activities and political information...'

'How does this code work?'

'It is very complicated and after we are through here I will do all that.'

'All right, Inspector,' said Hinchley-Cooke, inviting the police officer to continue reading.

' ... and I am also to have sole charge of all secret addresses of German agents in European countries and to be in charge of a bureau in England for the purpose of distributing information.'

'Where is that bureau supposed to be?'

'Well, wherever I wish. I could rent a room anywhere.'

'You haven't settled on that, have you?'

'No, as soon as I got all that I came right to you.'

The quality of information that Owens was promising far exceeded anything that he had offered hitherto, and must have been entirely new to the Security Service, despite the mail intercepts and surveillance. Of course, Owens' motives were far from clear and the reason for his visit to Scotland House at this time was hard to discern, although the deteriorating political situation in Europe made any clues to Nazi intentions a priority. Up until this point it would seem that all Owens really wanted was MI5's approval for his visits to Germany, holding out the prospect that this would yield more information which presumably he would continue to disclose. Although he had not mentioned the issue of money, a further motive would soon be revealed when Owens asked Hinchley-Cooke why his son had been questioned.

'Never heard of your boy. I don't know the first thing you are talking about,' replied the MI5 officer.

'You have a boy? A son?' asked the police officer.

'Yes. You sent him to a certain office in the city and he had quite a lot of questioning and was kept there for four hours.'

'What office?'

'Somewhere around the Monument district.'

'Who questioned him? For what purpose?'

'He was sent up there by the Labour Exchange.'

'And they questioned him?'

'They wanted to know all about me, my business and so on.'

'That's strange,' remarked Hinchley-Cooke.

'The strange part was that the names given to him were the same names – the same names as were given to me by a certain gentleman near Victoria Station. I came here on account of that.' Apparently the name used by the man who had questioned Owens' son was Jackson, this and the description of the man matched the identity of a German agent that Owens knew.

'Where are those names of the agents in Europe?' asked Hinchley-Cooke.

'They are to be given to me.'

'When?'

'When I go back.'

'When do you propose to go back?'

'I thought of going back next week, but I don't know, it all depends.'

The interview continued with a discussion about the type of information that Owens was being asked to supply in addition to the material that was to be transmitted, and this included the nature of photographs he had been asked to take, and the location of airfield plans he was to supply. Owens explained that he was to be informed which cities in England were to be the first to be bombed, and he had been asked to let the Germans know the location of power stations and steel works in these cities.

Owens was then questioned over what he knew about German agents already operating in England, and he revealed that he knew of two men. One was very dangerous and operated as a taxi driver in London, using a sweet shop as a cover. The other was a man who travelled around the country, only ever staying at hotels. Owens did not know their names but promised to find out. He then told them that he had seen the Luftwaffe's plans for a manned attack on British aerodromes.

'Did you see them secretly or openly?' challenged Hinchley-Cooke.

'I saw them openly. It is a kind of list, together with a map, and all those aerodromes are marked with two crosses. Others with one. I was told: "You need not be too particular about them. We want immediate information at once of these aerodromes. You go on a train to these aerodromes and get the men and machines concentrated there, and send them when we tell you." The ones to be attacked first are marked with three crosses.'

'The list was marked on the map itself?'

'They had a list here and a map there, regarding all these aerodromes.'

'Where were these aerodromes, do you remember?'

'There were a large number, including Mildenhall, Chichester – they were very particular about Chichester – and there were two aerodromes… Thornaby and Felixstowe.'

Owens then explained how the transmitter was to work, saying that it was portable and that he was to travel by train whenever possible. If he had to, he could hire a car and install the set in it by running two wires out of the window. He would then gather the information required and transmit it using the code. Owens said that he had not seen the receiver which was kept in a big office, but that the Germans had explained how it worked.

'You won't be able to receive messages?' asked the MI5 officer.
'No, not on that; that is merely for transmitting.'
'Where do you get your juice from?'
'From small batteries.'
'And it is all amplified up?'
'Yes, the machine is only about that big. You set whatever wavelength you want to transmit to, the forty meter band for example – it only takes about half a minute – and then you send to them.'
'And you do that by Morse?'
'Yes. There is a special key for it about that big and you cannot pick up the click.'
'Do you know Morse?'
'Well – in the Scouts – I knew a bit. I can learn, I know a few letters; I practise at all hours to work up a speed. They said you have to work up more speed than I had – about sixty.'

Having covered the matter of the radio transmitter, they then moved on to Owens' curious approach to the British Union of Fascists and, once again, Owens had an answer ready for the inspector.

'You mentioned the BUF?'
'I was rather interested in joining the BUF, which I did.'
'Did you join the BUF at the request of Hamburg?' asked Hinchley-Cooke.
'Yes.'
'Well, did they tell you why?'
'They were always interested to know things in England as regards the fascist organisation and it was possible to get a lot of information regarding the Communists because they have men in Communist organisations.'

Owens next went on to claim that the Germans employed a special method of bringing small documents across borders. Hinchley-Cooke asked if this was 'the old capsule?' but Owens said that this was not how the Germans did it, and neither did they write with invisible ink or use rice paper which could be swallowed. The German method involved writing ordinary ink on material that was similar to cigarette paper which went hard when folded up and could be put in the mouth. It was quite possible to talk with it in the mouth and could be swallowed if anyone became suspicious. Owens was also questioned about the use of cameras, and he explained that he had not been given one, as it was too easy to get caught using one. He claimed that the only time he did use one, he was sent to a reserve aerodrome which was little more than a field. An aircraft had crashed in the field recently so he photographed that. He had been told that there was another agent who would do any photography required.

Owens tried to raise the stakes: '… you understand that I am trying to work with you people and that my life is not worth two hoots if there is any slip made?' He proceeded to explain how the code worked and the meeting concluded with what was in effect an acceptance on the part of Hinchley-Cooke that Owens would carry on in the way he had been working with the Germans.

> 'Just carry on in the way you intended to,' instructed Hinchley-Cooke.
> 'It might be possible to get information regarding this transmitter.'
> 'Well, you might be able to collect your transmitter?'
> 'Well, that is a bit dangerous. There is a terrific lot of stuff coming in. If you let me carry on, I shall bring this vital information regarding the towns to be bombed. I am just wondering whether I had better leave at the beginning of the week.'

Here the interview ended, no doubt leaving MI5 perplexed about Owens' disclosures. He had admitted collecting information about RAF airfields, and was holding out the prospect of gaining access to a German wireless transmitter and some secret codes. By any standards, these were tempting prizes, but could the Welshman be relied upon? The other concern, perhaps the most significant of all, was the political dimension. With Prime Minister Neville Chamberlain convinced he had reached a settlement with Adolf Hitler, the government believed 'peace in our time' had been achieved. But if Owens' account was accurate, the Germans were on the brink of some major offensive involving an airborne attack on specific towns and selected RAF airfields. If his version was true, the implications were momentous indeed.

Only a few days later, Owens was again in contact with the police, this time with news of a leak. A Commander Kennedy, who worked for a camera company in London, had approached the Security Service with information about a German who was due to come over on technical work from Dusseldorf. Owens told the police the information given to the Security Service by Kennedy was now known in Germany, and moreover he said that the Germans were also in possession of a report on recent naval manoeuvres, and knew about a new method of artillery attack known as the 'Skip Method', where one line-of-fire leap-frogs the other. Worse still, they knew about the mass movement of troops from the east to the west coast, and the details of a tactical plan to funnel attacking German bombers towards British fighter aircraft. The plan involved creating a 'channel' through the defensive aircraft guns, lining it only with searchlights. The German bombers were intended to fly down this channel where the British fighters would be waiting for them.

According to Owens, the Germans wanted their agents in Britain to report daily on any changes to this arrangement. The Welshman insisted that his contacts were waiting for his instructions regarding the channel, and then added rather chillingly, 'To a degree my instructions will govern the position of attack on London, and I would like some advice on the matter.'

Owens also offered details of the location and personnel of Dr Rantzau's German Secret Service office, naming them as: Naval – Dr Becker; Army – Dr Laurance. Owens also promised to write to Dr Wentzel asking for details of their addresses, their call signs and instructions regarding the transmitter.

Now, for the first time, Owens was supplying tangible details about German personnel, and his warning about the leaked report proved that at least some of the information supposedly gleaned from his contacts in Hamburg was authentic. In political terms, Owens was now anticipating a massed aerial offensive aimed at London, and this was bound to be highly controversial. The German air-raids on Madrid, and the Italian air attacks on Barcelona during the Spanish Civil War, had moved modern warfare into a new realm, with centres of population enduring heavy airborne bombardments, and it was precisely these tactics that Owens was predicting would be applied to London. There had been much discussion about what protection could be afforded to the capital's civilian inhabitants, and the need to fortify certain key administrative centres, but the debate about the construction of deep shelters and the degree to which residential areas would become military targets in any future conflict was highly-charged. Once again, Owens had demonstrated a talent for making claims that were guaranteed to attract attention at the highest levels.

In these circumstances Owens was requested to stay in regular touch with Special Branch over the coming weeks as uncertainties grew during the crisis, and their meetings were usually arranged in public houses. At each encounter the opening gambit was to remind Owens that the caution given to him by Hinchley-Cooke still stood, that he was not employed in any way by the British Security Service, and that whatever he did was entirely on his own initiative. At these meetings Owens supplied information about individuals he described as German Secret Service personnel in Hamburg, and on one occasion he also showed the content of the letter he had written to Dr Wertzel, prompting the Special Branch officer to note that 'it appeared to me that S for reasons best known to himself, desires to ingratiate himself with the British authorities.'

Evidently preparations for the delivery of the transmitter were approaching completion, and Owens arranged a trip to Hamburg to carry out the final tests. Upon his return he arranged several meetings with MI5 and, after the usual cautions, revealed that the transmitter was to be delivered before 17 January 1939, and that he had received the code to be used. Owens described having seen a demonstration of the transmitter in action, explained how the code worked and offered copies of the transmitter's technical manual. He then produced a Victoria Station cloakroom ticket, numbered: k.7845, and the key to an attaché case, explaining how the radio could be redeemed.

Without Owens being told, the transmitter was recovered immediately from Victoria Station by Special Branch detectives and taken to Hinchley-Cooke who examined it and then had it returned. The ticket was then handed back to Owens, who declared his intention to go and collect the transmitter. Unaware that MI5 had already retrieved the case, Owens asked that someone should follow him at a discreet distance while he visited the cloakroom and claimed the case. Having signed a letter acknowledging receipt of the transmitter, Owens transferred it with its accessories to another case, and asked that it be delivered to Hinchley-Cooke.

This was an historic moment, for it was the very first time that MI5 had acquired a portable foreign transmitter capable of exchanging messages over quite long distances on variable frequencies. The hardware, ingeniously custom-fitted into a innocuous-looking suitcase, was far smaller than anything similar manufactured in England, and represented tangible proof that the Germans were engaged in espionage in London. This was significant because since Herman Goertz had been convicted in March 1936, not a single major spy had been detected and prosecuted anywhere in Great Britain. Years later it would emerge that Hitler himself, embarrassed by the sensational newspaper publicity attracted by Goertz, had placed a ban on all further risky operations that could jeopardise Anglo-German relations.

While MI5 was subjecting SNOW's wireless to a technical appraisal, and drafting a report detailing the information he said he had gleaned from his German contacts, he described a further dramatic development. Without any advance warning, while Owens had been walking home from the Underground station at Morden on the evening of 22 January, he said he had been approached by a stranger who had introduced himself by saying that he had brought a message from Dr Rantzau. He was to expect a telegram that would read 'Require samples immediately', and this would mean that Germany's frontier would be closed within forty-eight hours, and that he was to visit a series of aerodromes listed on a questionnaire and report on the state of their readiness. Now, it appeared, the Nazis were contemplating a surprise attack on Great Britain, in direct contradiction of the peace terms agreed by Neville Chamberlain only four months earlier in Munich.

Having dropped this bombshell on MI5, Owens announced that he would await further instructions at the Grand Hotel, West Hartlepool, one of his regular haunts when on his travels. He further explained that he intended to write to Rantzau saying 'regarding the samples, I have a car ready to call on all your customers' which would be his way of confirming to Rantzau that he was in place and ready to collect all the required information.

Later that very same day, MI5 received a report from the Air Ministry about a retired squadron-leader named Walter Dicketts who had reported having met the Welshman in a pub. Dicketts claimed that Owens had talked openly about his connection with 'a certain colonel of the CID, Scotland Yard' and that Owens had been heard to brag about how he was responsible for the arrest of a woman agent in Aberdeen. This, of course, was unquestionably a hideously indiscreet reference to Jessie Jordan, the Aberdeen hairdresser who had been identified as managing a post office for the German intelligence service, receiving mail from the continent and the United States, and then rerouting it to Hamburg.

Dicketts also alleged that further, when 'in his cups' Owens said that he held an SS badge, and that he was paid £5 per week from German sources. He went on to describe how 'some peculiar things have been happening.

Firstly, the gentleman in question arrived with a camera and told me that he was going to take photographs of certain coastal defence batteries here and when I asked him what for, he said "to take over to the other side."'

MI5 acknowledged the Air Ministry's report by declaring that Owens was known to be 'a bad lot' but asked that nothing should be done to draw him out, while requesting that anything else heard should be passed on. Meanwhile, MI5 developed the photographs that Owens had taken under German instruction and, returning them to him, cautioned that 'the development and the sending of photographs abroad may be construed as an offence against the Official Secrets Act.' As a result of this warning, Owens decided not to send the photographs and 'expressed his regret that the authorities did not want to use him'.

If Owens was disappointed by MI5's refusal to exploit his photos, he was certainly not ready to take the hint and abandon what was obviously becoming an increasing dangerous occupation. The international temperature once again was rising, with German troops moving into the Sudetenland.

The extent of Owens' dislike for those in power was made evident on 24 March when he was found to be trying to get hold of information about political scandals in which leading politicians, in particular Anthony Eden and Winston Churchill, were involved. Supposedly this information was to be used by the Germans as propaganda in an effort to destabilise the British government. Once again, SNOW had seized the initiative and taken MI5 by surprise, but was any case officer to distinguish between fact and fiction? It certainly occurred to MI5 that as a scientist, Owens was well-qualified when it came to collecting information regarding military innovations, and at one juncture he was thought to be seeking information on a new British explosive believed to be more powerful than anything yet invented. He was also after details of the new Sunderland bomber, and of secret experiments concerning 'the wireless cloud' which was to be used to bring down enemy aircraft.

Even if Owens was unable to supply the information requested, the very fact that the Germans were actively pursuing these topics was disquieting. Over the past year Hitler had annexed Austria in the *Anschluss*, occupied the Sudetenland, and most recently, in March 1939, seized Bohemia and Moravia. In doing so he had acquired a huge, modern, mechanised army, whereas the British army, still without conscription, could muster just two combat-ready divisions for deployment to France if necessary. If the reference to a 'wireless cloud' was an indication that the country's highly secret research into centrimetric radar was now a target for German intelligence collection, the implications were deeply troubling.

On his return from one of his trips to Hamburg, Owens reported to Scotland Yard that he had seen a letter from a man named Paddy from Ireland that had referred to an 'instrument' at Biggin Hill which was to be loaned to Paddy and then returned soon afterwards. At the same meeting Owens told Special Branch about the copy of a letter he had seen in Hamburg which had recommended that 'Lieutenant Stokes of Oldham aerodrome was a very good man to make contact with as he is in debt and lives above his means.' Once again, Owens seemed to be an enthusiastic informant, purveying information that contained leads to genuine counter-intelligence cases. This was MI5's lifeblood, but the doubts persisted.

On 11 August Owens was kept under discreet observation by Metropolitan Police detectives as he embarked on a steamer at Dover, destined for Ostend and, having ascertained that his final destination was Hamburg, MI5 learned that by the time he reached that city he was travelling with a woman whom he called his wife. This was an illusion that evaporated a week later, on 18 August, when Jessie Owens walked into Scotland Yard with her son Robert and denounced her husband, telling the police he was engaged in espionage for the Nazis.

This event was one of the many crucial turning-points in the SNOW case, and was entirely unexpected. According to Mrs Owens, she had wanted to tell the police about his activities for some time, but had restrained herself for the sake of her children. She told detectives that although they had quarrelled and he had left her, this altercation was not the reason that she had come to the police. She was informing on her husband because recently he had tried to persuade their son Robert, her brother's step-daughter and another friend to join him in what she called 'this despicable business' and that he had threatened to shoot Jessie if she reported him.

She also told the police that his business, the Owens Equipment Company, which had been established to sell his battery inventions, was now only a front for his other activities, and that Owens had been working for the British intelligence services when he was first approached by the Germans. He had set up a subsidiary of his company in Germany which was then used as a cover for his frequent visits to Hamburg, and she said that the letters he sent and received in the name of this company contained messages written in code. The company was, she alleged, also used as a method for paying him for services he performed for the Germans.

Jessie went on to describe the nightmares of her so-called holiday to Germany with her husband and their children. Initially they all had gone to Ostend, but Owens had received a letter instructing him to travel to Hamburg. They had been directed to leave their children Robert and Patricia in the care of the hotel manager and, having reached Hamburg they had met Dr Rantzau, whom she described as 'one of the chiefs of the German Secret Service'. Rantzau then had made what she described as 'feeble and amateurish' attempts to inveigle Jessie into becoming an agent. She also reported that in their absence a man named Peiper had visited the hotel in Ostend and had attempted to 'blackmail' the children. Alone, and far from home, it was only the protection of the hotel manager that had saved them. On her return, hearing what had happened, Jessie had threatened to have Peiper arrested.

Jessie also claimed that Owens then tried to recruit her brother's step-daughter and her friend Lily Bade, who had a German mother, and the step-daughter was now willing to give evidence against Owens. She alleged that Lily may well have believed her husband's extravagant promises, such as taking her to Germany with him, and expressed her belief that it was Lily who had accompanied Owens on his current visit to Germany, despite his assurance to Jessie that he was taking a brief holiday at the Golden Sands holiday camp in Great Yarmouth.

Jessie also reported that her husband had tried to entice his own son, then aged only eighteen, to go to Germany with him where he had told Robert that he would be employed as a draughtsman. She believed that this had been nothing more than a ruse because Owens' real intent had been to persuade Robert to work for the German Secret Service.

Jessie told the police all about the radio transmitter, and how Owens had put it in his car and driven to sensitive military sites and reported back information about them to his German masters. She also knew about the code that Owens used to send these messages, and she was able to give them details about his key word which she said was 'CONGRATULATIONS', the letters of which stood for numbers. Jessie claimed to have found some RAF codebooks in the house and told the police that she had destroyed them 'so that they should not fall into German hands'. She also alleged that Owens might still have in his possession other RAF codebooks which were recently reported as stolen. She warned that he was very clever, and that he carried coded messages in tin foil either in his mouth or in the cavity at the end of his cigarette lighter. She added that he was the chief of a group of agents who operated under his orders, and that he had even asked Jessie's brother, who worked for the arms manufacturer, Short Brothers, for secret information – a request that had been refused.

Unwittingly, Jessie Owens may have revealed what had motivated her husband's first approach to MI5 after he returned to Britain with information contained in the German mouth capsule. According to her, Owens had been warned by a railway employee that he was being followed and, fearing he was likely to be searched, had chewed up the incriminating evidence and spat it out of the railway carriage window. She said that he had been very scared by this incident and feared that he was about to be unmasked, so he had approached the police to pre-empt their intervention. She also asserted that her husband had been drinking heavily for some time, and had not been sober for weeks. She declared that she was willing to assist the authorities as far as possible, as she feared her husband might be violent. The police ended the interview with a promise that an eye would be kept on her home and, six days later, on 24 August, she sent a letter to the police with further information.

> Have received information re our talk that the two parties mentioned are now in Hamburg having gone via France no doubt they will return via Ostend, the later part of the week I also have the address of the man who is able to get any kind of passport which no doubt a certain Party may be travelling on as man and wife.

The Special Branch report of Owens' departure noted that when he left for Hamburg there was no mention of him having been accompanied by a woman.

Jessie's catalogue of complaints about her husband did not contain much that was not already known to MI5, but it did at least serve to confirm the depth of his duplicity, and seems to have prompted a general review of his current status. Not surprisingly, the recommendation was made that in the event of hostilities, Owens should be taken into custody as a self-confessed spy.

> This individual was originally employed by our Foreign Intelligence Section. It was subsequently discovered that he had betrayed his trust and gone over to the German Espionage Service operating against this country and that he was in fact double crossing. On his own admission he is still in the pay of the Germans and makes frequent journeys to Germany, no doubt taking with him any information he can get hold of.

As he is a most untrustworthy individual his activities should be curtailed immediately on the outbreak of hostilities.

MI5 and the Abwehr shared uncertain histories: neither had performed particularly well during the 1930s and neither had the complete trust of their political masters. MI5 began the war disastrously, completely unprepared, leading to Churchill's sacking of its long-serving founder Vernon Kell. It began to pick up momentum, running agents into the neutral embassies still based in London, but missed the presence of four of the infamous Soviet Cambridge spy-ring inside British intelligence, including Anthony Blunt as a senior officer within its own ranks. The Abwehr had been set up in 1921, taking its name, which means simply 'defence' in German, as a sop to the stringent restrictions imposed by the Versailles Treaty, which prevented Germany mounting any offensive military activity. It would fight a long and ultimately unsuccessful turf war with the Nazi Party's internal intelligence and security service, the Sicherheitsdienst, which would see the latter taking over responsibility for intelligence-gathering in 1944 after the 20 July plot to kill Hitler. While the Abwehr had some good successes against the Special Operations Executive in France, the British ambassador in Turkey and most spectacularly against the SOE in Holland, its operations against Great Britain were completely flawed, largely because having sent their agents into Britain, the Abwehr agent-runners believed them implicitly, a failing exploited brilliantly by the MI5 and MI6 officers running the double-cross system.

Upon the declaration of war on 3 September 1939, following the German invasion of Poland, Detention Orders under Regulation 18(b) of the Defence Regulations 1939, as predicted, were made against Owens and his girlfriend Lily Bade. A Special Branch detective, Inspector Holmes, visited Owens' home to arrest him, but he was not there and could not be traced. Then, perhaps sensing trouble, Owens contacted MI5 and once again offered his services to his country. A rendezvous was arranged at Waterloo Station, where Owens separated from Lily, and was approached by three detectives who arrested him. Seeing Owens being escorted by the policemen, Lily slipped away and returned to their flat in Parklands, the house in Surbiton where they had been living as man and wife. There the owner of the property, a 44-year-old Scot who had accompanied Owens and Lily on their recent trip to Germany, was asked by her to hide a parcel which she retrieved from the bathroom. This he did by burying it in the garden.

Meanwhile, Owens was taken to Wandsworth prison where the Detention Order was served on him formally. Initially, Owens refused to disclose his address but, just as he entered the prison, he revealed that he was living in Surbiton, adding that the transmitter he had previously shown to MI5 could be found in his bathroom.

On this occasion the police were accompanied by Major Tommy Robertson, the MI5 case officer who had exercised supervision over the SNOW case. A Scot who transferred from his regiment, the Seaforth Highlanders, to join MI5 in 1932 at the suggestion of his friend John Kell, the Director-General's son, Robertson had cut his teeth with the investigation of the Invergordon mutiny in which Royal Navy ratings had refused to obey orders for thirty-six hours in September 1931 in protest at pay cuts. Most recently he had been preoccupied by a case of Soviet espionage, a Foreign Office cipher clerk who had been suborned into betraying copies of sensitive telegrams. Angry at not being eligible for a pension, despite his creditable service in the First World War, Captain John King had opted to supplement his meagre income by selling secret correspondence to the NKVD. Finally identified by a defector who volunteered details of his treachery to the British ambassador in Washington, King had been confronted by Robertson in a Mayfair pub, and had confessed.

A kindly man with great charm and twinkling blue eyes, Robertson was an unconventional infantry officer and an inspired counter-intelligence professional. Far from being repulsed by Owens, whose behaviour appalled the staid Hinchley-Cooke, Robertson recognised a scoundrel and a not-very-lovable rogue. However, his style was very different to the older man. Robertson preferred to meet Owens in pubs, and was often accompanied by his wife Joan who was an exceptional judge of character. Although not formally employed by MI5, she was close to Lady Kell and would undertake voluntary work with her in the staff canteen. Always colourful, but not flamboyant, Robertson often wore tartan trews to his office, and was popular with his subordinates. While Hinchley-Cooke was confrontational, Robertson's approach was more subtle, and he at least gave the impression of being more pragmatic. He referred to the older man as 'Cookie' and was fond of him, as he might have regarded a past mentor. But Robertson also possessed a certain cunning, and never appeared hostile to Owens, thereby gaining a degree of co-operation that the half-German Hinchley-Cooke never achieved.

Known affectionately to colleagues as 'Tar', because of the initials with which he marked MI5 files under his supervision, Robertson was a shrewd operator, wise enough to realise that he still had not got the full measure of Owens, who never ceased to surprise. Indeed, when he visited Parklands, the couple living there initially tried to deny all knowledge of Owens, but Lily soon admitted that she and Owens had been staying there together. A search of the bathroom failed to turn up the radio, but the police did find a receiver which had been made by Owens himself. It was considered very possible that some of the more cryptic language found in Owens' correspondence with Rantzau, which MI5 had believed was a code, may have been references to this device, perhaps used to test whether the transmitter due to be sent to Owens would be powerful enough to exchange messages with Germany.

When questioned by the police, the Scot who owned Parklands revealed that he was also in the battery business, and that he had joined Owens on his trip to Germany in the hope of making some useful business connections. He said he had buried the parcel given to him by Lily because he thought he was doing a good turn for his friend Owens, who was undergoing some domestic trouble with his wife. When the parcel was unearthed it was found to contain the missing transmitter, and both Lily and her companion were escorted to Kingston for further questioning at the police station.

Under interrogation facts about Lily poured forth. She was a 27-year-old dressmaker, born to a German mother in West Ham. Introduced to Owens as 'Uncle Arthur' by a mutual friend, they had known each other for only a few months before Owens whisked her off on holiday to Germany. During the trip she and Owens had lived together, and while they were in Hamburg they met several people who had been introduced to them as 'doctors'. Then they had travelled to Berlin where in a beer-garden she had met a man known as 'the Doctor'. Lily insisted that throughout the time she had known Owens she had no idea that he had engaged in any business other than that of the Expanded Metal Company.

During an interview conducted by Robertson in Wandsworth prison, Owens explained that he could get another transmitter and receiver if he wanted. He disclosed that four o'clock in the morning was the time that Germany would contact him on the 60 metre wavelength, but that if necessary he could reach them at any time of the day or night. Soon afterwards Robertson returned to Owens' cell, accompanied by a radio expert, Colonel J. F. Yule, who asked him to make radio contact with – following the declaration of hostilities – now officially the enemy.

The decision to establish a radio link between the prison and Germany was truly momentous, for this represented the very first wireless contact of the war with the enemy. At the time MI5 had been preoccupied by the possibility of a hitherto unknown network of German spies operating in

Britain, and Owens offered the opportunity to be in direct touch with the Abwehr. If Owens could be manipulated successfully, there was a chance of learning more about the enemy's other networks, but his first attempt to send a signal failed when, as he examined the apparatus to make sure that it was properly set up, he pushed a switch at the base of the set which caused a fuse to blow. The transmitter was then removed for repair, and at six o'clock the next morning, on Saturday 9 September 1939, Owens keyed in his first message: ALL READY. HAVE REPAIRED RADIO. SEND INSTRUC-TIONS. NOW AWAITING REPLY.

MI5 monitored the signal strength, which was found to be poor, and no reply was picked up, so a further attempt was made at four o'clock when Owens had claimed that Germany would be listening for him. The second effort was again monitored and was found to have been jammed by a power-ful, unidentified station. Once again, no reply was received.

This failure prompted a late-night visit from MI5 officers who tried to persuade Owens that it was in his best interests to get in touch with Ger-many. They gained the impression that Owens had done all he could to make contact, but they were unsure whether he was still withholding some vital information. In casual conversation, while his guard was down, Owens revealed that he did not anticipate any air-raids because the Germans were expecting weather reports from him. He also let slip that if he was unable to make wireless contact, his instructions were to write to a pre-arranged address on the continent with a message that was to read 'the salesman will arrive (day) at (time).' The address was Dr Rantzau's, and the text was to tell him that Owens wanted him to get in touch. However, this version contradicted what Owens had said at an earlier interview, so the incident only served to heighten suspicions.

When Owens next tried to establish radio contact, a prison warder pushed the cell door open and asked those gathered inside if they minded anyone using the passage outside. At the thought of people being able to see him Owens paled, and was clearly terrified. He turned to the MI5 officer and begged 'don't let them see me – whatever happens don't let them see me.' He then explained that earlier the same morning a fellow prisoner had cornered him and said that he knew Owens had been 'quizzed by the intelligence cops'. Allegedly, the man had tried to find out what Owens had told them, and although Owens would not reveal his name to MI5, he claimed that the prisoner had just returned from Germany. When this story was relayed to Hinchley-Cooke, he recognised the individual immediately as someone about whom he already possessed considerable information.

Soon after this episode, on 11 September, Owens was moved from Wandsworth to Kingston police station where he was to be treated as a special prisoner, and was even allowed some liberty under MI5's supervision. On the following day Owens was taken flat-hunting by a police inspector, and found a suitable flat in the Kingston area. Top-floor accommodation was required to enable a concealed radio aerial to be strung on the roof and, having set up the transmitter, Owens made a further attempt, under MI5's supervision, to contact Germany and send a brief message: MUST MEET YOU IN HOLLAND AT ONCE. BRING WEATHER CODE RADIO TOWN AND HOTEL. WALES READY.

When challenged about this text, Owens explained that he was supposed to meet Dr Rantzau in Holland to pick up the code for transmitting weather details for areas in England that the Germans planned to bomb. The mention of Wales was a reference to Rantzau's desire to get hold of a Welshman who was a member of the Welsh Nationalist Party because he intended to establish a network of disenchanted Nationalists who would operate in Wales as saboteurs with arms which were to be brought up the Bristol Channel aboard a submarine. Owens suggested that MI5 should supply someone to go over to Germany with him who could fulfil this role. The reply was not immediate but then the letters 'O E A' were heard on his receiver. This was the call sign used when the Germans wanted to get in touch with the agent they knew as JOHNNY.

In September 1939, within days of SNOW establishing contact with the enemy by radio, his traffic had come under the scrutiny of a semi-independent intelligence organisation that worked in parallel with MI5 and offered technical support in the wireless field, an area of expertise rather new to MI5's staff. Based in a pair of neighbouring detached houses in Barnett, on London's border with Hertfordshire, the Radio Security Service employed a group of amateur license-holders, all volunteer members of the Radio Society of Great Britain, to scan the airwaves in the hope of detecting clandestine broadcasts. Upon the outbreak of hostilities there had been an expectation that several enemy spies might resort to the ether to exchange messages with Germany, but as it turned out, there were almost none. Nevertheless, the RSS experts who found themselves listening in to SNOW made an astonishing discovery. It seemed that his transmissions had been acknowledged by a German radio, but not one broadcasting from Hamburg, as had been expected. Bearings taken by British direction-finding stations calculated that his messages had been received by an enemy spy ship off the coast of Norway. Better still, his messages had been re-enciphered within a few minutes and then relayed to Germany. However, during this second part of their journey across the ether to the Abwehr's headquarters, his texts had been encrypted on a cipher generated on an Enigma machine.

Because SNOW's original messages had been drafted by MI5, the RSS cryptanalysts knew the plaintext version of the Enigma signals they were intercepting and were able to reverse-engineer the daily settings of the machine's rotors. By the end of 1940 the hand cipher traffic was being circulated by RSS under the codename ISOS, and the Enigma version as ISK. This remarkable breakthrough encouraged the codebreakers to extend their study of the enemy's Enigma traffic from the Abwehr to the Luftwaffe, and then to the many other circuits dependent on the device. Thus SNOW's morning broadcasts to his Abwehr controllers would become the daily 'crib' that helped the teams of RSS cryptographers to break not just his Enigma traffic, but all the rest of the Abwehr's most secret communications for the rest of the day, until the settings were changed again at midnight. While SNOW himself had no inkling of this vital game being played by an organisation he had never heard of, and was never let in on the secret, his contribution to the ultimate Allied victory was far, far greater than even his vivid imagination could ever have guessed.

***

After the success of his first transmission, it was decided that Owens should be allowed to make the trip to Holland. The detention order was lifted and Owens' passport was returned to him by Robertson. Arthur Owens was back in business and, on top of this, Lily was released from prison and given instructions to get everything she required for their new flat. Simultaneously, Hinchley-Cooke arranged with Superintendent Albert Foster of Special Branch for two police officers to keep a watch on the couple. MI5 also warned 'that on no account when he returns to this country is he to give the impression that he is on a special mission, but is to conform in every way to the requirements of the immigration authorities.'

Before his departure, Owens pointed out that Dr Rantzau would expect him to provide the name and address of a member of the Welsh Nationalist Party whom he could contact, and MI5 made arrangements to find a suitable nominee. The man they picked was Gwilym Williams, a retired Swansea police officer who had been born in Morriston near Swansea in March 1887 and had joined the police in Salford in 1907, where he remained for three years before transferring to the Swansea constabulary. During the First World War he had served with the 2nd Battery, the Royal Garrison Artillery. He had an imposing physical presence and was five foot ten inches tall, with brown hair and brown eyes. His police personnel file described him as having a 'fresh complexion' with three round scars on his right leg and a mole on his left elbow.

As a young man Williams had run away to sea where he had educated himself, having left school an illiterate. However, while away he was said to have picked up as many as seventeen languages, which included Welsh, French, Spanish and German, doubtless attributes that increased his value to MI5. He had often been employed by the police as a court interpreter, and his background, including his marine knowledge, would prove useful as MI5 tried to prepare SNOW's army of notional sub-agents. Physically strong, having been captain of the Swansea police's water polo team, he had been known to swim from Swansea pier to the Mumbles pier and back, a distance of six miles. He was also one of those likely to be called upon whenever there was trouble on the docks.

Williams had reached the rank of chief inspector when, in January 1939, he retired from the police, but within the year he was to begin a new career as an MI5 double agent. Part of Williams' task was to ensure that Owens was as loyal to the British war effort as he claimed, but before they left to see Rantzau, Owens went to Swansea to prepare himself for the encounter.

On his next visit to Hamburg, via Tilbury and Flushing, Owens gave the name of the Welsh Nationalist to Dr Rantzau who set about investigating his background. Rantzau wanted Owens to bring the man with him on the next visit, where a meeting would be arranged at the Savoy Hotel in Brussels. Owens was handed a coin to give to the man as a form of identification and in the meantime Rantzau was going to investigate the best way to ship the explosives, rifles and ammunition to South Wales by U-boat and Owens was to supply them with a suitable landing-site. Owens learned that the Germans had between three and four hundred submarines with a range of up to nine thousand miles, each armed with sixteen torpedoes.

During his visit Owens received an assurance from Dr Rantzau that, to protect him, he would be given advance notice of air-raids planned for his district. The Doctor also told Owens they intended to destroy the new

Hawkers factory near Owens' house in Kingston, and advised him to buy a gas mask. Although he had not been informed of any details, Owens later reported to MI5 that, if all else failed, the Germans would resort to bacteriological warfare.

Owens also learned that the Germans had information about transport aircraft and seaplanes based at Felixstowe where they were to have armaments fitted. From there they were to be taken to the Harland & Woolf shipyards in Belfast. Each plane was capable of carrying forty fully-equipped soldiers, and the Germans believed that they were to be used to deliver troops across their frontiers, so they were anxious about the numbers to be built. All this new information was relayed to the Naval Intelligence Division.

Owens also reported that the Germans could not understand why there was no heavy artillery supporting the British troops stationed along the Franco-Belgian frontier. When this item was passed to the War Office, the military intelligence analysts concluded that the Germans would take this apparent deployment of troops to mean that the British were planning to move these troops quickly through neutral Belgium or Holland. In consequence, the military intelligence analysts anticipated that the Germans might decide to move first.

The final piece of information that Owens brought home concerned a British pilot, Squadron-Leader Murray, who had made a forced landing near Hanover. In September 1939 Owens learned that he was being held in a concentration camp outside Hamburg.

The most consistent German demand was for weather reports, but the military authorities were reluctant to supply any information that would aid the enemy and encourage air-raids. When the Air Ministry was approached for advice on this sensitive topic, MI5 was informed that a decision on this matter was beyond its remit and was a policy issue which should properly be taken to the War Cabinet. Nevertheless, MI5 was anxious to build Owens' credibility and instructed him to send an immediate report on weather conditions in London.

On 26 September 1939 the Director of Air Intelligence, Air Commodore Buss, telephoned MI5 to say that the matter of the weather reports had been discussed, and that there was no objection to them being allowed to go out for the present, as long as nothing unusual happened. The information that they were to supply included an approximation of visibility at ground level; details of cloud cover including the height of any clouds; the velocity of the wind and its approximate direction; the temperature in degrees Fahrenheit.

MI5 wanted to avoid providing exact measurements, explaining that the information should appear to have been collected by an amateur observer, and not an expert meteorologist as this might betray the deception that Owens was working alone. The Air Ministry's nominee assigned the task of collecting the information would pass it on to Owens using the codewords 'Atmosphere Calling'.

Owens was instructed by the Germans to commence his transmissions at 10.00 p.m. exactly, but on 26 September there was quite a panic. On that evening MI5's radio operator, Maurice Burton, reported that he had made his way to Owens' flat carrying the key to the radio room which he kept so as to prevent SNOW from making unauthorised contact with Germany. On his arrival at 9.35 p.m. he had seen a car draw up outside the house and three men and a girl alight. He recognised two of them as Owens and Lily, but the identities of the other men were unknown to him. Accordingly, he had made his way to a nearby subway and telephoned Robertson, but while there, he had noticed a girl hanging about, and became aware that he was also being followed by a man. Robertson told Burton that the car was probably a police surveillance vehicle so, reassured, he had made his way back to the flat. As he returned he had made a note of the girl who was still hanging about and described her as fairly thickset, short, aged about 25–30, wearing a dark blue felt hat and dark coat.

Back at the flat Burton discovered that Owens' companions had indeed been Special Branch detectives, and was informed that the man trailing him was one of their colleagues who had been told to follow anyone acting suspiciously in the vicinity. By the time all this muddle had been clarified there had been only ten minutes left in which to prepare the equipment, so there had been a great rush to get the transmitter ready and it was only just in time that the message had been sent, using the CONGRATULATIONS keyword, which had read: LEAVING FOR WALES. WILL RADIO ON FRIDAY NIGHT AT 12. SEEING WW. PLEASE REPLY. The signal had been acknowledged, and the reply was: NEED MILITARY AND GEN-ERAL NEWS URGENTLY DAILY. Owens then sent the weather report, and Hamburg terminated the exchange of signals with 'Goodnight, old boy'.

This near fiasco, in the minutes leading up to an important transmission, had occurred because MI5 and Special Branch had failed to coordinate their activities, and the result was a large shiny car parked outside the house and seven people present during the vital transmission. The MI5 report on the incident noted that 'the good lady in the flat opposite did in fact put her head out of the door to see who all the people were going up and down her back stairs.' Accordingly, it was decided that in future only the minimum possible number of people should be seen entering and leaving Owens' flat.

To develop the link to the Abwehr further, MI5 told Owens to study a map of Wales and mark the likely places where arms might be delivered by U-boat. Owens explained that the Germans would make their first attempt once they were sure that conditions in the Bristol Channel were not too dangerous, and the landing would then happen somewhere between Penmaen in Oxwich Bay and Rhossili Bay, north of Worms Head. The Abwehr's objective was the sabotage of ammunition dumps and the steel works at Briton Ferry, near Port Talbot, and if this attempt failed the secondary task was to go further up the coast to Linney Head and sabotage military positions and supplies in Pembroke Dock and the Milford Haven seaplane base where there were believed to be large fuel stocks.

Owens then turned his attention to the Welsh Nationalist who would accompany him on his next trip to see Dr Rantzau. Insisting that the nominee should be able to speak German because he did not, and therefore was unable to understand Rantzau when he addressed his staff, Owens stressed that whoever MI5 picked should be able to 'look, speak and act like a Welshman, and should at least have a slight smattering of the Welsh language.' He had already ascertained through experiment that the Germans had no knowledge of the Welsh language, but they knew what it sounded like and would not be easily taken in by an imposter. To meet these requirements Scotland Yard suggested that a Special Branch officer who looked Welsh and spoke fluent German could go along, but it was considered unlikely that the detective would be able to learn enough Welsh in the fortnight available.

Owens then revealed that he had been asked by Rantzau for specific information about the number of troops heading for the coast that might indicate a large-scale deployment across the Channel. Having established that the majority of these troops had left England to join the British Expeditionary Force in France, Rantzau then disclosed details of a plan to drop German paratroops over England who would be lightly armed with machine-guns. Apparently Rantzau fully realised that these troops would stand no chance of victory, and would probably cause very little damage, but he believed the sight of enemy troops in German uniform on British soil would have an immense impact on morale. Owens explained that 'Rantzau has lived a lot in America and has acquired the American outlook of showmanship.'

Naturally, MI5 sought to learn as much as possible about the Abwehr's spymaster, and initially Owens was the organisation's principal source of information about him. He was described by Owens as six foot tall, well-built, clean-shaven, broad shouldered, with fair hair and a gold tooth on the top right side of his mouth. He had the general appearance of an American and his true name, as MI5 would eventually discover, was Nikolaus Ritter, a German who had emigrated to the United States but had returned to Germany ten years later after his New York textile business had failed in the Depression, but this was not the whole story.

While in the United States Ritter had recruited two important sources: Everett Roeder, who worked for the Sperry Gyroscope Company in Brooklyn, and Hermann Lang, an engineer employed on the design of the Norden bombsight, then thought to be the world's most accurate system of delivering bombs to their targets. The 27-year-old Lang, who had lived in New York since emigrating from Germany as a teenager in 1927, worked in Carl Norden's office in Manhattan and, when approached by Ritter in the autumn of 1937, had willingly agreed to copy the mechanism's blueprints at his home in Queens. The copies were then concealed in an umbrella and smuggled back to Germany by a steward aboard the *Reliance*, a Hamburg-Amerika line ship. Ritter's coup in obtaining the bombsight's plans established his reputation as the Abwehr's master spy.

Although both spies would eventually be compromised by another of Ritter's recruits, William Sebold, who acted as an FBI double agent, the technical information acquired by the Abwehr's network was considered by Berlin to be exceptionally valuable. Furthermore, by appealing to the patriotism of German emigrants, Ritter had accomplished his task without having to pay large sums to his subordinates. Thus, in the opening months of the war in Europe, Ritter's standing in the organisation was high, and he supervised a widespread spy-ring across the Western hemisphere serviced by a team of couriers based on German liners sailing to and from Hamburg.

Owens had developed a high regard for Rantzau and admired his intellect, sometimes appearing to be in awe of the Doctor's power both inside Germany and abroad, and he asserted that Rantzau had infested Brussels with his spies, and could do what he liked there. When asked by Owens how he crossed borders, Rantzau had laughed and said that he could go anywhere. His cover in Brussels was that of a director of a big hemp manufacturing company based in Germany who travelled to Belgium to sell his product. Recently, Rantzau had married his secretary, a Fraulein Busch, who was reputed to be as clever as he was and, known as 'the Baroness', was actively involved in her husband's work.

Owens had spent plenty of time in the Doctor's company, and their conversations had ranged widely, the two men appearing to have gained the other's trust. Owens recalled that on one occasion the topic of biological warfare had come up, and he described how he had been asked for the location of reservoirs, and especially those that supplied water to London. Although it would be very much a last resort, Rantzau had insisted that if all else failed the Germans were going to engage in bacteriological warfare, and they would drop bombs charged with bacteria into the selected reservoirs.

In preparation for his planned visit to Wales, Owens asked MI5 to intercept any letters arriving for him care of the Expanded Metal Company as these would contain the names and addresses of various agencies abroad which acted as 'spy bases'. Owens was also concerned for the safety of his flat while he was away, the presence of the girl spotted hanging about earlier made him very nervous and he asked that during his absence his flat should be watched.

Owens' trip to Swansea went well and he fulfilled his chief objective, to meet and approve Gwilym Williams, MI5's nominee for the proposed Welsh Nationalist agent who was codenamed G.W., and his friend W.W., both of whom Owens considered eminently suitable for the job. He also took the opportunity to have a drink at a pub in Pontardawe, not far from where he had been born, and he later reported being surprised to hear two people in the pub discussing the cost of living in Belgium, immediately jumping to the conclusion that one of them was a German spy trying to recruit the other who was a member of the Welsh Nationalist Party. On the following day the trio drove along the South Wales coast looking for places where a submarine might drop off arms and sabotage material and they all agreed that Oxwich Bay was the most suitable site. Content that the foundations had been laid for a sabotage organisation to wreak mayhem in the principality, the strange and uneasy partnership of SNOW and MI5 was ready to entrap Dr Rantzau.

Chapter II

The Welsh Network

BY OCTOBER 1939 the exchange of signals between Hamburg and the little flat in Kingston was well established, and Owens had even put Lily to work helping to decode the messages. She became so proficient that in some cases she had a better understanding of the system than either Owens or his MI5 wireless operator Maurice Burton. On one occasion she successfully worked out that the Germans had made a mistake and used the code for the second day of October when it was in fact the third.

One morning there was a knock on the door of the flat and a tall, thin-faced man wearing a hat and glasses asked, in a slight American accent, 'Are you in touch with the Doctor?' Owens confirmed that he was, and the man demanded to know Owens' telephone number. Owens explained that he had ordered a phone but was still waiting for the instrument to be installed, whereupon the man responded by saying that he would call back again, and that Owens could expect to be contacted in the streets or in a public house.

This unexpected incident demonstrated to MI5 that the Abwehr had the resources to operate independently in London, and even maintain a watch on Owens. There was a suspicion about the identity of this mysterious agent, but although a discreet alert was circulated to trace him, he was never found. Undeterred, MI5 proceeded with the preparations for the next step, Owens' mission to introduce the Welsh Nationalist and saboteur, Gwilym Williams, to Rantzau.

Placing another agent close to Owens had the benefit, from MI5's perspective, of providing an independent channel to report on his activities, far more reliable than surveillance and submissions made by those in whom he had confided. This role had been assigned to Gwilym Williams, codenamed G.W. by MI5, and shortly before their scheduled departure for the continent Williams travelled to London so that he and SNOW could spend some time together, and Owens could brief his companion on what to expect. Upon his arrival, Williams was met by Owens in a chauffeur-driven Daimler and, with the glass partition closed, Owens explained that they would be meeting 'the Doctor' who, he said, was in charge of the German Secret Service. Williams had been instructed to play up his cover, that as a retiree he now worked as a private enquiry agent investigating road accidents, an occupation that had led him to travel around Wales where he had witnessed the oppressive working conditions of the people and English exploitation. He should, he was told, dwell on his Welsh Nationalist political convictions, and appear pro-German.

To Williams' surprise, Owens told him that he should not be too surprised if the Germans addressed him as 'Colonel', asserting that he held that rank in the German army. Naturally, Williams did not know quite what to make of this extraordinary claim and tried to make a joke of it, saying that it must be difficult given that Owens did not speak German. 'Oh' said Owens quickly, 'they call me Colonel'. Changing the subject, Owens warned Williams that he was likely to be questioned about the locations of ammunition factories, oil refineries and steel works in Wales.

Owens told him that he might be expected to point out suitable landing-sites for U-boats on an Ordnance Survey map, and Williams said that he would attribute his knowledge to what he had heard from local fishermen. Owens concluded by telling him to show his approval of the project and to express his gratitude for anything that the Germans might send in the way of arms, explosives and money.

When they arrived at Owens' flat in Richmond, at 22 Cardigan Road, Williams was shown the transmitter and, on throwing the power switch, heard some very rapid Morse which Owens claimed was a transmission from Germany. Williams had asked if his host read Morse, and Owens claimed that he did, saying 'but they send it very slowly for my benefit'.

Owens then introduced Williams to Lily and took them to the Castle Hotel in Richmond, and later to a dance hall. During this encounter Williams and Lily got on very well together, and she described him as a grand man. However, Owens drank heavily all evening, enjoying whisky chasers with his beer, and at half past nine they made their way back to the flat for the nightly transmission. Williams was surprised that, despite all the alcohol he had consumed, Owens remained clear-headed, and he would later report that Owens possessed an extremely quick mentality and tremendous will-power.

The next morning Williams and Owens met in Trafalgar Square and spent the rest of the day preparing for their mission, acquiring visas and passport photographs. Then, on 19 October, the pair sailed from Folkestone for Ostend, their cover being a business trip on behalf of the Owens Battery Equipment Company. After arriving in Ostend they went on to Brussels where they were contacted by Dr Rantzau who told them to travel to Antwerp. Here Williams was introduced to Rantzau who was accompanied by a man known only as the Commander, who was said to be in charge of sabotage in the British Isles, and had travelled from Berlin to discuss the Welsh Nationalists with Williams.

After congratulating Owens on the quality of the information he had provided, Rantzau remarked that he liked Lily because 'she is on the side the money comes from'. Williams was then taken away and interviewed by the Commander who revealed that the Irish Republican Army was going to be run by the Germans. This was a curious disclosure, but not entirely surprising. Shortly before the war the IRA had mounted a campaign setting letterboxes alight, and it was to be expected that the Abwehr might try to create an alliance with republican extremists in Ireland. The Irish authorities had also anticipated such a development, but Williams' report was the first direct confirmation that the Abwehr was actively promoting the liaison.

The first item on the agenda for Dr Rantzau was the proposed U-boat landing-site at Oxwich Bay, and it was decided that it would be better to travel round the north of Scotland to reach the destination rather than risk the Bristol Channel. By consent it was agreed that the submarines would wait about a quarter of a mile out to sea and a motor boat would be used to collect the explosives.

Previously, it had been suggested to Owens that explosives and propaganda leaflets printed in Welsh might be delivered to Wales by parachute, but Owens had declined the offer. The Commander had also confided that he could smuggle explosives into England on neutral ships through Liverpool, and Williams had responded by saying that he had about thirty men in South Wales who were ready to carry out acts of sabotage and further the German cause. The discussion had then turned to the possibility of these men acquiring jobs in factories in England where they could carry out sabotage, and the Commander had observed that such incidents would have a psychological effect as well as causing some physical damage. He had expressed the hope that this might bring those responsible for the conduct of the war in Britain to a state of mind where they might be willing to listen to reason.

Part of the plan, it was explained, was to school Williams in the preparation of chemicals to make explosives, based on a mixture of three parts potassium-chlorate to one part sugar, which would be ignited by concentrated sulphuric acid. Williams was given various instruments for weighing and measuring these ingredients, after which the Commander gave him a demonstration.

In addition, Williams was instructed to take up stamp-collecting as a means of concealing microdot communications, a method of reducing a photograph to a tiny size so it could be concealed in an otherwise innocuous item that would go unchallenged in the regular mails. Owens was given several microdots, and on one of them was the name of a man who lived in Liverpool and, it was claimed, was a Fellow of the Royal Photographic Society. The others contained detailed instructions about how they were to send information out of Britain by sticking these microdots onto the back of postage stamps.

At that time, the use of microdots for concealing clandestine communications was quite an innovation and one relatively unknown to MI5, so this intelligence would prove exceptionally valuable to the Security Service whose counter-espionage division was in a relatively embryonic state.

Whilst Owens was in Brussels the subject of money had come up. Told that a woman in Bournemouth was to be his paymaster, he was handed £500 and Williams £250, and Owens was also offered £20,000 in U.S. dollar bills for the Welsh Nationalists. Owens declined the foreign currency, as he said it would be too dangerous to handle in England because of the difficulty in exchanging dollars, but he suggested that the money should be paid into a bank account so he could pay the Welsh saboteurs in English currency. Finally, the meeting ended with instructions about changes to the wireless frequencies. Like Owens, Williams was to be given a short-range transmitter and was told to brush up on his Morse code so that he could contact the U-boat when it arrived. Owens was to remain the general organiser of agents and the only radio link between the United Kingdom and Germany. They were also told that a man coming over to meet other agents in Britain would visit Williams. Then, out of the blue, Dr Rantzau announced that he was contemplating coming over to Britain himself.

Guy Liddell, the Director of MI5's B Division, recorded the progress of the SNOW case in a personal diary he kept every day during the war. On the return of Owens and Williams he noted that the case looked promising, with Gwilym Williams starting a stamp business so that the Germans could send messages on the backs of stamps. Owens was also to offer £50,000 to anyone who could fly 'one of our latest aircraft to Germany'.

Liddell had also received a visit from Brigadier Kevin Martin, the Deputy Director of Military Intelligence at the War Office, who had been in contact with a representative of the *News Chronicle* reporting what he thought was an illicit wireless station. Martin wanted to trace the transmitter and then announce this success in the press, but Liddell was of the opinion that the Germans should be encouraged to think that MI5 was grossly inefficient, because if they thought that MI5 was capable of tracing these broadcasts then they would wonder how SNOW's messages were managing to get through. In fact, it was perfectly possible that the messages detected by the *News Chronicle* were Owens' own nightly signals.

On their return to London all the banknotes were taken away by MI5 and the serial numbers checked to determine their origin before being restored to the two spies. During his debriefing, Owens revealed that he believed there was a German agent in the Air Ministry and one in the Admiralty, but did not know their identities. He also brought with him wooden slabs containing detonators and, perhaps most important of all, the microdots which contained the details of the German agent operating in the Manchester area.

On 4 November 1939 MI5's Richman Stopford, adopting the alias of Mr A. Head, went to Manchester to interview one of three brothers with the surname Eschborn. According to Stopford's preliminary research, two of them lived in Britain and the third was still in Germany. The man Stopford met was codenamed CHARLIE by MI5 and, according to his official file, he was 5'10' or 11', stout, with a round face, pale complexion, clean-shaven, dark hair, brown eyes, straight nose and looked like a respectable business-man. He was of a nervous disposition and Stopford succeeded in thoroughly frightening him by revealing that the Security Service knew everything about him and his family. The reason that CHARLIE was working for the Germans, or so he claimed, was that they had threatened to harm his brother Hans, still in Germany, if he did not do what they told him. Now Stopford explained that if he did not co-operate with MI5 his other brother in England, who like CHARLIE was working for Germany, would be 'put inside'. Stopford also instructed him not to breathe a word of their conversation to anyone or he would make sure that a copy of his confession fell into the hands of the German Secret Services.

CHARLIE assured Stopford that he was entirely British in his sympathies as he had lived in England nearly all his life, and would be happy to help MI5. Stopford was confident that CHARLIE was indeed an unwilling agent who had been frightened into working for the Nazis. The reason the Germans found him such a useful agent was that he had a British passport and therefore enjoyed freedom of movement, and because of his expertise in photography. CHARLIE confessed that his German controller had asked him whether he could reduce photographs to a size small enough to fit on the back of a stamp. He also admitted that his contact, whom he named as Georg Hansen, had told him to expect a visit from a German agent who would introduce himself by mentioning his family. Stopford told CHARLIE that if he was contacted by a German agent he was to carry on acting as if he was working for them, but that he should contact MI5 with a simple letter mentioning that 'Mr Roberts' had been to see him.

MI5 decided to cement the relationship with CHARLIE by sending Owens to Manchester to make contact with him. Owens was instructed to get in touch via the Manchester Photographic Society, rather than going directly to CHARLIE's house, in case he was being watched. On his mission to Manchester to approach CHARLIE, Owens would use the name 'Thomas Graham', but would register at his hotel under the name of Thomas Wilson, an alias he occasionally adopted. He was to tell CHARLIE that if he wanted to make contact he could do so through a cover address, at British Colombia House in London. 'Graham' was also to tell CHARLIE that he must not jeopardise his position in any way, and that this included trying to obtain information from the War Office. This warning was based on a claim made previously by CHARLIE to the Abwehr while on a visit to Cologne, when he had told the Germans that he could get information from such a source.

MI5 made the decision not to tell CHARLIE that 'Graham' was one of their own agents, and had deliberately left SNOW with the impression that CHARLIE was an authentic enemy spy. This strategy was intended to test the true loyalties of both spies, but it was a tactic not without risk. The intention was to test the integrity of both men and see who reported contact with the other, but, with the survival of his brother at stake, the options were not quite so clear-cut for CHARLIE, who had no reason to suppose that 'Graham' was not precisely who he claimed to be: a representative of the German Secret Service.

Lily accompanied Owens on the mission to Manchester and he duly checked into the Queen's Hotel under the name of Thomas Graham. He chose this alias because his father's name was Thomas, and his own middle name was Graham. Owens then contacted CHARLIE by telegram, asking him to come to the hotel as soon as possible as he had a message from his family. CHARLIE understood the coded message instantly, made his way to the hotel and on arrival was told by Owens that he had come from 'the Doctor', whom CHARLIE had met in Cologne, when apparently he had called himself 'Reinhart'. CHARLIE replied that he did not know anyone by that name, but he did know a Doctor Hansen, prompting Owens to explain that he knew the Doctor under a variety of names.

Owens briefed CHARLIE on a mission he was to carry out which involved going to Liverpool to photograph the docks and other strategic sites which he was then to reduce in size and send by post to 'Mr T. Graham, c/o British Columbia House, Regent Street, London W.1'. The package was to be accompanied by a covering letter bearing the date written in full. However, he was instructed to abbreviate the month if there was a problem. The conversation then turned to CHARLIE's brother whom CHARLIE said had been sending material to Germany for the past eighteen months, and had been taking too many risks by sending the information he collected too openly. Allegedly, the brother had claimed to have plenty of sources and that he could get any information he wanted.

Owens gained the impression from CHARLIE that the two brothers had been active spies for a very long time, and that although each knew what the other was doing, up to a point, they were in fact acting independently. Considering that CHARLIE had been under the impression that Owens was a genuine Nazi spy, it is easy to see how both sides reported equally distorted versions of the encounter. Upon his return to London, Owens telephoned the War Office extension 393, the number he had been given for Robertson, and asked to speak to him so he could submit his report. However, the man on the other end had replied 'Is that you Lynovski?' so Owens had put the phone down and reported the incident later to MI5. The episode served to unnerve Owens, or so he said, but there was no obvious explanation for what had happened.

Despite this minor mishap, MI5 encouraged the link between CHARLIE and Owens, and when CHARLIE reported the visit he was told that he would be given suitable information to pass on to Thomas Graham. He was assured that MI5 knew the address at Columbia House and had a good idea who Graham might be, without disclosing that 'Graham' was actually an agent operating under control. At this point CHARLIE confessed that he did not much care what happened to his brother, whom he knew to be pro-Nazi, and that he would be willing to sign an undertaking to prove his own loyalty to Britain. CHARLIE was then told to arrange another visit from Graham so he could pass on the information that MI5 would give him.

Once again, adopting the guise of Thomas Graham, Owens duly went to Manchester in mid-November 1939 and met CHARLIE again. His information included items about a change in the secret arrangement for grain convoys, and details of recent troop movements from Ireland to England. The troops were believed to be mainly Royal Engineers and Royal Artillery who were destined for training centres in England, and he also revealed that eleven ships escorted by two destroyers had left Liverpool on 19 November. This material had been provided by CHARLIE on his own initiative, and in the circumstances would have been bound to give cause for doubt about his true loyalties. Even having been reassured that MI5 was on to 'Mr Thomas', CHARLIE had persisted in passing him potentially valuable military information.

During their second encounter, CHARLIE complained that his photographic equipment was not good enough to produce the required microphotographs, but he gave an assurance that he would experiment with it and see what he could do. When a further meeting with CHARLIE was scheduled, Owens decided that instead of going up to Manchester himself, he would send Lily and a girlfriend of hers instead. She duly reported back that CHARLIE was worried about taking the required photographs because a member of the local press had recently been in trouble with the authorities for taking a harmless photograph of a sunset.

Baffled by this unexpected development, MI5 called Owens in to explain his decision to send Lily to Manchester in his place, and to point out that this could have been risky. Owens replied that he did not enjoy the journey, and that he wanted to be in the flat in case a radio message was received that night. He also said that he had total trust in Lily not to discuss sensitive matters with CHARLIE in front of the friend. Finally, Owens was told that if he intended to do anything like this again, he should inform MI5 first, and it was also pointed out to him that as the head of the organisation in this country it was his responsibility to get things moving and if necessary he should radio Germany to ask permission to progress matters. As a result of this episode, Owens was told that MI5 intended to keep a watch on both his flat and his movements and, ever one to put a positive interpretation on matters when his faults were exposed, he agreed that this would be a good idea in order to verify the identity of any enemy agents who might try to reach him.

On 12 December 1939 CHARLIE was once again visited by Stopford in the guise of 'Mr Head' to check up on any contacts he may have had. He was also given a roll of photographic film containing a plan of an aircraft factory in Speke and two aerial views, and was instructed to develop the film and report to 'Graham' that he had received the plan from a friend, a draughtsman in Liverpool. He was to say that he had asked the friend if he could copy it for the records of the Manchester Amateur Photographic Society, on the understanding that it would not be published until after the war. If 'Graham' asked where he obtained the aerial photographs, CHARLIE was to refuse to say, claiming that the source was too secret. CHARLIE said that he did not want to take any German money from 'Graham', but it was agreed that any cash should be put into a fund from which he would buy himself some photographic equipment once the war was over. CHARLIE then asked for £50 to buy a Leica camera and lens for the microphotography, and he was given some more shipping information, which he was to say had come from someone at Morris & Jones, the tea merchants with offices in Liverpool and Cardiff. Thus, having received a comprehensive briefing, CHARLIE then wrote to 'Graham' asking him to come to Manchester as 'he had some especially interesting photographs from the exhibition that he would like to show him'.

MI5 persisted in encouraging the link between CHARLIE and SNOW because it was judged that for as long as neither realised the other was working for the British authorities, the reporting of each could act as a litmus test to ensure each other's integrity. However, human nature being what it is, and the two putative German agents each anxious to impress the other, the operation was not going entirely according to plan. However, SNOW's value lay in the many sides to his character, and one of the benefits derived from tolerating his unpredictable behaviour was the occasional solid counter-intelligence lead. One of them, a dividend derived from SNOW's visit to Rantzau, was a reference to a woman who was the Abwehr's paymistress in Britain. All money paid to Owens by mail was the subject of scrutiny by MI5 and it had been noticed that on a recent £5 note there was a rubber stamp mark 'S. & Co. Ltd'. In researching the origins of this note Richman Stopford visited the department store Selfridges in Oxford Street, London and met the chief cashier, Mr King, in an effort to try to trace the note's history. Stopford learned that the note had arrived in the store on the same day that Owens had been paid, and there were only three ways this could have happened. It was either paid out against a cheque or draft, given in exchange for higher denomination notes, or given in exchange for notes or coins of a lower denomination. Having checked with Selfridges' bank, Stopford concluded that the note had not been paid out against a cheque. Stopford then questioned the four head office cashiers who could have changed a note of a higher denomination, but none of them remembered having done so. The only option left was the three store cashiers whose numbers were marked on the rubber stamps. One of them remembered taking in a £5 note at about that time in part payment for a purchase from an assistant. Having found the assistant in question, Stopford discovered that the note had come from a tall lady with grey hair who had been wearing spectacles. She had been dressed in black, with black furs and had carried a large dark attaché case. The assistant had found the lady to be particularly charming and well-spoken, and this description was confirmed by another assistant who had handled the stamped note. She worked in the underwear department and told Stopford that on the day in question a lady, aged about sixty and six feet tall with grey hair, of rather stoutish build, who was very charming in manner and well-spoken, had taken seven £1 notes out of a purse which she had concealed in her stocking. The woman then asked if she could have a £5 note in exchange for five ones, as she was anxious to send it away by post. A third assistant told Stopford that the lady had a rather full face but did not use lipstick or nail varnish 'as she was not that type'. The lady had told her that she was doing her Christmas shopping early, and had bought a pair of pyjamas for her niece and a slip for herself. She had then put the items into a cheap-looking case which was probably bought from a shop like Marks & Spencer.

Two of Owens' previous payments had been mailed from the Bournemouth and Southampton area, so a picture was emerging of someone who drew £1 notes from her own bank and then travelled up to London to launder the money by changing it into £5 notes. MI5 then made a comparison between the Selfridges list of customers with addresses in Bournemouth and Southampton, and traced the note's serial number to the Midland Bank branch at 59 Old Christchurch Road in Bournemouth, and found the name of Mrs Mathilde Krafft, a local resident whose telephone number was Parkstone 893.

Mrs Krafft was then placed under surveillance, her mail was intercepted and she was observed to visit her niece, Mrs Editha Dargel, on the continent for eight weeks. According to MI5's records Dargel had been deported earlier in the year because of her pro-Nazi activities. On 4 December 1939 Krafft received a letter from Wm H. Muller & Company, a travel and shipping firm of Electra House, 78 Moorgate, London, EC2, which requested a meeting. Three days later when Mrs Krafft visited the offices of Muller & Company, Stopford was in a car parked outside, accompanied by two of the sales assistants from Selfridges. They positively identified her as the woman who had changed the banknotes. Stopford later reported:

> I should describe Mrs. Krafft as being of rather above medium height and probably taller than she looks owing to the fact that she is decidedly thickly built and has something of a flat-footed walk giving the impression of being stiff at the hips. She is full faced with pale complexion and has a typical German Hausfrau appearance. She gives the impression of being moderately well dressed for an elderly lady, but is certainly not smart. She has rather an active look in her eyes, and I should say that her eyes, though not beautiful, are somewhat striking. She had dressed in a very dark fur coat and wore a bunch of violets. She had rather pointed black shoes. Her toes being a little turned out. She wore a black felt hat with a high crown with a big floppy brim which turned down. Her hair is dark, going grey, and dressed in a bun at the back. She was not wearing glasses, and carried a medium sized black ladies handbag.

A widow of German extraction, Mrs Krafft was discovered to have made bank withdrawals coinciding with the cash payments received anonymously in the mail by SNOW. Interception of her mail revealed that she was in correspondence with a niece in Copenhagen and planned to travel to Fiji, where she had inherited a coconut plantation from her late husband. Then there was an embarrassing fiasco when, at MI5's request, the Secret Intelligence Service made some not very discreet enquiries about her niece in Denmark, which would become a great cause for concern. Guy Liddell noted in his diary that:

> There has been a bad slip-up in the SNOW case. Some time ago Jock Whyte wrote to SIS asking for enquiries to be made about Editha Dargle in Copenhagen. The Danish police blundered in and asked her whether she knew a Mrs Krafft, hence a letter from Editha Dargel to Krafft telling her not to correspond in future.

This awkward incident could have had disastrous consequences for SNOW, and for a while his transmissions were closed down, but after a short period of inactivity, contact was resumed. Meanwhile, the surveillance on Mathilde Krafft continued until she was later arrested and detained at Aylesbury prison.

* * *

In early December 1939 Owens moved into a new flat in Richmond and, after consultation with MI5, made arrangements for a further visit to Brussels. His instructions were to complain that he had only received £50 in the last two months, and as he was performing a dangerous job for the Germans he did not consider the pay adequate. Owens had been asked by the Abwehr to take his accounts with him on the trip so MI5 went through them, and the accountant reported 'from what I can see he has done England for as much money as he can.'

SNOW was instructed that if anything went wrong on the mission he was to send a wire to Lily, signing himself as 'Owen'. He was to ask for instructions concerning CHARLIE, and to query why things were moving so slowly.

When Owens arrived in Brussels, Dr Rantzau told him that he had been called to Berlin to explain why the weather reports had been so poor. Rantzau had made excuses for Owens by saying that his agent could not be expected to give accurate reports at night in the black-out, but it had been pointed out that the reports had not matched those transmitted from Ireland and Holland. As a result, Owens was instructed to gather his weather data between 12 noon and 2 p.m. Owens was also told that his signals had not been coming through well so his call sign was to be changed to OIK, with the German station using CTA. He was to start transmitting again at 7.15 p.m. on 26 December, and the weather code would also be altered to five letter groups where the first and last group were to start and end with the letter X. Finally, Owens was given 'CHRISTMAS CAROL' as the new codeword to indicate wind speed. Wind direction was to be indicated by A for North, B for South, C for East and D for West.

As instructed, Owens raised the issue of money and Rantzau explained that there had been trouble with his agents in Britain, and that they were making new arrangements for payment. He was given £215 as an advance, which had been collected in Holland as £1 notes and then changed into £5 notes at a bank in Antwerp. Referring to CHARLIE, Owens informed Rantzau that he had written to him and told him to get the apparatus he needed to make microphotographs.

In his subsequent report to MI5, SNOW stated that the Germans were keen to know about plans to lay mines in the Irish Sea as they wanted to disrupt traffic around Liverpool. As soon as CHARLIE was ready to commence operations, Owens was to inform Rantzau who would start putting his agents in touch with him. Owens was told that these agents would use the phrase 'greetings from Auerbach' as their recognition code.

Apparently the Germans had not been too impressed by Gwilym Williams, as they had found him to be too nervous. Owens said that he was satisfied with him, but if they wanted to carry on making use of Williams it would be best to contact him direct. Despite their concerns about Williams, the Germans still intended to send explosives by submarine to South Wales as arranged previously, but now they would wait until Owens had given them the go-ahead.

Owens was also to make arrangements to receive a new kind of explosive that had been designed to sabotage shipping. The bombs were to be concealed in electric accumulators which neatly fitted with Owens' battery business. Each of the accumulators would contain a bomb but, although charged, in case they were checked by customs they would not contain any distilled water, which rendered them safe. Detonation would be controlled by a small timer which could be set to go off at any time from one hour to seventeen days. When he was ready to receive the bombs Owens was to write to the Societé de Consignation et Affrètement (SOCONAF), at 25–27 rue Jesus, Antwerp. He was also told about a new type of incendiary device which was to be packed in Swedish bread. When the bread was opened it would reveal a small ring which, when pulled, would ignite twenty seconds later.

MI5's interest was caught by a further item reported by SNOW. Allegedly a man codenamed LLANLOCH was to stand as a candidate at the next elections. He was described as exceedingly influential, especially in high military circles and may already have passed on a good deal of information to the Germans. This man would write to JOHNNY and arrange to meet him at his club. After this meeting, Owens was to go to Antwerp to collect the names of other Members of Parliament who were alleged currently to be helping the Germans. If Owens' information was true then the Nazi infiltration of British society had reached levels more worrying than MI5 had previously realised.

Rantzau also informed Owens that he might be needed in Canada as the Germans were very interested in war materiel produced there. In particular, they wanted to find out about the production of artillery shells by the

Canadian National Car Company of Hamilton, Ontario. The Germans were also keen to discover what they could about new aircraft manufacturing plants in Toronto and Montreal, and the names and particulars of the firm producing Bren guns. They also wanted to contact someone in Canada who would be prepared to put explosives on board cargo ships destined for Britain.

On his trip to Brussels Owens also met 'the Commander', but this time he was accompanied by a woman whom Owens described as being fairly tall, with medium hair, who spoke good English and was well dressed. She was about thirty-eight years old and wrote shorthand. Before the war she had lived in Farnborough and London, and had collected information from officials based at the Royal Aircraft Experimental Establishment. She also had contacts with important British fascists and was disappointed that she had not heard from her friends in the BUF. She had said that if she did not hear from them soon, she would give JOHNNY the names of some of them so that he could contact them. MI5 suspected his description of the middle-aged woman fitted Lisa Kryger, a German who had come to their attention in 1936 because of her frequent contact with Nazis and her association with the notorious William Joyce, aka Lord Haw-Haw.

Finally, Rantzau had returned to the subject of his proposed visit to Britain. Apparently the Germans thought it was easy to smuggle contraband in through England's east coast so Owens had been instructed to find a reliable fisherman who was prepared to hire out his boat. Once he had found his man Owens would be sent a set of special signals to be used at night at a prearranged location to make contact with a submarine carrying a cargo of explosives. This would be the method Dr Rantzau would use to visit Britain.

The prospect of the head of the German intelligence service coming to Britain, or meeting a ship in the middle of the North Sea, presented MI5 with a golden opportunity to prove how valuable their system could be to the war effort, as it raised the possibility that they might destroy the submarine he was on or, even better, capture him. Once again, Arthur Owens would have to be integral to any plan and, as ever, this meant that MI5 had to try to predict all the possible outcomes. Accordingly, three options were considered. The first was to acquire a fishing-boat and man it with its own crew of trusted nominees. The advantage of this was that the crew would be reliable and the possibility of a leak was lessened. However, it was acknowledged that the unexpected arrival of a complete crew of strangers in a fishing port might itself arouse suspicions amongst the locals and cause loose talk.

The second option was to employ a trustworthy fisherman and his crew. However, this would have meant placing complete faith in an unknown quantity, but at least if this alternative was adopted there would be no problem about them fitting in, or causing the locals to become suspicious.

The third option was to get hold of a group of naval ratings who were from the area and perhaps had worked in the fishing industry before the war. This would mean finding an explanation for why these men were all suddenly discharged.

A final decision on this plan was delayed until MI5 had consulted the Admiralty which, it was hoped, might be able to provide a boat and crew without raising suspicion. As so many fishing trawlers were employed as auxiliary minesweepers in the area, this had appeared quite possible.

Owens reported that he had also been asked to recruit a lorry driver who regularly travelled to aerodromes and dockyards. Equipped with a transmitter in his vehicle, he could maintain touch with the German submarine when it brought over explosives or agents, and when he was not performing this function he could let the Germans know anything of interest. Owens believed he knew someone who fitted the bill, and so had recommended a friend of his named Phillip to MI5 instructed SNOW to warn Phillip that he might be contacted, and to await instructions before he took any action. MI5 was attracted to this scheme as it offered the chance of access to new radio frequencies, call signs, transmitters and possibly even a new code. Control of a large network of agents was one way that Owens could increase his importance to both MI5 and the Abwehr, and he seems to have had his friend Phillip ready and waiting for the role, so it may be that the original idea was his, and had not come from the Abwehr as he claimed.

Owens' perceived status in the eyes of MI5 was important to him, as it was one way that he could gain control over his own affairs. Owens had given assurances to Dr Rantzau that he controlled a network of Welshmen ready to undertake sabotage missions, and he had convinced MI5 that this was a useful way to discover the Abwehr's intentions. MI5 decided to earmark individuals in relevant factories who would stand up to any scrutiny that the Germans may put them through should Owens, JOHNNY to the Germans, be asked for their names. Once again, MI5 considered the options: working with a completely notional group, or employing reliable men and placing them as agents in the chosen factories. The MI5 report on the plan concluded: 'It will naturally be necessary to have an actual explosion at each of these factories in order to instil confidence into the enemy. These explosions should be followed by the necessary amount of publicity in the Press.'

Since the episode when Lily had been sent to Manchester in SNOW's place, MI5 had increased its surveillance on him, and the move to a new flat in Richmond had given the organisation an opportunity to improve its technical coverage by installing a microphone in the dining-room. Unfortunately, Owens seemed to conduct most of his conversations in the kitchen, and since moving in Owens had purchased a radio which had been placed in the dining-room. The staff monitoring the microphone noted that the radio was turned up to full volume on almost every occasion there was a lengthy conversation. The officer supervising the operation reported that 'I am unable to resist the conclusion that it is done with the purpose of drowning the conversation.' It was also noted that Owens had begun to travel by taxi or car, which made the task of watching him more difficult. Although there was no firm evidence that Owens was doing anything that he should not, his behaviour did little to allay the concerns that MI5 had about him.

***

Although a question arose as to the extent MI5 was manipulating Owens, or vice-versa, MI5 now had several schemes in play designed to persuade the Abwehr to show its hand. However, it was also true that the organisation was under some pressure to obtain results at a time when information about the enemy was at a premium and SNOW represented a unique source of potentially valuable intelligence about espionage and sabotage. If SNOW was to be believed, he had adopted the role of a German master spy, in regular wireless contact with his controllers, in command of a network of saboteurs and enjoying Rantzau's confidence.

In an attempt to make progress, Owens was instructed that in his next transmission to Germany, amongst the usual information about troop movements, he should inform the Abwehr that he had found a suitable lorry driver who was now ready to receive the new transmitter. He was also to say that he had not yet been contacted by LLANLOCH and would like instructions by return. In the case of the proposed Welsh network of saboteurs, Owens was asked to go over the arrangements that had been made, and he revealed that he was supposed to steal sticks of dynamite from friends of his working in the mines of South Wales, which he was to use with the detonators he had brought back from Brussels, although he still had no instructions as to when this was to happen.

Another tactic employed by MI5 in the hope of forcing the Germans to disclose their intentions was through CHARLIE, but first he had to perfect the process of reducing photographs to a small enough size.

The intention was that CHARLIE could master the process in time for Owens to take the microdots with him on his next trip to see Rantzau. He used a Zeiss Super Ikonta camera which was placed at a distance of three feet from the object to be copied, and had experimented with exposures of one second, half a second, one fifth of a second and one tenth of a second. Through trial and error he had found that an exposure of one second had produced the best results. The lights used were 250-watt lamps placed twenty-five inches to either side of the camera, but slightly behind the lens so as not to cause any reflection. The background was a dull black surface which CHARLIE considered to be very important. He had also experimented with a pantatomic film, but found that autochrome film was best suited.

At the start of 1940 SNOW was called to a meeting by MI5 in Victoria Street to discuss his recent visit to Manchester, in the guise of 'Thomas Graham', to see CHARLIE. He reported that CHARLIE had been keen to find out how he might be approached by other German agents and had been advised by 'Graham' that they would probably bring him greetings from his friends in Germany, but there would be no mistaking it when it happened. CHARLIE had given Graham the photographs of Speke aerodrome, and had explained that he had received them from an official there. When the matter of money had come up, Owens had showed his usual reluctance to part with any of his own cash. He explained this to MI5 by saying that he believed CHARLIE was being paid directly from Germany, but MI5 pointed out that he was doing dangerous work and had to be refunded for all the equipment he had bought.

All of CHARLIE's photographs were shown to the Air Ministry and the Director of Air Intelligence, Archie Boyle, determined that there was no reason why the photographs should not be sent to the Germans. However, Squadron-Leader Plant, who had previously expressed concern about sending weather reports to the enemy, also objected to sending the photographs on intelligence grounds. Another problem was that the photographs had been taken since the start of the war, so the city lights were blacked out. Photographs of this type would have been very difficult to take and they might raise suspicions because of the ease with which CHARLIE had been able to obtain them. At this juncture SNOW had pointed out that if CHARLIE really was in touch with Germany independently, and had told his German masters that he had given the photographs to his English contact, it would create further suspicion if JOHNNY failed to pass them on. As for where CHARLIE had obtained the photographs, Owens could tell the Germans that CHARLIE was unwilling to reveal his source.

When the MI5 officers closely examined the list of questions delivered to SNOW on the microphotographs they were struck by the evidence of a considerable leak about the deployment of RAF squadrons. They were also surprised by the expectation that questions of such scope and detail could be answered, and pointed out that in order to address the questionnaire a source would either require access to the Air Ministry's Operations Room or to the confidential papers issued from there. MI5 also noted that there were a vast number of locations listed in the questionnaire, and that unless SNOW had told the Germans that he had a contact at the heart of the Air Ministry, it would involve a huge amount of travel which realistically would take a good deal of time. However, the meeting finally concluded that as squadrons were moved around frequently, disclosing their current location to the enemy at a particular moment might appear to be useful information, but in fact would quickly be out of date.

When SNOW was questioned about the level of detail in the questionnaire and the expectation that such questions could be answered, he admitted that he had 'shot rather a line and said that he had a number of contacts in the Air Ministry in the Contracts Department'. He also revealed that he had claimed similar contacts at the Admiralty and the War Office. When dismay was expressed at this disclosure, Owens reassured his audience that the questionnaires were only guides, and that Rantzau did not really expect him to be able to answer them all.

In an attempt to acquire a fishing-boat MI5 approached the Admiralty and was informed that SIS already possessed a trawler which they used for 'certain work' on the east coast. However, MI5 declined this offer because the ship would only be available for two months. As an alternative, it was suggested that MI5 should contact the Chief Inspector of Fisheries at the Ministry of Agriculture and Fisheries. A Mr Thompson was said to be very discreet and had done work previously for the Admiralty so, on 17 January 1940 a visit was made to 10 Whitehall Place and Thompson was informed of MI5's problem. Thompson supplied the name of Mr T. S. Leach of the District Fisheries Office in Cleethorpe Road, Grimsby, explaining that the fishing-grounds were restricted by the Admiralty, so any vessel outside the allocated area would raise suspicion. This news was vital information for SNOW and something that he would have to relay to the Abwehr so, with this in mind, Owens was given £30 in petrol vouchers and told to go to Newcastle, Grimsby and Lowestoft, a journey that would take him at least a week. In addition, MI5's reason for sending him to Newcastle was to have him learn what he could about 13 Fighter Squadron RAF. Although this information could have been provided instantly by MI5, in the interests of verisimilitude it was considered important to have SNOW find it out for himself. MI5 felt that this material was essential so that, in the event an agent falling into enemy hands, he could not make damaging admissions while under interrogation. If the agent had actually been to the places claimed, and made all the observations mentioned, they would be more likely to add the irrelevant small details that emerge under intense questioning and help establish authenticity.

In mid-January 1940, when Owens set out on his trip to the north of England, his progress was handicapped by severe weather which prevented him from reaching many of his objectives. Nevertheless, despite the adverse conditions, he was able to gain an impression of just how generally lax the standards of security were. On one occasion, while dining at the George Hotel in Grantham, he overheard a conversation between an RAF pilot officer and his woman companion. She was well-dressed, wore spectacles and was about thirty-five, and Owens decided she was trying to extract as much information as she could from her host.

Having failed to reach the coast, Owens made his way south and stopped to see a friend at RAF Wattisham where he had no trouble at all in gaining access to the aerodrome. He was then told by his friend that recently a man wearing an RAF uniform had walked all around the airfield, and it was not until he had left that it was realised he was bogus.

Apart from this snapshot of the deplorable state of security at RAF bases, the trip was of little use and on his return from London Owens learned of MI5's dissatisfaction. He was instructed that on his next visit abroad he would have to tell Rantzau that a great many of his contacts within the Expanded Metal Company, on whom he said he relied for information, had been called up, as had a number of his friends who worked in the militarily-sensitive contracts departments he had boasted of previously. As for the agents in South Wales, Owens was to say that many of them had been called up, but some had worked their way into factories in the region. Consequently, he would pledge to do his best, but his only real source of information was CHARLIE. Owens was also told to suggest that if the Germans could put him in touch with other agents he could distribute the questionnaire and achieve much better results with less delay.

Unbeknownst to Owens, CHARLIE had been trying to contact him and had sent two letters which appeared to be about a business deal, but were in fact asking Owens to come and see him in Manchester urgently. Owens had not received the letters because they had been addressed to 'Thomas Graham', and this alias had not been included among those to be forwarded from his old flat at 9 Norbiton Avenue, Kingston to his new address. Thus it was not until late January that 'Thomas Graham' made his visit to CHARLIE in Manchester.

On his trip to Manchester Owens carried the photographs of the RAF aerodrome at Speke and asked CHARLIE if he could reduce them further, but was advised that this would mean a considerable amount of work, so it was decided to take them as they were. CHARLIE offered some pictures of the Manchester Ship Canal, and said that he could easily obtain photos of the Manchester and Birmingham water supplies. Another useful development was CHARLIE's decision to join the Police Photographic Organisation which photographed air-raids. CHARLIE also confided that he had acquired an informant at the Cammell Laird shipbuilding yard who could access secret documents. Between them, Owens and CHARLIE arranged that they would no longer write to each other, but instead 'Graham' would visit once a fortnight. Owens had always reported that CHARLIE was trustworthy, but the feeling was obviously not entirely mutual because, at the next MI5 debriefing conducted by Stopford, CHARLIE asked whether MI5 could devise a means of safeguarding him should anything emerge about 'Graham' that he did not know. His principal concern seemed to be that Graham might incriminate him. He also suggested that if MI5 wanted to keep an eye on his home, and monitor the movements of any enemy agents, the house opposite was available for let. Stopford, still using the alias of Mr A. Head, said that they would consider the idea, and might even use infra-red photography at night.

When Owens was next contacted by the Abwehr he was asked to go to Antwerp on 8 or 9 February 1940. CHARLIE was keen to send a letter to his brother so MI5's Richman Stopford was put in charge of writing something for CHARLIE to give to Owens, which CHARLIE could photograph and then reduce to a microdot. Naturally, MI5 was keen not to make it seem too easy for CHARLIE to independently communicate photographs or information, such as the documents from Cammell Laird, so Owens was to be vague about this sort of information and hope to draw the Germans into giving him a name or two of other hitherto unknown contacts. Owens was also told to try to persuade the Abwehr to put agents in touch with CHARLIE, and to provide the names of agents who could help in gathering the information requested on the questionnaire. MI5 held the opinion that 'the more people we had working for CHARLIE who were nominated by Rantzau and company, the better from our point of view.' MI5 would also let Owens take a camera with him on his next mission in the hope of seizing a photograph of Rantzau or other Abwehr staff.

In the days before Owens left for Antwerp, CHARLIE came to London in order to deliver the microphotographs to 'Graham', and copies of them to MI5; among them was the letter for his brother. Owens then met Stopford to be given the answers to his questionnaire that, after lengthy negotiation, had been cleared by representatives of the armed forces who, understandably, had been somewhat reluctant to disclose material that would go straight to the enemy.

As Owens made his way from Victoria Station on 8 February, en route to the continent, he was about to take his seat in the first-class carriage when he noticed a man standing in the corridor. As Owens sat down the man entered the compartment, sat opposite him and engaged him in conversation. They were soon on friendly terms, and Owens learned that the man's name was Samuel Stewart. When they reached Folkestone there was a delay in the flight's departure due to fog, and Owens and Stewart stayed overnight at the same hotel. When, the next afternoon, Owens finally reached the Hotel de Londres in Antwerp, he noticed that Stewart was staying there too, so they dined together and went to the cinema. His new acquaintance would not allow Owens to pay for anything, and the following day JOHNNY asked Rantzau about him. Rantzau responded by describing Stewart as extremely reliable and a man who could be trusted, and said that Stewart had run a shipping business with offices in Antwerp, London, Belfast and Dublin, adding that he had access to the Ministry of Shipping. Owens became convinced that Stewart was already very well-connected with the Abwehr and was probably responsible for giving the Germans information about ships sailing from Britain and Ireland. Owens noted that when he had first mentioned Stewart, Rantzau immediately said 'Oh yes, that reminds me about your wireless', and from this it was postulated that Stewart might know something about mystery signals that had been detected from a transmitter located in Belfast.

JOHNNY's meeting with Rantzau had been arranged after he had contacted the SOCONAF, and had also been attended by Mrs Keller. JOHNNY handed over the photographs and gave Rantzau the information relating to the questionnaire, and the German appeared to be very happy with the weather reports, and especially with the material relating to the armaments fitted to Hurricanes and Spitfires. Apparently the Germans had learned that the new fighters were being fitted with four machine-guns and Rantzau had been anxious to find out the calibre of these weapons. It seemed likely that the Germans had learned about this improvement to the RAF's fighters after a visit by a group of Members of Parliament to the aerodrome at Northolt.

During their meeting Rantzau gave JOHNNY new instructions concerning the use of his wireless and explained that he could now get through between 6 p.m. and 1 a.m. at night, and between 1 a.m. and 6 p.m. during the day. The difference was that during the night there would be a permanent watch, while it might take a little longer to establish radio contact in daytime. Rantzau was also pleased with CHARLIE, so JOHNNY asked if there was any interest in colour photographs, which Rantzau said could be very useful in identifying the types of camouflage being used. The Germans were also keen to acquire details of the water supplies to Birmingham, Liverpool and Newcastle.

For his efforts JOHNNY was given twenty-four £5 notes and three bundles of dollar bills which added up to a further £500. JOHNNY was now on the Abwehr's payroll and was informed that he would in future receive £250 a month from Berlin. He was also handed a further, detailed questionnaire and was asked to find out how and where Canadian troops were being trained in Britain. At this point Owens complained about the amount of information that he was being asked to collect and the travel involved. However, Rantzau took the wind out of his sails somewhat by saying that they did not expect him to answer them all completely, and told him to carry on as he was doing and travel as much as he could. In time, he added, they would put people in touch with him. JOHNNY also reported on his attempts to find a trawler on the east coast and was told that this was still needed. Rantzau then revealed that he was going to America on a long visit, and would not be back in Europe until the middle of the year which was when, he claimed, the real war was going to start.

When JOHNNY mentioned the batteries it was explained that they intended to send over some trial shipments from Holland via Belgium, and that if these trial runs were successful the Germans would begin sending explosives and parts for wireless sets. During his stay he was taken around the SOCO-NAF factory, where it was arranged to send him details of freight rates, and the prices of batteries and accumulators. There was very little mention of the South Wales sabotage plot on this trip, but that was put down to the fact that no method had yet been established of making the necessary deliveries of materiel.

While he was in Antwerp, arrangements were made for JOHNNY to meet Mrs Keller alone at the railway station, where she told him that she had visited England and knew a number of people in Farnborough and in what she termed 'the Fascist Party'. Having explained this, she entrusted him with an open envelope containing a typewritten card addressed to Eugen Horsfall, Wyke Cottage, Wyke Corner, Feltham, Sussex. The letter gave Horsfall details of a new address for a Mrs Whinfield, and referred to books which he was going to discuss with her. JOHNNY was instructed to post the letter when he returned to England, together with an unsigned postcard. He was also given a piece of paper with a request for a copy of *Raphael's Astronomical Ephemeris of the Planet's Places*, which was to be sent to SOCONAF in Antwerp. Naturally, MI5 assumed that this was all some sort of code, noting that Mrs Muriel Whinfield was the wife of Colonel H. G. Whinfield, a retired officer who had stood as a BUF parliamentary candidate before the war.

This link appeared to confirm a connection between the Abwehr and the BUF, and MI5's files included a dossier on the Whinfields' son Peter who had been arrested in Switzerland and detained in January 1940 because of his activism on behalf of the BUF.

When in conversation with Rantzau, Owens later recalled that he could hear the voices of other agents coming and going but, frustratingly, he said he could not see them. Many of the voices had spoken in French and were assumed to be agents working in France, but on one occasion, on Saturday morning, he did see the arrival of a French girl. He reported that she was very good-looking, about 26- or 27-years-old, 5'7' to 5'8' with very dark hair, brown eyes, slim build, a very good figure and wearing a small black hat. She was said to be on very good terms with Rantzau, and Owens thought that he would recognise her if he saw her again.

Owens returned to England on 13 February 1940 and, when questioned by MI5, produced his new questionnaire concerning troop movements and deployments, the whereabouts of shipping and details of aircraft at RAF aerodromes. The Germans were also still keen to know about Canadian armament factories, personnel in Toronto and Ottawa, and the training that Canadian soldiers received in the United Kingdom. The other matter that concerned MI5 was the possibility of the Germans breaching the reservoirs mentioned in the questionnaire, but this was later ruled out due to the technical difficulties of having to deploy a torpedo launched from an aeroplane. The pressures involved would mean that the weapon would probably explode before reaching its target. This did not eliminate the possibility of sabotage by a ground-based agent, or the use of weapons laced with bacteria that could be dropped into the water.

Upon being shown a photograph by MI5, SNOW immediately recognised the subject as Sam Stewart and he was warned to exercise the greatest caution in his dealings with him. SNOW was told to befriend Stewart in order to earn his confidence and collect as much information about him as possible. So a week later, on 20 February, Owens visited Stewart at his office where he was plied with cigarettes and treated like a millionaire.

Once again, back in Britain, Owens adopted the role of 'Thomas Graham' and contacted CHARLIE in Manchester to ask him to attend a meeting in Matlock on very short notice. When CHARLIE reached the rendezvous he found that Graham was accompanied by his wife and had news from Germany. Graham told CHARLIE that the Doctor was going away for about two months so it would be April before Graham had any further contact with him, but assured him that when the Doctor returned he might have something for CHARLIE to do. In the meantime, CHARLIE would be contacted by someone called the Commander, and that he had received a message by wireless instructing him to destroy airfields. Graham also told CHARLIE that he wanted to hire or purchase a small boat, and gave his approval to his request to buy whatever camera equipment he needed to produce the required documents. In return for all this CHARLIE supplied Graham with information about shipping movements in Liverpool and a list of ships presently in the docks.

Upon his return to London Owens reported his activities in the north to MI5, and it was decided that a message should be sent to Germany: 'Satisfactory trip North. Am expecting to arrange for boat at Hull soon. My

Welshmen have been called up; must have explosives and assistance with regard sabotage at airports. Am ready.'

This message was MI5's way of finding out what the Abwehr had planned in terms of the delivery and use of explosives for acts of sabotage. In an effort to make the sabotage plan viable, MI5 contacted Air Commodore Archie Boyle and asked if he would mind an explosion at one of his aerodromes in the near future. His reply was that, as far as he could see, there would be no objection at all.

On the night of 27 February, Owens' wireless set burnt out due to dampness caused by snow blown into the flat. It was too badly damaged for Owens' wireless operator, Maurice Burton, to repair, so it was sent to the Post Office Research Station at Dollis Hill where technicians worked on it. The next day, 28 February, Burton monitored a signal from Hamburg which expressed concern because of a lack of response from JOHNNY and in an effort to avert German suspicions MI5 instructed Owens to send a cable via SOCONAF in Antwerp which read: 'Business satisfactory. Technical fault developed. Machine being repaired.'

Owens was also to get in touch with Sam Stewart and arrange to meet him, so that he had an eye-witness to corroborate his report that all was well and he was still at liberty.

In a further attempt to support SNOW and to facilitate the import of German batteries and accumulators containing bombs and transmitter parts, it was decided that Owens should establish a firm in London to import these items. Owens was to be joined in the company by a man picked by MI5 who had experience in this line of work. Owens then sent an order on 4 March 1940 to SOCONAF in Antwerp which was to be censored in the usual way to avoid suspicion:

Dear Mr Caby

Many thanks for your letter and sample battery the price is a little high for this country as there are large importations of American batteries here. However I am opening an office and will employ help. And will as a trial take 1,000 batteries as per sample and please Inform me all the requirements and cost etc. To London.

As soon as possible I will forward you my business address, and I would be glad if you could show this letter to my friend and impress on him that I require the batteries and electrical equipment he has left for me very urgently, also if he can find out if the special car accumulators are made for me yet.

In preparation for the sabotage plot, MI5 again contacted Air Commodore Boyle to ensure everything was ready once the explosives arrived and asked if he would agree to three separate explosions at three different aerodromes over a period of a fortnight. Undeterred, Boyle replied that he would get onto it straight away.

In early March 1940 Major Robertson arranged to meet SNOW at The Barn public house below the Star and Garter Hotel in Richmond. Robertson took his wife Joan with him and, because he was in uniform, he sent her in to ask Owens and Lily to come out and see him. The pair duly appeared and it was arranged that Owens should follow Robertson in his car. As Robertson drove off slowly, waiting for SNOW, a car got between him and Owens. In an effort to let Owens catch up with him Robertson pulled over and as he did the car pulled in behind him. Robertson noticed that the young driver of the car got out and went to examine his petrol tank, but as he did so Robertson gained the impression that his real reason for leaving his car was to keep an eye on Robertson through his back window. At this point, as Owens had nearly caught him up, Robertson drove off leaving the young man behind, but nevertheless convinced that the young man had been following him.

Robertson later discussed the matter with his wife and Owens and established from Owens that the young man had entered the public house two or three minutes after his arrival, had ordered a beer and sat at the window overlooking the car park where Owens was parked. The young man then left but some time later, when Robertson's wife arrived, the young man had once again entered the bar and sat in the window seat with a view of the car park. Later he left, leaving some of his beer behind, which Robertson's wife found odd. What worried Robertson most was Owens reaction to all this strange behaviour, which was an attitude of complete calm. Robertson simply could not work out how an enemy agent would know to follow him unless someone had tipped them off that he would be there, and the only person who knew that he was going to be at the public house that day was Owens. As a result of this episode Robertson began to wonder whether Owens was double-crossing him.

Chapter III

The Dead Don't Care

DURING EARLY 1940 a number of articles were published in the British press on the theme of illicit wireless broadcasts and the measures taken by the authorities to detect clandestine transmitters. This campaign provided MI5 with the opportunity to persuade the Abwehr that Owens should be entrusted with new codes. The plan called for SNOW to express anxieties about his safety in his messages, and to include the claim that he had seen a mobile GPO detector van near his flat.

SNOW was expected to go to Antwerp on 4 April and he intended to take the relevant newspaper cuttings with him. He had recently been to see Sam Stewart who had said that he would travel with Owens when he next went abroad, but MI5 decided that Owens should not tell Stewart that he intended to go to Antwerp as a test to see if Stewart found out about the trip from some other source.

This mission would be critical, for as well as delivering answers to the Abwehr's questionnaire, Owens would have to remember the explanation for the failure of his wireless. He was also told to pretend to be angry because of the Abwehr's failure to deliver any explosives, and to point out that an opportunity had been lost because the importation of accumulators into Britain had recently been banned. He was also to tell them that petrol rationing was restricting his movements, and that the sources he had in place at aerodromes and factories were being called up and moved frequently, making contact with them difficult.

MI5 realised the danger that Owens was putting himself in by making yet another visit to the continent, and through continual, almost daily, contact with him the consensus was that he could be trusted, with one officer reporting: 'He is a stupid little man who is given to doing silly things at odd moments, but I am perfectly convinced that he is quite straightforward in the things which he gives me and the answers to my questions.'

SNOW flew out of Shoreham airport to Brussels on 4 April 1940 and, having landed safely, made his way to Antwerp where he booked in at the Hotel de Londres. He was then picked up by a large green American convertible and driven to a flat outside Antwerp where he met Dr Rantzau who was back from his long trip to America, and had quite a few changes to announce in the way he wanted JOHNNY to operate. However, before he could outline these changes, JOHNNY complained about not having been given spare parts for his radio, which were supposed to have been sent in the accumulators from SOCONAF. He also explained about British measures to find illegal transmitters and asked for a change in his wavelength. He was told by the Commander that spare parts such as valves would be delivered to him at his Sackville Street offices by an Indian. The parts, he said, would either be left in a wireless that would be brought to him for repair, or delivered in an ordinary parcel.

According to SNOW's subsequent report, the Commander always stayed at the Taverne Sonia when he visited Antwerp, where he would become tremendously drunk.

Rantzau had new security procedures for JOHNNY which involved changing his call sign every day. In order to make this possible JOHNNY was given the Methuen edition of *The Dead Don't Care* by Jonathan Latimer which would act as his key. Rantzau then explained that JOHNNY was to add the day's date to the number of the month in order to produce a page number. By taking the last three letters of that page and reversing them, he would acquire the daily call sign. Rantzau also tried to allay JOHNNY's fears concerning illicit transmissions by asserting that radio direction-finding was a very difficult undertaking, and mentioned that the Germans had been trying to trace a short-wave transmitter operating from Wilhelmshaven without success. He also explained that it was difficult to change the wavelength because to do so would require an adjustment to the length of his aerial. A compromise suggestion was that JOHNNY could move the dial on the transmitter by a degree or two, which should help disguise his position from anyone trying to track a particular signal.

The Germans claimed they were still very keen to carry out the sabotage of an aerodrome or an arms factory and had found a way of smuggling the explosives into Britain. The idea was that SOCONAF would purchase twenty batteries from a company in Denmark. These would then be imported into Belgium via Hamburg and there the Germans would substitute twenty different batteries which contained explosives. JOHNNY would then buy these batteries from the Belgum-based firm and import them into Britain. JOHNNY pointed out, as had been suggested by MI5, that many of the people whom he had recruited as saboteurs had now been called up, leaving him short-handed. Rantzau responded by revealing that he had arranged for JOHNNY to receive some help from a South African whom the Germans had trained. This man was to work his way into an aircraft factory where he would try to obtain plans and aircraft parts, which he would then deliver to JOHNNY. Having collected the information or aircraft parts, a trawler would set out for the North Sea which would be met by the Germans. Rantzau disclosed that since the *Kriegsmarine* only had ninety U-boats left, and it was proving difficult to train replacement crews, it would be dangerous and expensive to deploy a submarine and instead he intended to use a seaplane.

Rantzau then turned to another way of communicating with JOHNNY which would involve the use of microdots concealed in SOCONAF's headed paper. One would be placed in the top loop of the '&' between 'Consigna-tion' and 'd'Affrètement' which would be virtually invisible to anyone casting a casual eye over the letter, or even to someone who was looking for cryptic messages or codes in the body of the letter.

There was also to be a change in the way that JOHNNY was paid. He was given £369 in cash but was informed that an account had been opened in his name with the Guaranty Trust Company in New York with a deposit of £750, on which he could draw using a cheque book. The reason for this was apparently Rantzau's concern that JOHNNY should not spend too much German money in England, thus helping the British economy.

JOHNNY tried to draw Rantzau out on the matter of Samuel Stewart whom, he said, he had seen in England twice; Rantzau said that he did not have any specific business for the two men to do together but suggested they should of course stay in touch. Rantzau apologised for not having a reply from CHAR-LIE's family, but said he could pass on the news that they were all well.

SNOW later reported that the Germans intended to start bombing activi-ties in the North Sea, and as such would welcome any shipping news from the Liverpool area. Rantzau told JOHNNY that they also intended to carry on their attacks on neutral shipping because 'a sailor who has been attacked by machine-gun fire from an aeroplane would not be very willing to return to his job.'

SNOW came to believe that part of the reason that the South Wales sabo-tage plan had gone quiet was that the Germans had become suspicious about Gwilym Williams, and he was asked a number of questions concerning a letter he had written which contained language that was considered to be of a quality far above the kind that the Germans would have expected a man like him to write.

The biggest surprise for JOHNNY occurred when he was asked to find someone who could become his replacement. He was to groom this individual who, having been proved trustworthy, would go to Germany where they would be trained in general espionage and in particular sabotage. Having completed the course this person was to return to Britain and take over the reins from JOHNNY. As for JOHNNY himself, he was to be given an espionage-related job in Germany, and Rantzau pointed out to JOHNNY that he 'cannot last forever.' When Owens returned to Britain, he did so carrying a new questionnaire, and a new job offer.

Owens also reported that two bombs had been placed the *City of Sydney* when the ship had docked in Amsterdam, and it was now en route to Mauritius. Owens had been asked to find out the position of the ship and to wireless her course to Antwerp, but was instructed by MI5 to say that the steamship's owners refused to give him the information. However, Guy Liddell ascertained that the ship was never in Amsterdam and advised that they should not act on Owens' information.

Upon his return to London SNOW underwent a lengthy debriefing by MI5, and one of the issues he raised was bomb damage sustained recently during an RAF night raid on Sylt and the Hindenburg Dam, a causeway which linked the island to the mainland. The attack had lasted several hours and the House of Commons had been informed about the progress of the mission by the Admiralty which had been in direct touch with the bombers taking part in the raid. Publicly, the Germans had downplayed the raid's impact, even arranging a tour of the mainly 'undamaged' site to a group of selected journalists. Having put so much effort into this massive attack, and having made sure that Parliament had been aware of it, it was considered important for morale and the hopes of the British people that the attack on Sylt should be deemed to be a success. Accordingly, it was left to Owens with his access to the Abwehr to bring home the answer, and on 16 April T. A. Robertson wrote a memo to Air Commodore Boyle:

> In case you have not already heard it, or received any information on the sub-
> ject, our informant has recently been told that the raid on Sylt was effective in
> that a considerable amount of damage was done to a number of towers on the

Hindenburg dam. This information was given to him by a reliable informant and I have no reason to doubt its accuracy.

This item is of particular interest because it is an early example of SNOW's information being circulated in Whitehall as part of the intelligence picture of Germany, and he himself is obviously being characterised as a trusted individual acting as a conduit to a reliable source offering accurate data about bomb damage, an important topic at a time when the RAF's aerial reconnaissance capability was in its infancy.

It was clear from Rantzau's renewed enthusiasm and his previous threat that on his return the war would really start, that the Germans were edging closer to mounting sabotage missions in Britain. However, Owens' supply of information, while certainly useful, posed some problems. For instance, Owens' report about German plans to attack Britain's water supply created a dilemma. If the military authorities suddenly decided to guard previously unprotected reservoirs, German suspicions might be raised. The difficulty lay in the vague nature of the report which left it unclear whether a particular reservoir had been made a target, or if the threat was more general. Furthermore, there was a question over the type of attack to be anticipated. Would there be an explosion or a bacteriological contamination? Detailed analysis of the questionnaires that Owens brought back from his visits with Dr Rantzau would perhaps supply the answers, but more importantly these questionnaires gave MI5 the opportunity to include fabricated material in the prepared answers. It was through this planting of fake information that MI5 could gain the military advantage and prosecute their fight against the Abwehr's sabotage campaign.

The questionnaires disclosed not only the Germans' priorities but also indicated some vulnerability in the enemy's knowledge, and these weaknesses could be exploited in the answers that SNOW passed on to the Germans. MI5 realised that this process would also work in reverse, and that if SNOW were to tell the Germans that the British wanted particular information, then this was likely to be treated as significant by the enemy. MI5 put this strategy into action in April 1940 when it was decided that SNOW should communicate to the Germans that the War Office had just made an urgent request for photographs showing the area surrounding Bergen in Norway. In fact, the British planned to land troops at Trondheim, some 665 kilometres north of Bergen, so the purpose was to deceive the enemy. Owens was to receive this information from CHARLIE who supposedly was ideally-placed to hear of such requirements. To facilitate the transaction, Richman Stopford contacted CHARLIE and told him to reach 'Graham' with a message that 'he had heard confidential gossip and gave it as such for what it was worth, that the War Office were urgently asking for detailed photographs of Bergen.'

By sending this information through JOHNNY, the Abwehr's most trusted agent in Britain, it was hoped that the Germans would believe it and concentrate their troops around the Bergen area, thus allowing a relatively easy landing for the actual attack on Trondheim. To ensure the trail of information was covered as carefully as possible, it was left to Stopford to first give this information to CHARLIE and tell him to pass it on to 'Thomas Graham'. The expedient of employing SNOW as a cut-out meant that he could stand up to cross-examination about CHARLIE's source if he was challenged. Furthermore, Owens was to be away when the attack actually took place, so CHARLIE was told to try and phone Mr Graham at home during this period to tell him that the information about Bergen was false and that the attack would actually be on Trondheim. Of course, MI5 knew that it would be impossible for CHARLIE to get hold of Graham, but this ruse was intended to ensure that his credibility was preserved.

The cover-plan, to misdirect the enemy away from the true British objective, was an early example of strategic deception, a concept that would later be adopted by the Chiefs of Staff and their planners as an essential component of operations to engage the enemy in the build-up to D-Day. In this instance, however, the Norwegian campaign ended in a chaotic withdrawal across the North Sea and the occupation of the entire country by the Nazis. Despite the fact that it was Winston Churchill who had been the driving force behind the Norwegian campaign, the failure of this mission led to the collapse of Neville Chamberlain's government in London. Ironically when Chamberlain stood down it was Winston Churchill who replaced him as Prime Minister. Once again, MI5's handling of Owens, the organisation's first double-cross agent, would have an impact on the course of the war that was far greater than anyone could have imagined at the time.

However, not everything was going Owens' way, and he was soon to be reminded of the precarious nature of the business in which he was involved. On his latest mission to see Dr Rantzau, Owens had said that he feared the authorities might be closing in on his illicit transmissions. Coincidentally, on his return the British received an intercept from France which appeared to come from the area of London where Owens was based. The French were told that the British knew all about the source of the transmission, but for Owens the insecurity of his position can only have been amplified.

* * *

On 23 April 1940 a copy of the *Daily Mirror* was delivered by an Indian sailor to Owens' offices in Sackville Street where it was handed to his new business partner, William Rolph. Also presented with the newspaper was Owens' business card, which he had given to Dr Rantzau in Antwerp. Wrapped inside the newspaper were radio valves, the wireless replacement parts Owens had made such a fuss about when in Antwerp.

The man who delivered the newspaper was a Lascar or Indian sailor who disclosed to Rolph that he had travelled to Britain on the *City of Simla* which had left Antwerp on 19 April, and had arrived at the Albert Docks in London on the following day. Naturally, MI5 was anxious to trace the seaman so the ship's chief engineer and captain were invited to an interview at the Admiralty. There were over 160 Indians on board the vessel but MI5 calculated that the valves had probably been brought aboard in Antwerp. Apparently the ship had taken on its crew in Calcutta but one Indian, who was married to a German, had come aboard at Antwerp and had enquired about precisely when the *City of Simla* would sail to London. As for smuggling the valves off the ship in London, it seemed likely that they had been hidden under the fez that the Indian sailors tended to wear.

At MI5's request Rolph agreed to visit the *City of Simla* on 25 April 1940 to identify the Lascar. Rolph was well-placed to participate in the operation because he was himself a former MI5 officer who had served in the organisation during the First World War, and had remained in contact with his colleagues.

Rolph, wearing a boiler suit, was given a pass and escorted aboard the ship where the Certificates of Service for all the Indian and black seamen were made available for inspection. From these documents Rolph picked out Mohideen Coonjee as the sailor who most resembled the man who had delivered the valves. In order to confirm his identification a lifeboat drill was arranged, and while the men were putting on their life-belts, Rolph spotted Coonjee supervising a winch party and took his photograph. MI5 later concluded that Coonjee, born in 1897 in Bangalore, probably had acted for Obed Hussein, who ran a home for Indian sailors and a courier service in Antwerp, and was married to a German woman.

As a result of this investigation Obed Hussein was put under surveillance for a period of two months in an effort to pick up any of his contacts. Arrangements were also made to watch the Commander at the Taverne

Sonia and the Hotel de Londres, and consideration was given to the idea of putting a girl in touch with the Commander. According to one of MI5's Belgian contacts, it was likely that a man named Ullrich of the German Consulate in Antwerp was the go-between with Obed Hussein.

* * *

In an effort to move the sabotage plan forward, two airfields, at Martlesham and Farnborough, were selected by MI5 for a fire or explosion. The scheme was to damage an aircraft and a hangar, thus ensuring there would be a Court of Enquiry and plenty of publicity, and since this might lead to questions in Parliament it was felt that the Secretary of State should be informed. For an even better effect, there was a suggestion that two or three aerodromes should be attacked at roughly the same time over the course of a fortnight. It was felt that once accomplished, there would be little pressure from the Abwehr to repeat the exercise as Owens could protest that these events were not easy to arrange. One benefit, it was hoped, would be an improvement in security at government establishments. Of course, none of this could happen until the Germans finally managed to smuggle the explosives into Britain.

SNOW had also been asked to supply secret documents from aerodromes, although the exact nature of these secret documents had not really been defined. After consultation it was decided to include RAF instruction manuals and papers routinely carried in aircraft. Acquisition of such items would, it was thought, enhance SNOW's status, although there was no wish to compromise the most recent editions of the documents, so some slightly out of date, non-classified, versions were specially prepared so they would appear current and secret to the Abwehr.

Meanwhile, in Manchester, CHARLIE expressed concern that he had no sort of written sanction for the work he was doing for MI5, but it was explained to him that MI5 never provided that kind of documentation. He had perfected the production of the microphotographs to the point that they matched the German versions, and CHARLIE declared that he intended suggesting that his microdots would be a good method for sending reports to 'Graham', with whom he had agreed a telephone code to facilitate more direct communications from Manchester. In reply, it was suggested that Graham would write to CHARLIE using invisible ink. In one conversation with MI5, CHARLIE wondered whether all his work would earn him any recognition, such as a medal once the war was over, but there were no assurances on that score either.

By May 1940 the escalation of the war and associated travel restrictions had made it increasingly difficult for Rantzau to meet Owens in person, but he remained keen to begin training a replacement who would require coaching in sabotage techniques in Germany. This meant finding a new method of delivering his candidate to the continent, and attention now concentrated on arranging a rendezvous at sea with a fishing-boat.

Chapter IV

Rendezvous in the North Sea

On 15 May 1940 two MI5 officers, T. A. Robertson and Richman Stopford, travelled to Grimsby to meet Mr Leach of the Board of Agriculture and Fisheries, who was told that there was a need to hold a rendezvous with a German submarine or seaplane somewhere in the middle of the North Sea. Mr Leach took them to see the owner of a trawler, the *Barbados,* registered as GY.71, which could be ready to sail by Saturday, 18 May.

The *Barbados* was predominantly black with a red, white and blue flag on the funnel. The MI5 officers revealed that they wanted the vessel to keep to its normal fishing routine and suggested the operation could be postponed until she returned from sea if she was engaged in fishing on the relevant date. The fisheries official explained that the trawlers generally fished in groups, and that if any of them strayed outside the permitted fishing grounds, suspicions would be raised. The two intelligence officers also learned that the crew boarded the ship in their everyday shore clothes carrying a seaman's kitbag and oilskins. When the trawlers returned with their fish they used a different quay and then came ashore once they had docked.

The captain of the *Barbados,* who was believed to be entirely trustworthy and would be fully informed about the true purpose of the voyage, was assured by MI5 that there would be no risk to his ship or crew. The crew themselves were told rather cryptically that they might see 'funny things on this trip, but whatever they see will not be what they think it is'. Their silence was to earn the crew members a bonus of £5, the mate £10 and the skipper £20, if the trip was a success – money that would be provided by Snow. The skipper was asked to remember everything that happened during the voyage, and told that if MI5 needed to meet him, a discreet rendezvous would be arranged.

Owens himself was briefed on the mission on 17 May by Robertson who suggested that Sam McCarthy, whom he had recently met, accompany him on the voyage. Although Owens did not know it, McCarthy was already working for MI5, codenamed BISCUIT. As soon as the need to find a replacement for SNOW was first mentioned, MI5 had acknowledged the need to control the candidate, and McCarthy was the chosen nominee. McCarthy was a reformed petty criminal, a conman who had been involved in drug smuggling and more recently had worked for the police as a stool-pigeon. However, as with CHARLIE, MI5 had decided against letting Owens in on the full plan, so he was to remain unaware that BISCUIT was actually working for MI5 as a loyal double agent. This expedient was intended to give MI5 an opportunity to check on SNOW when he thought himself free of his handlers.

Earlier in May, Robertson had invited BISCUIT to his club where he had been given the mission of gaining Owens' confidence by befriending him, apparently by accident, at the Marlborough public house in Friarstile Road, Richmond, where the Welshman was a regular. He was given a description of Owens and was told that he was 'a tremendous talker'. By the time the trawler mission became a reality, BISCUIT had managed to make contact with Owens, and the two of them were to be treated as special observers, with the skipper kept in the dark about the exact nature of their mission. SNOW was to say that he was a friend of the owner of the *Barbados,* to whom he had paid £150 for his services. Robertson could not guarantee 'that the crew of the trawler would keep their mouths shut but that we would have to take a risk on that'. He informed SNOW that the trip had many potential problems because they did not know what type of vessel Rantzau was planning to use, so they could not predict whether the meeting would actually take place on the trawler, or on Rantzau's vessel. Finally, SNOW was given the information relating to his questionnaire and told that when the mission was completed he and BISCUIT were to come ashore to be paid off in the normal way, and would be left to fend for themselves.

The suggested rendezvous was 53 degrees 40 minutes north, 3 degrees 10 minutes east, at 26 fathoms at midnight on Tuesday, 21 May or Wednesday, 29 May. The destination was chosen because to stray any distance outside the permitted fishing grounds could arouse suspicion and might even leave them open to attack from British aircraft. Once in the correct position, the trawler was to use special recognition signals supplied by Rantzau.

MI5 had invested a good deal of time, resources and trust in Owens and it appeared that this operation might achieve the capture or eradication of Dr Rantzau. On Saturday 18 May, MI5 asked SNOW if he had made his mind up about taking McCarthy on the mission, but he expressed some reservations and was not sure that he was the right sort of person. Accordingly, he was invited to a meeting in Richmond Park at four o'clock that same afternoon where the two men agreed a cover-story to explain how Owens had met McCarthy, and why he was the right man for this mission. At the end of this discussion SNOW was asked privately if he had made up his mind about McCarthy, and he agreed that McCarthy appeared to 'fit the bill admirably,' and then he added that 'it was just as well that he was a greenhorn at this type of work.'

Before parting, Owens took McCarthy aside so that the two could talk things over, and MI5 was keen that they should learn more about each other. After their chat had concluded, BISCUIT was driven away by MI5, and at this point he revealed that he and Owens had already spoken earlier that day, and during this conversation BISCUIT had said that he was willing to go into Germany for Owens, but had wanted to know how much money he was going to make. Owens had told him not to worry because the Germans were fine people who would look after him. Owens then told BISCUIT that he was going to introduce him to someone from MI5. BISCUIT had said that he thought this might be a dangerous thing to do, but Owens had insisted that there was nothing to worry about because the Germans already knew all about his connections with MI5. BISCUIT observed that his impression was that Owens was extremely pro-Nazi and was being paid vast amounts of money for his work. BISCUIT also accused Owens of trying to get as much money out of MI5 as possible and said that Owens had told him that MI5 'were for it as soon as the Germans started landing in this country'. Owens had then accused MI5 officers of pocketing money they had been given to pay him.

This revelation immediately threw the trawler mission into doubt but, for the moment, BISCUIT was instructed to carry on as if nothing had happened. In the meantime, MI5 hurriedly organised a series of meetings to discuss the development. If Owens was arrested the whole of the double-cross network could collapse, but BISCUIT's disclosure had led the officers gathered to believe that SNOW was double-crossing them; that he was working for the Germans and had revealed everything that he was doing for MI5. Guy Liddell was of the opinion that Owens treated 'the whole business as a money-making concern and gives a little to both sides. Probably neither side trusts him.' He was relieved that the only information he had was planted on him by MI5.

The results of their deliberations were pragmatic, for they knew that they had the chance to capture Rantzau alive and this was an opportunity they could not pass up, and even if they could not take him alive they could eradicate him.

MI5 consulted the Admiralty and, working on the NID's advice, came up with a plan codenamed Operation LAMP, which involved the trawler going out as if it was on a normal fishing trip, with SNOW and BISCUIT on board, until the afternoon of 23 May. At this point they would head off so that Owens would think they were sticking to the original arrangements to meet Rantzau, whereas in reality they would sail in a direction that would take them away from the rendezvous location. Meanwhile, another trawler which had been made to look identical to the *Barbados,* but manned with naval personnel and under the charge of a naval officer, Commander Argles, was to wait at the rendezvous. This trawler would be equipped with depth-charges, hand grenades, an anti-aircraft gun and a wireless set. Accompanying them out of sight was to be an S-type submarine, HMS *Salmon,* which would lie in wait in the hope of capturing Rantzau. Having loitered for an hour or two at the wrong location, the *Barbados* would make its way back to port. Upon arrival, Owens would be arrested and charged with being a German spy, and it was planned to round up all those connected with Owens, including Mathilde Krafft, Eugene Horsfall, Mrs Whinfield and Samuel Stewart. Stopford telephoned Grimsby in order to inform the captain that Owens was double-crossing MI5, but that McCarthy was working for MI5.

Having arranged Operation LAMP, MI5 took precautions not to tip off Owens and called at his flat to give him the information he had been asked to supply and the money needed for the mission. MI5 also met BISCUIT and he was told to get as much information as possible out of Owens on the journey up to Grimsby and when they were on the trawler. It was also arranged that BISCUIT should make contact again when they arrived in Grimsby, if he could get away from Owens.

Thereafter BISCUIT duly contacted MI5 daily and reported that during the train journey from King's Cross to Grimsby, Owens had been making notes about things he had seen from the train, including aerodromes and power stations. He had also said that he thought MI5 was a rotten organisation and was keen to get his own back on them but, most worrying for MI5, was that in addition to the information and photographs he was supposed to take with him, Owens had a document that they had not given him and which could seriously jeopardise the whole of the British Security Service. While still on the train Owens had produced a menu card for the fortieth anniversary dinner of the Important Persons Club, a dining-club run by MI5 at the Hyde Park Hotel to maintain links with retirees and other useful intelligence contacts. The menu included a seating plan identifying all the guests, and BISCUIT said that Owens had told him that he could show him 'the bastard's name who I introduced you to'. At this point, BISCUIT said Owens turned to the page with the name T. A. Robertson on it. Owens then said that the Doctor will be glad because 'when our advance guard get here they will know who to get and where to get them'. BISCUIT also told MI5 that Owens did not want the Doctor coming aboard the trawler because there was always the chance of a double-cross or someone photographing him. When they were in the hotel BISCUIT had seen Owens going through the pockets of two naval coats hanging on a rack, but when he had not found anything he had said 'we failed Hitler' and gone to bed.

Despite the latest report from BISCUIT, MI5 decided that the current plan could still go ahead and so the *Barbados* set sail from Grimsby in the very early hours of the morning of 20 May. During the voyage Owens spent much of his time asking the captain and crew lots of questions about convoys, what arms were at hand and whether there were any flashlights on board. He even asked the mate if he was in the German Secret Service. BISCUIT grew more suspicious when he gained the impression that Owens was expecting an early contact to be made because he was continually searching the skies. Owens only left the wheel-house occasionally to go below for a cup of tea and at about 4.30 in the afternoon, when BISCUIT was below deck, a seaplane circled the vessel and then flew off. The captain thought that the aircraft had British markings, but that they were in the wrong place, on the tail rather than the fuselage. The plane had flown away westwards, the direction from which it had appeared, and shortly afterwards two explosions were heard from the north-west, about one and a half miles away. Shortly after midnight the captain decided to cast his nets and do some fishing, so Owens retired to his cabin, but after only ten minutes the amphibious aircraft returned. This time the captain identi-fied it as a seaplane and, as it circled them, it dropped green starlights from both port and starboard and flashed a Morse signal to heave-to. The captain went to tell BISCUIT about the plane and asked him what to do and, from the captain's report, BISCUIT became convinced that this was a German plane and was sure that Owens expected something to happen imminently, even though the rendezvous was not scheduled for several days. Worried that Owens might go up on deck and signal the plane, BISCUIT ordered the skipper to haul in the nets, switch off the running-lights and head for home at full speed.

When Owens heard the nets being pulled in he became concerned that something was wrong, but the captain told him that the nets had become fouled and had to be recovered. When they had been sailing for about two hours Owens asked where they were going, and was told that they were going to a location near the rendezvous spot to wait.

From all that had happened BISCUIT concluded that they were being followed by a German plane. BISCUIT was keen to keep Owens below deck, so with the help of the captain and the mate, Owens was tied up, searched and locked in the captain's cabin. Then Owens accused BISCUIT of being a German agent adding, 'I am a mug – I thought so and my man in London warned me about you'. He then told BISCUIT that he was making a mistake: 'it's not me you want, it's the other fellow, my agent in London. If you let me go we will get him.' Then came BISCUIT's famous retort: 'Heil Hitler... you bastard'.

On Tuesday the ministry fisheries official Leach telephoned MI5, announcing that he had received a signal from the *Barbados* saying that she was returning to Grimsby and that 'she had important information.' On arrival, the crew was paid off, MI5 asked the owner if he would mind going out again and he agreed.

Meanwhile Owens, who had been detained aboard HMS *Corunia*, was challenged with having double-crossed MI5, a charge he denied. He claimed that he was never going to let the meeting take place because he thought that BISCUIT was a German agent who was leading him into a trap. Owens was then asked about the Important Persons' Club list, and why he had been taking notes during the train journey. He claimed that he had been given the list by Rolph who did not hold MI5 in very high regard, and had confided to Owens that he wanted to go to Germany as an agent because he was short of money. Apparently, when he had shared this ambition with MI5, he had been told that he could not go because he was a Jew, which had made him very angry and prompted him to produce papers that proved he was not Jewish. Rolph had given Owens the I. P. Club document to sell to the Germans for £2,000. Regarding the notes he had taken on the train,

Owens reminded his MI5 interrogator that he had previously been told by them that he should make notes of anything he saw that might be of interest.

Based on Owens' responses during the interview, and his explanation for his suspicious behaviour, MI5 concluded:

> His mind is a very odd affair and it does not work on logical lines and the arguments which he put up for the things which he had said to BISCUIT were not exactly convincing but at the same time seemed to hold a certain amount of water... I find it exceedingly difficult to make up my mind one way or another as to whether SNOW is in actual fact double-crossing me.

Despite these doubts about SNOW's reliability, it was decided to continue with the operation in the hope of seizing Dr Rantzau. A conference was held to discuss the plan at the Royal Hotel in Grimsby, attended by BISCUIT, his MI5 handlers and Captain Cowan, representing the Royal Navy's flag officer for the Humber estuary. Owens was told that MI5 was convinced that he had tried to double-cross his handlers, but nevertheless he was going to be given one more chance. He would be accompanied on his new mission by seventeen naval ratings, the *Barbados* was to be fitted with a concealed Oerlikon, and Owens was warned that if there was any sign of duplicity on his part when they reached the rendezvous he would probably never come back to England. The captain was told that he was not to trust Owens for one moment; if he thought Owens was trying to double-cross them he could take any action he thought suitable. However, MI5 agreed to reconsider SNOW's case if he proved instrumental in persuading Rantzau to come aboard the *Barbados* where he could be captured.

The *Barbados* returned to Grimsby from its second voyage at 6.20 p.m. on 24 May. It was met by MI5 officers who had been alerted by a message transmitted as the ship approached the port, declaring that 'the action had been completed and there was one cot case.' The cot case was Owens who had experienced a rough passage and, complaining of a duodenal ulcer, looked desperately ill. According to Lieutenant-Commander Argles, Owens had appeared most anxious to get hold of Rantzau, alive or dead, but when he was questioned Owens said nothing new, apart from his claim that he had been living in fear for many years as a result of some photographs he had taken of Kiel Harbour in the mid-1930s. He revealed that he had been confronted with this evidence some years later in Germany and, under duress, had revealed that he had been acting on behalf of British Intelligence. According to Owens, the person who had confronted him had been Dr

Rantzau, and he had discovered that Owens was working for the Admiralty in the mid-thirties and had used this against Owens in order to get him to work for Germany.

Owens, however, denied that he had ever betrayed MI5, insisting that he had never given any details of individuals who worked for MI5 to the Germans. He also claimed that he was unsure about Sam McCarthy and suspected that he was working for the Germans, and was leading him into a trap. When he asked why a German agent would want to be taken to Germany to become a German agent, Owens had no answer. MI5 also pointed out that if he truly believed this scenario, he should have reported his suspicions. Owens begged to be given one last chance, asserting that he had drawn Rantzau out and was confident that he could help MI5 capture him.

After this incident MI5 requested the Home Office for a new Detention Order for Owens, but his interrogation had not elicited enough evidence to justify his arrest. The real issue was whether MI5's best link to the Abwehr should be sacrificed, putting at risk all that had been achieved thus far. Accordingly, with some reluctance, MI5 decided that if Owens was going to be released from custody then it had to be done quickly so as to give him enough time to return to London and send a message to Rantzau. Back in his flat, and under strict MI5 supervision, Owens sent a wireless message to Germany asking why Rantzau had not been at the rendezvous, and demanding money to pay the captain's wages. The message was acknowledged, but there was no immediate reply. In these inconclusive circumstances Owens' telephone was disconnected and he was banned from leaving his flat without permission, his career as a double agent now hanging in the balance.

Immediately after the interview with Owens, MI5 crashed in on his business partner in London, William Rolph. He was known to be short of money and had already approached MI5 for cash, so Owens' story that he had been asked to sell the list of members of the Important Persons Club to Germany for £2,000 was considered highly likely. Owens had also claimed that Rolph had developed a code with which he could communicate with the Abwehr, and that Rolph had shown Owens a blueprint of MI5's internal structure and organisation. Rolph was also said to have voiced his dissatisfaction about the way that MI5 was being run by Colonel Hinchley-Cooke and Captain Robertson. Until Owens had offered this information, MI5 had not entertained any inkling that Rolph could be anything other than loyal. However, the detail of Owens' confession was supported by what MI5 now knew about Rolph. As soon as the list of I.P. Club members had been mentioned by BISCUIT, MI5 instantly considered Rolph as a likely culprit for the leak. MI5 also knew that Owens had met Rolph on 18 May, just before his departure for Grimsby, which lent further credence to his allegations.

When Robertson and Stopford confronted Rolph with the charges he expressed astonishment, but was asked to turn out his drawer and open his safe, where Owens had told MI5 he kept his organisational chart of MI5's structure. In the safe were several old I.P. Club lists, but the 1939 version, found on Owens, was missing. At this discovery Rolph became evasive and flatly denied having met Owens on Saturday 18 May at seven o'clock. MI5 knew that the two of them had been together in his office at this time because they had been under observation by watchers. When confronted with this surveillance detail, Rolph changed his story and remembered that Owens had visited him that evening with Lily. MI5 then threatened to bring Owens to the Sackville Street offices for a confrontation, and at this development Rolph became agitated and paced from room to room.

Also present in the offices was a cleaner named Stokes, and Robertson saw Rolph trying to pass something to him. Then Rolph was spotted taking something out of his drawer, ripping it up, and concealing it in his hand. As he walked out of the office, he was then seen to throw something into the bin. Stopford asked if he had thrown anything of importance in the bin but Rolph denied it. Stopford then took Rolph to the bin and asked him to turn it over, while Rolph insisted there was nothing there. Stopford put it to Rolph that he had thrown his code in the bin, and at this point, with the torn pieces of code staring him in the face, he admitted it.

Rolph was questioned for several hours during which he conceded that he had met Owens before he went away and, in an attempt to prove his credentials, had shown him the I.P. Club lists from his safe. However, Robertson remained sceptical about this as Rolph and Owens had been working together for the past two months. Rolph said that he had left the 1939 list on his desk and that Owens must have picked it up when they had left the room with Lily. However, at a later point in his statement he claimed that the list was still on the desk when they had all come back into the room. Rolph then speculated that Owens must have returned to the office after he had left, but the steel gates that guarded the office would have made this impossible. Robertson and Stopford were unimpressed by Rolph's testimony and believed that he had changed his story on countless occasions and had lied to them. They came to the conclusion that Rolph probably had given the list to Owens in the hope that he could extract some money out of Rantzau for him.

On 30 May 1940 Robertson visited Owens at his home and told him that he was unsure whether Owens had already betrayed him, or was just about to. Owens protested his innocence and Robertson told him that, against his better judgment, he had been persuaded by BISCUIT to give Owens another chance. Robertson professed his faith in BISCUIT who, he declared, would henceforth be reporting on Owens. Robertson also warned that if he suspected that Owens was double-crossing him or BISCUIT, he would not be responsible for the consequences. Owens asked if he could have protection but Robertson told him that he wanted to have nothing further to do with him personally, and that in future he should only contact him through BISCUIT. Robertson also informed Owens that he had a complete statement from Rolph, but he was not going to read from it. As he left the room, Robertson informed him that Rolph was dead. In his subsequent report Robertson noted that 'I left before he had any chance to question me or show any surprise.'

Rolph had taken his own life by gassing himself in his Dover Street flat, but MI5 could not let his suicide become general knowledge in case the news aroused the Abwehr's suspicions, so the local coroner was persuaded to record the cause of death as a heart attack.

Once again, Owens had survived a situation that could have seen his career come to an end. On 13 July 1940 Guy Liddell recorded in his diary that people seemed to think that Owens was 'on the straight and narrow path'. However, Liddell also mentioned that he still had his doubts about Owens, although he had to admit that some of the information that Owens had provided had 'proved to be reliable.' He was referring to the *City of Sydney*, a ship which Owens had previously told MI5 had two bombs planted on it in Amsterdam. MI5 had checked up on the veracity of this claim only to find that the ship had never been to Amsterdam. Nevertheless, when the ship docked in Mauritius it was searched and the bombs were duly discovered.

* * *

Because of the failure to hold a rendezvous in the North Sea, at which Sam McCarthy was to be introduced to the Abwehr as JOHNNY's successor, a new meeting was arranged in Lisbon for 24 July. Across much of Europe, the military situation had deteriorated dramatically over the previous weeks, with the British Expeditionary Force evacuated from Dunkirk, and the Nazis in occupation of Paris. With German troops in control of Belgium, travel to the continent from Britain was severely restricted. Ostend, Antwerp and Brussels were now in the hands of the Nazis, thus denying them as convenient locations for a *tref* with Abwehr agents.

It was in these circumstances that McCarthy, codenamed BISCUIT, flew to Portugal and checked into his prearranged room at the Grande Hotel Duas Nacoes. Here, of course, he was under constant scrutiny by enemy agents, by the PVDE secret police and even the hotel's proprietor who routinely passed on information about guests to the Germans.

McCarthy had hardly arrived before the proprietor offered him a share of 30,000 escudos to help two Jews escape to America, but he did not trust the man, suspecting that he would probably double–cross both McCarthy and the Jews. Accordingly, he turned down the offer but did manage to profit from it by reporting the incident to Henri Doebler, his Abwehr contact and link to Dr Rantzau.

According to BISCUIT's report, Doebler was about forty years old and had been born in Hamburg. He was six foot tall, with blue eyes and grey hair, held an Argentine passport and spoke Spanish, French and German, but his English was not very good. Doebler's flat was in the Rue Santa Maria, and McCarthy and Doebler were to become very friendly.

Doebler often visited the bars and hotels frequented by the British and American residents, and his espionage duties involved sending explosives to America and recruiting agents. McCarthy's standing with Doebler was greatly enhanced by his recruitment of Rene Emmanuel Mezanin, a steward on the *American Clipper* whom he met in a bar one night. Doebler had suggested that McCarthy should approach the man, Mezanin was eager to make some easy money, and McCarthy found that he had recruited a German spy.

BISCUIT also reported that as they were driving through Lisbon, Doebler had pointed out the head of British Intelligence and claimed to know where he lived and ate. Apparently Doebler's lady friend, who accompanied him everywhere, moved in very elevated Lisbon society and was in contact with President António de Oliveira Salazar who, she had claimed, was becoming very pro-German.

McCarthy and Doebler spent a whole week together before Rantzau arrived and as they had got on so well he put in a good word for BISCUIT. When they met Rantzau, he was posing as a diplomat under the alias 'von

Jorgensen' and although he was only in Lisbon for twelve hours, he had a series of questions ready for McCarthy about his relationship with Owens. McCarthy gave Rantzau fake details about British defences, information which was designed to give the impression that the British were ready for a German attack. Rantzau was interested in JOHNNY as, he said, his work was falling off, and McCarthy pointed out that Owens was worried about his wife and troubled by the need to remain close to his transmitter, thus preventing him from leaving his flat. Rantzau seemed to have a high opinion of Owens' son Robert and knew that he was a good draughtsman with an extensive knowledge of aircraft. The Doctor thought that it would be a good idea for Owens to find him a job in an aircraft factory where he might prove useful. He also questioned McCarthy about the North Sea trawler incident, explaining that he had been at the rendezvous and that it had been his seaplane that had circled the trawler two days before the agreed date.

Rantzau also gave McCarthy some useful information regarding new German technological advances, and these included an attempt to make parachutes invisible. Allegedly, the project had failed because the chutes were too heavy. Rantzau arranged for Doebler to show McCarthy how to make invisible ink, and gave him a lengthy intelligence questionnaire concealed in five microdots. He was handed 3,000 dollars which he was instructed to pass to JOHNNY, keeping £400 for himself. Most importantly for MI5, BISCUIT was also given a suitcase wireless set and instructions on how to use it.

Before his departure Rantzau told McCarthy that Reichmarshal Hermann Göring was to 'open the bird-cage on 14 August but that the big show would not begin then but would start later'. This, in retrospect, would be the first indication that the Luftwaffe would initiate what became the Battle of Britain, an intensive conflict fought over the skies of southern England in anticipation of what was intended to be a Nazi invasion across the Channel.

Upon his return to London, when McCarthy was debriefed by MI5, he recalled that he had detected some friction between Doebler and Rantzau, despite the fact that they worked together. Apparently Doebler could not understand how Rantzau had climbed to such seniority in the Abwehr, and he had even accused Rantzau of being a liar, but McCarthy found Doebler himself to be rather gullible and thought that it would be easy to plant an agent on him.

Whilst in Portugal BISCUIT had been asked to find somewhere in Britain where explosives could be dropped by parachute, so on his return he visited the Quantock Hills in Somerset. However, BISCUIT was not comfortable in the countryside, because he lacked a sense of direction, and was so disorientated that on one occasion he missed his train because he had to return to the farm where he had lodged in order to retrieve his revolver which he had left under his pillow. Eventually a suitable site was found and the location passed on to the Germans with the suggestion that it would make a good place to drop agents.

MI5 had learned that three German agents would be sent to Wales so Major Ford, the Regional Security Liaison Officer based in Cardiff, had obtained a house in the Swansea area that could serve as a safe-house. Gwilym Williams had received instructions to make the house ready for occupation by the trio and a Mr Doust of the Post Office Research Station at Dollis Hill installed microphones so all the conversations could be recorded. In addition, SNOW was told to go to Swansea, accompanied by his supervising radio operator Maurice Burton, to establish contact with Williams, but Owens was advised not to let him know about the three German agents. Instead, Owens was ordered to tell the Germans to contact Williams direct, and he was then to tell the Regional Security Liaison Officer (RSLO), Major Ford, once they had done so. This expedient was intended to enhance G.W.'s role and status, and give him an independent communications link with the Abwehr, thereby increasing his value to MI5 and reducing the burden on SNOW. MI5 was also keen to use G.W. to keep tabs on SNOW.

The other unfinished business from BISCUIT's visit to Lisbon was his questionnaire, which included a request for JOHNNY to pick up information about aerodromes and air-raid damage. Although MI5 had previously expressed concern about his independent collection efforts, Robertson authorised him to accept the task and assured him that anything he spotted could be reported to the Abwehr. Adopting this policy meant that if anyone checked on his information, it would stand up to scrutiny, but it would also include some 'chicken-feed', false information about an anti-aircraft device that shot wires into the sky to ensnare aircraft.

During his travels in search of information, Owens reported seeing thirty-three Spitfires, three Hurricanes, two Blenheims and one biplane under cover at Northolt. All were visible from the road and, as MI5 had already obtained a clearance from the Air Ministry's Intelligence Directorate that anything which could be seen from a public road could be given to the enemy, a request was made for this item to be transmitted. The response from the Ministry was that 'under no circumstances' was the information to be sent. Whilst this ban was respected, the location of the landing-ground in the Quantocks was sent and the response from the Germans was a request for continuous reports on several aerodromes. The actual reply ended with the ambiguous order 'Let BISCUIT do nothing else' which Burton took to mean that BISCUIT should only concentrate on aerodromes, but Owens interpreted it to mean that McCarthy should cease everything.

However, SNOW's interpretation of this ambiguous message may have been connected with a recent incident. Owens claimed that BISCUIT had turned up drunk at his house and threatened to murder him, Lily and their new-born baby Jean Louise, unless he was given some money. Lily had almost died giving birth so emotions were already high. Owens, who was usually the person accused of drinking too much, had taken the threat seriously and had written McCarthy a cheque for £200. As McCarthy was occasionally seen to suffer from delirium tremens, MI5 tended to believe SNOW's version of events. Thereafter, BISCUIT's behaviour became increasingly erratic and he missed an arranged trip to the north, claiming that he had misunderstood the instructions. McCarthy was also confused over how much he and CHARLIE were meant to know about each other, despite having been instructed to speak quite freely and mention the proposal to have an Abwehr radio expert lodge with him.

Due to the concern within MI5 about the nature of the German message regarding BISCUIT, Robertson decided that the best policy was to ask the Germans what they meant when they said that 'BISCUIT should do nothing else'. Burton suggested it would be simpler to tell the Germans that BISCUIT was going to Manchester to concentrate on aerodromes, his reasoning being that if the Abwehr did not want him to do anything then they would tell him not to go.

No such message was forthcoming, and a day later BISCUIT was sent to Manchester to see CHARLIE in order to ask if he would be willing to have an enemy radio expert lodge with him, the idea being that the radio expert would operate the new transmitter that BISCUIT had brought back from Lisbon. Burton received a call from BISCUIT in Manchester reporting that everything was alright up there, although there were conflicting reports from displeased MI5 sources that BISCUIT was mostly to be found drunk in the local pub and that his cross-examination of CHARLIE over the latter's knowledge of Dr Rantzau was entirely inappropriate.

On 2 September 1940 Robertson met BISCUIT and was told about the location that had been chosen for the landing-ground in Somerset. It was decided that a transmission should be sent to the Germans with a request that JOHNNY should let McCarthy know when the drop was to be made so that he could be in attendance. McCarthy also reported that CHARLIE did not think much of Owens as an agent. The growing number of agents in the network was beginning to produce rivalries between the double-cross spies.

Despite BISCUIT's behaviour in Manchester CHARLIE still expressed himself willing to provide a room for the new German transmitter and its operator. There were domestic difficulties to overcome as CHARLIE was concerned that his sister-in-law might become suspicious, and MI5 realised it might be difficult to keep an eye on him in CHARLIE's house. An alternative was simply to arrest the man on his arrival and take him to London for interrogation. If he could be turned, MI5 could then take him back to Manchester where he could operate under supervision. The difficulty with this option was that if other agents wanted to contact him and he was not available, suspicions could be aroused. It was therefore decided to establish a safe-house in Manchester and install the operator there. Accordingly, instructions were sent to Germany to inform the Abwehr that CHARLIE intended to find a house for the radio expert, but on 9 September, before the message was transmitted, a further problem arose. During an enemy air-raid a bomb was dropped near Owens' house which failed to detonate, but damaged local power cables and cut the electric current so the signal had to wait.

Such delays were frequent. The management of SNOW had been relatively easy when he had worked alone, albeit with his imaginary network of Welsh saboteurs, but the recruitment of BISCUIT and CHARLIE had complicated matters, especially as Owens had been led to believe that CHARLIE was an authentic German spy in direct contact with the Abwehr. For instance, when MI5 wanted to send information regarding Canadian aircraft which had recently arrived in Britain it was decided that this information would have to come from SNOW via CHARLIE, who had been asked to obtain it by BISCUIT. It was then necessary to wait for CHARLIE to come to London so that he could pass it on. MI5 considered the time-lag to be necessary as it made the whole process more plausible.

In Manchester CHARLIE was given the task of acquiring a safe-house in Salford, the cover for which was a photographic studio. The radio operator's cover was that of a man from the south whose house had been bombed, but CHARLIE was always nervous and concerned about how much help he should give the new German agent. What if he was asked to take photographs of an aerodrome or even help blow one up? MI5 instructed him to co-operate with the man and gain his confidence, and to bolster his nerve the local police were briefed and asked to watch the new agent when he arrived. CHARLIE then declared that he had arranged to decorate the flat, a cause of some dismay at MI5 because of their plan to install microphones. CHARLIE was persuaded to delay his redecoration and, with the cover story intact, a message was sent to Germany that the transmitter and safe-house were in place.

* * *

During the invasion in the summer of 1940 the Germans asked SNOW for details of British plans for a counter-attack, and requested information about the new fortification of the south coast. He was also warned about the arrival of new agents, and in early September 1940 he received an urgent signal:

Swedish friend in fields near Oxford. How can he contact you at once please. Answer at once he is also standing by for your answer.

MI5 immediately responded with:

Can meet booking office High Wycombe Railway Station. Will wear white button hole. Password, have you seen the station master. What time?

The Germans then replied:

Trying to make arrangements tonight at 2 a.m. for tomorrow at 11 a.m. Man is 5ft 11in. Slender, mostly glasses. Can you come again tomorrow at 7 a.m.

SNOW then answered: O.K. will call at 7p.m.

MI5's responses to the German message were in fact an act. In reality, an Abwehr parachutist had landed in Northamptonshire and soon afterwards had been arrested by the Home Guard and delivered to Camp 020, a secret detention centre at Ham Common in west London, for interrogation by MI5.

When questioned, the agent, Gösta Caroli, said that he was quite prepared to be shot as a spy and was not interested in his own life but merely that of another spy whom MI5 said they knew would soon be joining him. He claimed that he had been reluctant to become a spy, but having taken the job was prepared to see it through and was determined not to give away his friend. The skilled MI5 interrogators succeeded in persuading him that the Germans had given him a very raw deal and had sent him over here ill-equipped and under somewhat false pretences. He came round eventually to this view and agreed to work his wireless and under supervision transmitted a 'safe-arrival' signal to his controllers, explaining that he was living rough in the countryside. Having turned Caroli, MI5 codenamed him SUMMER and devised an elaborate plan to make use of the opportunities offered by a new transmitter and a new double agent.

In response to the Abwehr's request that Owens should help Caroli, whom they still believed to be in hiding, MI5 decided that the rendezvous should actually take place in case the Germans had arranged to be at the railway station in order to watch the meeting. However, it was also agreed that Owens should not attend the meeting himself. Ever since the trawler episode those supervising the operation had not felt they could trust Owens as before. MI5 was also keen to separate the various spies now in harness so that if one was compromised the whole system would not collapse. Instead, the plan called for Sam McCarthy to be deployed as he was someone who could be trusted. McCarthy was to meet SUMMER and walk with him until they were picked up by MI5 cars. He was warned that this could mean quite a bit of walking and therefore he should not visit any public houses en route. This left MI5 to decide what they should tell Owens, and in turn what he should tell the Abwehr. The very fact that the Abwehr had put SUMMER in touch with Owens showed how important he was to them, and as SUMMER might only be the first of many spies intended for Britain this was an operation that had to be undertaken with care.

The meeting between McCarthy and SUMMER duly took place at High Wycombe railway station, but nothing unusual happened and no German agents were present. MI5 now had to work out what story would be given to Owens to pass on to Germany about the arrival of SUMMER. Due to the length of time it had taken to break him, SUMMER theoretically had been on the run for about a fortnight, so an explanation was prepared for what would have been said to McCarthy when the two men had met. As his needs would have included shelter and a new identity, the message was prepared claiming that he was hiding in the countryside.

SUMMER presented the possibility of extracting new information about the impending invasion, but his mission's exact purpose remained unknown and it was decided that Owens should ask for advice as to what he could do for SUMMER, the hope being that in their response the Abwehr would reveal what they had in mind for him. JOHNNY was still the sole line of communication between the Abwehr's agents in Britain and Germany, but it was becoming increasingly difficult for MI5 to co-ordinate all the stories required to keep the deception credible. Thus far, the Abwehr had appeared to believe everything that Owens had told them about the meeting with

SUMMER, and evidently the Germans were keen to put him to work, as was indicated in the next message:

> Thanks for help to friend. Won't forget. Expecting reports of his trip… Please try and give daily reports no matter how little. Paramount importance constant observation air ports, planes, new A.A. locations fortifications, troop movements and concentrations.

During SUMMER's interrogation he revealed that he was soon to be followed to England by a friend about whom he was willing to talk if MI5 undertook to protect him. With this assurance Caroli disclosed that a Dane, Wulf Schmidt, was scheduled to be dropped imminently into Cambridgeshire, and accordingly MI5 circulated a warning. Sure enough, a second parachutist was taken into custody soon after landing in a field near Cambridge and, after a period of interrogation at Camp 020, was assigned the codename TATE. When searched, TATE was found to be carrying a forged ration book that bore a bogus serial number that had been supplied to the Germans by Owens. The number was part of a four-numeral series, but the one on the ration book began with the letter P, which was never used on the genuine article.

TATE's insertion into Britain had involved a parachute jump from a height of 3,500 feet, and for a few moments he had been caught in the beam of a searchlight. He'd then become entangled in some telegraph wires and injured his foot when he hit the ground. MI5 decided to run TATE as a double agent alongside Owens and SUMMER, knowing that he would have to be turned and persuaded to make contact with Germany as quickly as possible before the Germans realised that he had been caught. Any delay might compromise SNOW, and indeed the whole embryonic double-cross system.

The speed with which German agents were turned was impressive, and depended on the use of subtle psychological methods rather than more physical means. MI5's strategy was to undermine an agent's confidence in his controllers by manipulating the information gained from other sources to make it appear that the interrogators knew rather more than they really did. When questioned, bulky files were placed on display to convey the impression that the organisation had already accumulated large amounts of intelligence on their subject. Apart from the threat of execution, violence was eschewed, although on one occasion there was a lapse in discipline and TATE was physically assaulted by Colonel Alexander Scotland, a visitor to Camp 020 from another intelligence branch, MI9.

Scotland was discovered attacking TATE, who defended himself by hitting back, and the incident was reported by Malcolm Frost, the MI5 officer who intervened. Appalled at Scotland's behaviour, and convinced that 'Gestapo methods' were not the way to acquire reliable information or co-operation, Liddell banned the officer from seeing TATE again. Nevertheless, Scotland turned up again, this time carrying a syringe supposedly containing a drug that would induce the prisoner to speak. Scotland was told that he could not see TATE, who was not in a fit state to be interrogated, although in reality there was nothing wrong with his health.

Meanwhile, as TATE was coaxed into collaborating, Owens was becoming increasingly concerned about his safety during the Luftwaffe's air-raids on London, so he asked the Abwehr whether he should move from his flat to somewhere safer. Having been informed by the Abwehr that this was acceptable he was told by Robertson to look for a house in Oxford. However, he was not the only one looking for accommodation – the raids on London meant that there were few houses available in the area.

When Owens' search for accommodation proved fruitless, he was allowed to rent the home in Addlestone, Surrey, of Jock Whyte, the MI5 officer heading B Division's B23 sub-section. Under the agreement he paid four and a half guineas a week, plus the housekeeper's and gardener's wages, in return for which Owens, Lily, baby Jean and Burton could eat the vegetables from the garden. Meanwhile, JOHNNY was still receiving almost nightly requests for detailed weather reports and information about aircraft movements.

One of Owens' missions involved a trip to Kent to collect information about the bridges over the Royal Canal between Appledore and Hythe. This he effected by the cunning method of approaching a sentry and asking him what he knew about the bridges. The sentry gave him all the information he required, though Major Scotland of the War Office vetoed the transmission to Germany.

On 24 September Owens received a message telling him that 'Man for Manchester coming, possibly beginning next week.' From the interrogations of SUMMER and TATE, MI5 believed that this was a man named Reisen, a German. If the intelligence was correct, they would be on the look-out for a man from the United States who spoke English with an American accent. He was described as being thirty-seven, with black hair, clean-shaven, of medium height and of medium build. Upon contact with CHARLIE he was to be taken to 20 Rock Street, Higher Broughton in Salford, where a wireless had already been installed. Robertson talked over the arrival of this agent with Owens, in particular the nature of his identity and his password. His National Registration card was to have the letters CNFS, which was a variation of CNFV, a bogus series that Owens had previously sent to the Abwehr. Owens was told to tell CHARLIE all he knew about the new arrival and the way he was going to work. However, MI5 was not willing to sacrifice the entire operation for this one man, and it was decided that if he should be arrested before he could contact CHARLIE, he was to receive no special protection. Inspector Page, who was the local police contact, was told to deny all knowledge of the man even if the arrest was made by one of his own men, and was advised that the man was to be treated in the same way as any other unauthorised alien.

In the same message with the information about the imminent arrival of the Manchester agent, the Abwehr told JOHNNY that the Swansea agents would also be arriving soon. As a result, two MI5 officers were sent to Wales to contact Major Ford and Gwilym Williams, and on their arrival the officers were installed at the Osborne Hotel in Langland Bay, about five miles outside Swansea.

Meanwhile, MI5 was engaged in developing SUMMER, who was released from Camp 020 and accommodated in Cambridgeshire with a handler named Theakston who was instructed to gain his confidence. This he did, but his assessments of his charge were rather different from the conclusions reached by his interrogators. When Owens heard that SUMMER had left BISCUIT's home he was surprised and pointed out that Germany would be expecting to hear from SUMMER. MI5 did not want Owens and SUMMER to meet, so in order to prevent any direct contact between the two men, they sent Owens to Hythe on a reconnaissance mission to keep him occupied.

Meanwhile, McCarthy had been to Manchester to see CHARLIE who was expecting the new agent, and on his return he had passed on CHARLIE's concerns regarding the agent. Apparently CHARLIE was willing to take some time off work in order to look after the man, but could not stay with him all the time, and wondered whether he should leave him alone for long periods. He was also in need of money and wanted to know whether to write to Owens or get some from the new agent. It was decided that due to the growing expense of running an ever-increasing number of agents, Owens should ask Germany for more money.

TATE, the latest addition to the network, had also been moved to Cambridge, and was starting to transmit but his signals were not getting through.

He believed that the Abwehr would listen out for him for up to six months so MI5 did not give up. Under interrogation he had told MI5 that two other Abwehr agents had been trained at the same time as he and SUMMER. One was Danish and the other Canadian, and the intention was for them to be dropped in Somerset and in South Wales. In anticipation of the arrival of a new agent in Wales, another MI5 officer, Richard Brooman-White, was sent to assist the Cardiff RSLO, Major Ford.

When the expected agents failed to arrive at the allocated time SNOW's radio operator Maurice Burton was instructed to ask the Abwehr for an explanation. The reply informed JOHNNY that both the men were ready, and were just waiting for the right weather conditions. They also informed Owens that the man destined for Swansea had the money that had been requested, acknowledging Owens was supposed to be receiving £250 a month plus expenses, which included everything except food, drink, clothes and his rent. Naturally, MI5 was keen to take advantage of this arrangement and certainly enjoyed the irony of having the enemy pay for their operations. Accordingly, Owens was encouraged to invent false journeys which were legitimised by sending information that was already known to the enemy. This added to the potential to claim even more expenses.

At the height of the Luftwaffe raids on London in September 1940 McCarthy was instructed by the Abwehr to report on their effect, and once more it was agreed that MI5 could transmit whatever information could be gathered by ordinary observation. On the night of 9 October 1940 McCar-thy reported that Cambridge Circus had been wrecked and that Whitehall, Charing Cross, the Palace Hotel, Gray's Inn Road, the Saville Theatre and departmental buildings had all been hit and had suffered considerable damage. However, the Germans had other plans for some of their bombs. They offered various options for smuggling more money to their agents in Britain, and these included another meeting with McCarthy in Lisbon, a rendezvous at sea near a Scottish port, or putting the money inside a dummy bomb which would then be dropped at a pre-arranged point.

In dealing with the request for details of aircraft and weapons factories, MI5 noted that within a ten mile area of Swansea docks there were factories involved in the manufacture of 'every possible implement of modern warfare'. This report was shown to DMI Home Forces who did not have any objection to this information being handed over, but expressed his sympathy with the people of Swansea.

On the same day that Owens sent his message asking about the two agents he was expecting, a letter was sent to Gwilym Williams from a man identifying himself as Miguel Piernavieja del Pozo stating that he had just arrived in London from Spain. He claimed to have met a friend of Williams, by the name of Mr G. Kettering, who had wanted to pass on his regards and some news. However, he explained he was having trouble getting to Swansea and so was eager to meet Williams at his London flat. The bona fides of Mr Kettering were checked in the nightly message to the Abwehr, which confirmed that 'Man with password Kettering is OK. Is man of Captain for propaganda and sabotage.'

Williams then travelled up to London from Wales by rail and was met at Paddington Station by BISCUIT who took him to the Bachelors' Club with instructions to make sure that they were not being followed. At the club they went through Williams' story, and he was then sent to meet the Spaniard at the planned 5.50 p.m. rendezvous.

Williams went to room 117 at Athenaeum Court, 116 Piccadilly, where he was met by the Spaniard who was keen to check his identity and proceeded to quiz him about his age and occupation. It was when Williams mentioned the Welsh Nationalist Party that the Spaniard seemed to accept him as genuine. The Spaniard then produced a tin of talcum powder which he gave to Williams saying 'it is full of pounds for you' and advised that as the money had come from abroad, all the serial numbers were likely to be known to the authorities, and it would therefore need to be laundered.

The Spaniard explained that his mission was to send reports back to Madrid, so he wanted to learn about the Welsh Nationalist Party and places in Wales and England where weapons and aircraft were manufactured. Williams was asked to find someone reliable in London who he was to bring with him to the Spaniard's flat. This man's role would be to deliver Williams' reports from Wales to the Spaniard in London so he could send the information back to Madrid. Williams then asked about the visitors he was expecting in South Wales but, much to Williams' surprise, the Spaniard seemed to know nothing about them, saying that he was connected with the Spanish embassy and that he was leaving for Glasgow that night on diplomatic business. Accordingly, MI5 arranged for the Glasgow police to keep del Pozo under surveillance. Williams described him as being aged between twenty-eight and thirty years old, about five foot eight with a sallow complexion, slim, with a small black moustache. He had black hair, dressed in dark clothes and was described by Williams as being obviously Spanish.

After the meeting Williams was eager to open the tin of talcum powder, but waited to meet his MI5 handler before doing so. He had been told that he was to keep £200, which would be used to pay for the Spaniard's expenses, and the tin was found to contain £3,900. Although Williams was unaware of this, he was unwilling to part with the tin, complaining about the way that he had been treated concerning his own expenses, and even went so far as to say that he was no longer willing to work for MI5. Williams was eventually pacified when it was agreed that the matter would be looked into but as a result of this episode another MI5 officer, John Marriott, described him as 'an opinionated mercenary Welshman and needs to be thoroughly frightened. I think he is a dangerous man, potentially, as he is no fool.'

Owens' interest always increased when money was involved and he claimed to have been told that Williams should not be allowed to handle large sums of money, suggesting that MI5 should tell the Abwehr that Biscuit had handed the money in the talcum powder tin to him, with only a small amount having been given to Williams. However, Owens had recently been noticed using the telephone in his house while Burton's back was turned and, ever wary of Owens' activities, MI5 decided that when he moved into his new house microphones would be installed. Burton reported that 'after a long period of quiescence, Snow appeared to be feeling his oats again' and should be watched very carefully.

The double-cross system got underway in the person of Arthur Owens and it had grown with British-based agents like G.W., Charlie and Biscuit. Now, with the arrival of Summer and Tate, there was the possibility of controlling further agents who either had been, or were to be, despatched by the Abwehr. However, a German invasion was expected at almost any moment, so time and information were at a premium. With its growing stable of double agents, MI5 hoped that the imminent arrival of agents for Swansea and Manchester would improve the volume and accuracy of information obtained from the enemy, especially if they could be turned. However, despite the elaborate preparations that had been made for the new arrivals, none materialised although, according to Snow's wireless traffic, a South African agent, whom Biscuit had been told about, was dropped at some point during the last week of August and the man for Manchester was dropped on the night of 15 August.

What had happened to these two spies? MI5 considered it possible that they had come down in the sea or that some other disaster had befallen them. It was also thought that three Cubans, named Robles, Martinez and

Hechevarria, who had arrived in Fishguard carrying sabotage equipment, were the agents intended for Swansea. The Spaniard del Pozo, who had contacted G.W., was also a candidate as he used the password that the Swansea agent was supposed to mention. All MI5 could do was wait and hope that the Germans had not become suspicious, and that the network of double agents in Britain could start to reap the rewards of all their hard work.

Whilst the slow pace of developments was very frustrating for MI5, the next major development in the Snow case would come from a completely different source, would leave the entire double-cross system teetering on the brink of catastrophe – and have disastrous consequences for Owens himself.

Chapter V

CELERY

IN NOVEMBER 1940 Walter Dicketts, a former First World War air intelligence officer who had been cashiered from the RAF for dishonesty, was sent on a mission to an aerodrome near Grantham to collect information for SNOW.

MI5 was surprised at the ease with which he managed to retrieve a considerable amount of information and that he seemed to have no difficulty gaining access to the establishment. He entered the aerodrome by buying a works badge and was able to learn a good deal of useful information. He did this by engaging people in casual conversation and was surprised that even though he told them he had a Swedish mother, they were still willing to tell him all manner of things. In all he spent three hours walking around the facility, including visits to the secretary's office and the drawing office, without once being challenged. He then walked around the airfield perimeter without being stopped and challenged, and gained a good deal of gossip with an intelligence value by visiting the local pubs in the Grantham area and talking to airmen he encountered.

Codenamed CELERY, Dicketts had been put in touch with Owens by MI5 to find out whether he was double-crossing his case officers. As far as Owens was concerned, Dicketts was a disgruntled MI5 agent whose contact with MI5 depended on Owens himself. However, as Dicketts came to know Owens, he developed the opinion that Owens was exceptionally artful, often attempting to check upon his new friend to establish what, if anything, lay behind the relationship. Dicketts gained the impression that Owens may have learned a great deal about him from sources within Special Branch, with whom he appeared to be very friendly. According to Dicketts, Owens drank very heavily, remarking that he saw 'bottles of whisky disappearing like magic'. He also claimed to have seen Owens pouring himself a drink as early as half past seven in the morning. Owens was also very free with his money, and at one point spent £1,500 on a fur coat for Lily. Dicketts also seemed to have little regard for Owens' wireless operator, Maurice Burton, whom he thought liked and trusted Owens rather too much. Dicketts reported that the two men were becoming close, often indulging in private conversations, and that they frequently visited the local pub together. Burton was also said to be involved with a girl, someone he claimed to have known for a long time, although he sometimes passed her off as a cover to obviate suspicion amongst the locals.

From MI5's viewpoint, Dicketts represented an opportunity to check up on Owens, and establish an independent channel of reporting on his activities, and indeed those closely associated with him, such as Maurice Burton, Lily and the others. His principal objective was to solve the continuing mystery of precisely where the Welshman's true loyalties lay. If he really was a reliable double agent, firmly in MI5's camp, then the intelligence rewards could be considerable, whereas any suggestion that he had switched sides and was collaborating with the Abwehr would put lives at risk, and the entire double-cross system in jeopardy.

Dicketts suspected that Owens had lines of communication with Germany outside MI5's ken, a view reinforced by his knowledge that Owens had been able to alert his son Robert about an imminent Luftwaffe air-raid on London. How could he have done so when there was nothing in his declared signal traffic to show the source of his warning? Dicketts had a very low opinion of Owens and told MI5 that he was 'an inveterate liar and lies even to his wife about everything. He is terrified of air raids and is bone idle.'

On 18 December 1940 Owens and Dicketts were sent to Manchester to see CHARLIE in the hope that the wireless agent or his replacement might still appear, but upon their arrival they found him in a very anxious state and Dicketts thought that CHARLIE's demeanour would be likely to give him away to the German spy if he ever turned up. Whether Owens had developed any suspicion that CHARLIE was really under MI5's control is unknown, but McCarthy's unfortunate visit to Manchester earlier that year was now to have further repercussions for the SNOW network because CHARLIE revealed that BISCUIT had informed him that Owens had sold him out to MI5. CHARLIE also said that he did not know who he was working for, and that he had been present when Burton had installed listening equipment at the Manchester address, and that he knew exactly how it worked. All this made Owens very suspicious of CHARLIE, and threatened the unity of the developing double-cross system. Once MI5 became aware of Owens' suspicions the decision was taken to tell CHARLIE to let Owens know the truth about his position, that he was in fact pro-British and had been contacted by MI5 and turned into a double agent before Owens had first gone to Manchester to meet him. This revelation must have come as a surprise to Owens, and perhaps created doubts in his mind about exactly how much control he actually exercised over his network. Combined with CELERY's appearance, Owens must have been aware that his role at the heart of the double-cross system was not quite what it once was, or indeed what he *thought* it was.

With Owens now apparently able to trust him, CHARLIE was instructed to take the wireless agent, when he arrived, to 20 Park Street and to keep him there until Owens could see him. CHARLIE was also directed that if he was asked any questions he should tell the man that he had been ordered not to discuss anything with him. This arrangement suited both Owens, as it put him back at the centre of the operation, and CHARLIE, whose nervous disposition would not enable him to withstand much cross-examination.

On 28 December 1940 Robertson wrote to the DMI, General Davidson, enquiring about high poles joined by wire in the fields between Aldington, Stowting, Lyminge, Hawkinge and Folkestone. He wanted to know about the materials used on these anti-glider obstacles, the distances between the poles, the gauge of wire, and how they were arranged. This need to canvass the armed services every time an item of information needed to be cleared before it could be conveyed to the enemy became an increasing burden for MI5, and the solution was the establishment of a permanent sub-committee of the Wireless Board, to process requests for permission to transmit authentic data. However, the Wireless Board, consisting of the three intelligence service directors, the Chief of MI6 and MI5's Director-General, was found to be established at too exalted a level to respond quickly to the increasing demands of MI5's double agents, so in December 1940 a new body, designated the XX Committee (for double-cross, but usually referred to as the 'Twenty Committee' after the Latin numerals XX) was created under J. C. Masterman's chairmanship. A respected Oxford don, fluent in German and exuding a natural authority, Masterman had not yet found his niche in the Security Service, but his appointment to run the XX Committee was an inspired one.

Representatives from the Air Ministry's intelligence branch, the Naval Intelligence Division, the DMI, Home Forces, MI5 and MI6 assembled for the first time in early January 1941 and thereafter met weekly to discuss the performance and needs of the growing stable of double agents operating under MI5's control. This excellent innovation offered a practical solution to give Robertson's team of case officers the support deemed essential if SNOW and his subordinates were to fully exploit their status.

* * *

At the beginning of 1941 Owens received a signal from the Abwehr instructing him to meet Dr Rantzau in Lisbon. Evidently the failure of the North Sea rendezvous had not deterred him from setting up a further meeting with his main agent in Britain in person. This development was important as Owens still believed that whoever accompanied him on this mission would be appointed his replacement, and that he would then take up his post in Berlin. This time, however, it was decided that it would be Dicketts, rather than BISCUIT, who would go with him. In order to travel, Dicketts would need a Portuguese transit visa and he suggested that the best way to acquire one would be to apply for an ordinary visa for Colombia, which he thought he could obtain from a friend, which would help him with the transit papers required for Portugal. As the plan called for a sea voyage, no exit permit was required, and Dicketts travelled to Newport, South Wales, to secure a berth. The arrangements for Owens' travel, including letters of introduction from the London Chamber of Commerce, were also left to Dicketts, but time was precious because Dicketts was due to travel in less than a fortnight by boat, with Owens flying to Lisbon soon after.

During this final period before their departure, Dicketts reported that Owens was 'running with the hare and hunting with the hounds' and warned Robertson that Owens was likely to question him about whether Dicketts was trustworthy, to which Robertson confirmed that he would most certainly reply in the affirmative.

Prior to SNOW's departure MI5 undertook some housekeeping to ensure his safety, and reviewed the Abwehr's traffic with SUMMER to determine precisely what the enemy knew of his circumstances. MI5 had attempted to keep the agents separate but a study of the messages suggested that the Germans must have known of the links between them, so it was agreed, with some reluctance, that SUMMER should be terminated.

> It is generally agreed that SUMMER must be eliminated. If this necessity is agreed it is essential that he should be finished off as quickly as possible, so that the other side may suppose that he has been executed before he could be induced

to disclose all the small details and traces falling within his knowledge. If this is done it ought to be fairly easy to retain their confidence in SNOW.

MI5's objective in promoting the mission to Lisbon concerned the planned German invasion of Britain and the acquisition of any information about German secret weapons, to which Hitler had taken to referring. Robertson asked Owens whether he thought he could persuade Rantzau to take Dicketts to Germany for training, saying that if he could, then he might be able to pick up a great deal of information. To assist in communications, Dicketts was to be given a plain language code which could be transmitted from Hamburg, with certain words having a pre-agreed secret meaning which would let the British know his progress. As for Dicketts himself, he asked for some kind of insurance letter, and Robertson assured him that if anything went wrong MI5 would take care of his wife and child.

As they prepared for their mission, Owens appeared to be having second thoughts and told Dicketts that if he decided not to go he would cable him and also send a message to Dr Rantzau. Owens also advised Dicketts that if the Doctor produced a message from Owens containing the word 'Dicky', that would indicate that he was authorised by Owens to work 'hand in glove with the Doctor.' The true meaning of the message was not entirely clear to Dicketts so he passed it on to MI5. But the organisation was equally puzzled by its ambiguity. Dicketts believed that Owens probably would not tell them its real meaning. And before anyone could get to the bottom of Owens' cryptic words he received a message from Germany that added further intrigue: 'Friend in England has secret material re infrared detector. Can you bring this to Lisbon? How can he be sent to you without knowing your identity?'

This reference to infra-red technology was remarkable, as the secret equipment, still in its infancy, was employed by the Admiralty to detect shipping and by the Air Ministry for tracing illicit infra-red beacons. There was also an infra-red telescope under development by EMI which was fitted to Defiant aircraft to assist in the identification of enemy night-fighters. MI5 suspected a leak, and as far as could be ascertained from the Admiralty, there was only one document which detailed the apparatus, and that had been compiled by the Royal Aircraft Establishment at Farnborough. Dr Hill, the scientist supervising the RAE's experiments, had been to Eindhoven before the war where he had discussed infra-red technology with the Philips company, which had its own system that, it was claimed, had only been offered to the Dutch navy. However, it was later learned that Philips had also been dealing with the Germans, and that the device did not work very well because the lenses were the wrong distance apart, a problem that had subsequently been rectified by EMI, thereby producing a much better infra-red telescope. Hill reported that if he saw the leaked document he might be able to identify its source, although the issue had been further complicated – the devices were now operational so there were plenty of potential sources of the leak.

This new and unexpected last-minute request from the Abwehr prompted Robertson to meet Owens and Dicketts at his club where they discussed the implications. Their objectives were first to 'keep the SNOW party going' and 'at all costs to identify the individual who had managed to obtain this information.' Robertson stressed that under no circumstances could information about infra-red, which was considered vital to the war effort, be passed on to the enemy, and he made two suggestions. One was that Owens should ask the Germans to tell their agent to deliver the information to a known address so it could be taken to Manchester and turned into micro-photographs. The second was that the Germans should instruct their source to send an intermediary to meet Owens or his nominee. Owens thought that as the information was so important to both Britain and Germany, it would be best if he attended the meeting himself, but before doing so he would confirm that the Germans had total trust in their source. Accordingly, following a conference attended by Guy Liddell, Dick White, Felix Cowgill and John Marriott, a message was sent to the Abwehr:

> Informed infra-red stunt vital importance and great hope here. Am afraid employ contact or use mail to get papers. If you trust your friend and he is safe, suggest he put material through letter-box at specified address at specified time when I can arrange to receive it. As time important for me prefer 9.15 tomorrow morning in time for material to be taken Manchester 10.15 train. Have phoned CHARLIE standing by.

On 28 January Dicketts met Robertson at his club to agree final arrangements for his mission to Lisbon, and he handed back all the documents that he had been given to memorise. During this encounter, Dicketts confessed that he had become convinced that Owens was mad and was double-crossing MI5.

The next day, Robertson met Sam McCarthy at his club, where he was asked to keep a sharp watch at his home at 14 Craven Hill, Bayswater, which had been designated as the drop-off point for the infra-red information. He was instructed to note any people who seemed interested in the address, but Robertson did not mention that he had also arranged for a man to be positioned in the house opposite with instructions to contact Robertson if anything suspicious happened.

Before his departure for Lisbon, it was agreed that Owens should see the reports written by Gwilym Williams for the Spanish journalist, Miguel Piernavieja del Pozo, now codenamed POGO. Williams, of course, was supposed to be one of JOHNNY's sub-agents, so Robertson gave Owens a summary of the case which, Owens thought, showed up the Germans' lack of professionalism. MI5 was keen to know whether POGO was linked to Rantzau's operation, and Owens suggested that when he met the Doctor he would complain about the Abwehr's practice of putting agents in touch with his men without previously warning him that they were coming. This, it was hoped, would draw the Doctor out on the subject and reveal whether he was aware of POGO's activities. Robertson told Owens to be prepared to discuss what had happened during the North Sea incident, and advised him that before he left Owens would be given the answers to the questionnaire that BISCUIT had brought back from his last mission to Lisbon.

Despite Owens' increasingly erratic behaviour, Robertson thought it unwise for him to run BISCUIT down as he had made a good impression on the Abwehr during his trip to Lisbon. Owens should also expect to discuss what had happened to SUMMER, who had disappeared. In reality, SUMMER had attempted to escape from his MI5 safe-house at Hinxton in Cambridgeshire, and then tried to take his own life, so he had been returned to Camp 020 for permanent isolation. However, Owens was instructed to tell the Doctor that SUMMER had taken his wireless to Cambridge railway station and deposited it at the luggage office. He was to say that the cloakroom ticket had been sent to Sam McCarthy who had been asked to collect the wireless. Owens was also to raise the issue of the agents destined for Manchester and Swansea, and was to point out that it had been very difficult to get hold of safe-houses, and that to keep them unoccupied for any length of time would arouse suspicion.

SNOW was due to fly to Lisbon on 14 February 1941, so on 8 February it was his turn to meet Robertson at his club. There Owens expressed a wish to be present at 14 Craven Hill when the infra-red documents were delivered. In mentioning this, Owens said, he was only quoting MI5's policy that, if he was expected to give Dr Rantzau a believable account of the meeting, he would need to be present. He also made great play of his ability to identify anyone who turned up to make the delivery, or even question the individual concerned. Robertson was uncertain and put Owens off for the moment. Another matter to be considered was the Abwehr's request that Owens should bring his identity card and ration book to Lisbon. Normally such documents were deposited with the port authorities on departure but, given what the Germans knew about Owens, it would be only natural that he would have several of these documents in different names, so if he did not bring them with him it might be difficult for him to explain.

The question whether Owens should be present at the Craven Hill safe-house for the drop of the stolen infra-red documents was a cause for much debate within MI5. Robertson felt Owens should not be present because the Germans originally had been very insistent that he should not reveal his identity. Their reasoning, he believed, was that they realised the danger of letting different cells within the organisation learn too much about each other in case one was compromised. The domino effect of exposure could be devastating, so in his response to the Abwehr's initial message, Owens had replied that the matter was of such importance that he should handle it personally, but Robertson thought it was an unnecessary risk to allow an unknown agent to gain a description of him. Contact between Owens and the agent might also have consequences for future MI5 operations for if the need ever arose to arrest the agent, there might be repercussions for Owens as it might reveal that he was working for MI5. In his deliberations, Robertson believed that it might be worth sacrificing McCarthy, but not Owens. Robertson thought that it was probably vanity that motivated Owens' wish to be involved, but concluded that if he decided to stay away the Germans would be less likely to become suspicious. In short, a safety-first attitude would be the most effective.

Robertson also deliberated over whether to arrest the mystery agent or leave him at liberty. He knew that if the agent was let run there would be no chance of compromising Owens, and that his status might even be enhanced. He also recognised that MI5 was already going to retrieve the stolen documents, so there was little to gain from holding the delivery-boy who may be nothing more than a minor agent. Allowing him to leave after the drop might offer the opportunity of following him and observing his movements over an extended period, a strategy which could lead to further gains. An arrest was irrevocable, and would end any possibility of future action. It was also possible to adapt the plan as it developed, if the agent was let run and kept under discreet observation. Furthermore, there was also the possibility that the agent would be followed to the drop, so any arrest would be likely to scare off the whole organisation, thus preventing MI5 from ever discovering how the infra-red documents had been stolen.

On the other side of the equation, Robertson acknowledged that the agent could be an important member of an enemy organisation and this might be the only chance to get hold of him. Following such an individual would be difficult, especially at night in London during the black-out. Even if the man was only a minor agent, an interrogation might be a quicker way of finding out about his organisation than following him for weeks. Robertson was also aware of the kudos that would be gained from an arrest of this kind which would be a much-needed boost for the double-cross system that had yet to prove its worth.

Robertson wanted to keep Owens onside before his trip to Lisbon and therefore gave serious consideration to his views. Owens had suggested McCarthy's address for the drop, and Robertson took this as a sign that Owens trusted McCarthy, and was less likely to run him down when he met Rantzau.

Robertson's conclusion was that an arrest would offer a small but certain gain, whereas letting the man run was essentially a gamble, so he was in favour of taking what they could get. He was aware that more experienced MI5 officers did not share his opinion, and an alternative plan had been proposed whereby they would follow the agent in the hope that he would lead the watchers to his base of operations, but that if this had not happened before darkness fell, he should be arrested. They knew that if the man was crafty enough to stay on the move until it was dark, then he was likely to be dangerous and might escape altogether, in which case they would move in and arrest him. This time-scale also gave MI5 the opportunity to read the documents and re-evaluate the advantages of arresting the man or letting him run.

After much deliberation it was decided that McCarthy should be the man present at the drop and he was instructed to ask the agent into the house, but not to press him if he appeared reluctant. He was to ask the agent if he wanted the plans back and, if so, how this was to be done. He was also to add that he was not very technical and ask whether there was any explanation that should be conveyed to make them more understandable. Owens wanted McCarthy to try to engage the agent in conversation and thereby establish his identity, and it was agreed that if anything went wrong at the drop Owens was to blame McCarthy when he reached Lisbon. However, Owens was warned not to denigrate McCarthy too much because it could backfire on him. The infra-red document drop was to take place at McCarthy's house on Owens' advice, and if the agent noticed that he was being followed and reported this back, then this would cast suspicion on McCarthy and, by association, have implications for Owens himself.

In the house opposite the drop MI5 installed a cine-camera fitted with a telephoto lens to capture images of whoever turned up, and placed a microphone to record the conversation. To assess the value of the documents quickly, J. C. Masterman spoke to the Director of Air Intelligence, Archie Boyle, to acquire the services of a boffin with the relevant technical expertise. Owens was due to leave for Lisbon with the documents on the afternoon of the drop, so a quick decision about the status and sensitivity of the material was essential.

Robertson was aware that Owens seemed to think that he could 'get away with most things with the Doctor' but MI5 wanted their agents' background stories to be as believable as possible, so Robertson arranged for Owens to lunch with Lieutenant Richardson, the personal assistant to the Vice Chief of the Imperial General Staff. Owens would then be able to tell Rantzau that Richardson was his source of information inside the War Office, and their meeting would enable Owens to learn about Richardson and offer Rantzau a coherent story.

At one o'clock on 2 February, Owens went to the Criterion Restaurant to lunch with Richardson, but the latter reported that they achieved nothing more than arranging that they would say they had met through the Expanded Metal Company before Owens started talking about himself. The only other thing Owens was interested in during the lunch was Richardson's address and telephone number, which he did not disclose, and whether Richardson was in a position to obtain information about anti-aircraft defences and troop positions. He had seemed very pleased when Richardson told him that he could probably get this sort of information, and he then invited the officer to dine with him and his family that same evening. Owens was living at Ottershaw in Surrey at the time, so he sent a 1934 Austin 12 to drive Richardson to the Anchor Hotel, Shepperton, where he was introduced to Lily and Walter Dicketts' wife Kaye. Owens was a regular at The Anchor and, according to Richardson, the fact that he and Dicketts were spies appeared to be general knowledge among the rest of the clientele.

During the meal they drank toasts to Owens and wished him luck on his trip to Lisbon. Owens told Richardson about his troubles with his first wife Jessie, and claimed that she had tried to betray him to the Germans. Richardson noticed that Owens had a peculiar habit with regard to his false teeth, noting 'he only wears his false teeth when he is eating and he has a sort of sleight of hand trick of slipping the dentures into his mouth under cover of a handkerchief before a meal.'

At the end of dinner Owens invited Richardson to meet him the next morning for a cocktail, but Richardson excused himself because he felt that he had done enough. It later emerged that Owens was not just travelling to Lisbon on MI5's behalf; Marika, The Anchor's barmaid, had given him a note to deliver to Coronel A. Pinho Ferreira, at 10 Rue Palmeira in Lisbon:

Cheri, Apres si longtemps une petit note de moi c'est d'introduire un tres bon ami de moi soyez gentile. Je t'aime comme toujours et après la guerre je retourne te voir et te baiser. A toi Marika.

Whether Owens understood the content of this vital note is not known.

On 13 February 1941 the cine-cameras were in place and microphones had been installed at 14 Craven Hill where Dicketts and a team of MI5 officers waited for the arrival of the enemy agent delivering the stolen infra-red documents. At 8.40 a.m. a man approached the house and, when he was directly opposite, took out his handkerchief, blew his nose and looked over his shoulder twice. He was wearing a dark overcoat, no hat and had a stiff white collar. He carried a canvas bag of the type used for large gas masks, but he left without approaching the house. When this same suspicious-looking individual was spotted the next morning at the same time, he was followed to Whiteley's department store in Queensway where, it was discovered, he was employed as a floor-walker.

On the following day Guy Liddell recorded a further incident in his diary, although the version declassified by MI5 remains heavily redacted:

There has been an interesting incident in the SNOW case. Last night a man giving his name as Robert Livingstone turned up [material removed] and asked for Mr Wilson. He gave as his address the Cumberland Hotel, London. Enquiry there shows a man of that name was there on the night of 12 February and he had come from Ayr, so enquiries are now being made in Ayr. We have not yet been able to ascertain whether SNOW knows this man.

[four lines deleted]

On the whole I am inclined to think that the infra-red man lost his nerve and knowing that SNOW was leaving Bristol this morning thought he would try and get in touch with him at the [material removed]. This may on the other hand have been a plot by the other side who suspected that there might be a trap in the project for a meeting place in London.

Eventually Owens was informed that no one had turned up at the rendez-vous and he became worried about the implications for his imminent trip to Lisbon, suggesting that a message should be sent that evening telling the Germans that he had waited for hours but nothing had happened, and this had made him extremely annoyed. Owens' anxiety gave him cold feet about the whole Lisbon mission, and he told MI5 that he would rather not go at all, but finally he agreed not to back out at this late stage. Some MI5 officers, mistrustful of Owens, believed that he knew that no one was going to turn up and as he was leaving for Bristol to catch his flight from Filton, John Marriott arrived saying that a message had been received from the Abwehr telling Owens not to worry, and that the drop would be rearranged on his return from Lisbon. On hearing this news the watchers were called off and Owens departed for Lisbon.

During his time in Portugal it was recognised that communications would be difficult but, on 22 February, MI5 received a message from Owens:

'Dicketts not arrived, worried, can you help.'

MI5 then contacted the Admiralty for news of Dicketts' ship, the *Cressada*, which had departed the previous week, and learned that it was due in Gibraltar that same day before making for Lisbon. Accordingly, MI5 arranged for Lily to send a cable to Owens informing him that all was well, and that Dicketts should be arriving shortly. The next day Lily received a cable from Owens telling her that he had found Dicketts in bad shape, but everything was now alright. MI5 told Lily to pass the message on to Dicketts' wife to put her mind at ease as she had been very worried that her husband might have to go to Germany. Robertson had told her that he could not say whether this would happen as it was a decision that would have to be made by Owens and Rantzau, but if he did go Robertson doubted that he would be detained for any length of time.

Meanwhile, on 9 March, MI5 received an enquiry from the Home Office regarding the Detention Order issued in May 1940 and still outstanding on Owens. MI5 replied that Owens was currently behaving himself and was even proving useful, adding that the order should remain in force. A few days later, on 16 March, MI5 made an arrangement with Owens that if he brought an enemy agent to their attention he would receive a bonus payment of £50.

On 23 March 1941 Felix Cowgill wrote to Robertson with what he described as 'disquieting news for you about SNOW', revealing that on his arrival in Lisbon Owens had been informed that the Germans had known for the past few months that his messages had been faked. Apparently Owens had not denied this but had told Rantzau that he had been found out by the British and had been forced to continue sending the messages. Rantzau, apparently accepting this explanation, had given him £10,000 and a new set of instructions. Owens had also told the MI6 representative in Lisbon that he had convinced Dicketts that he was really working for the Germans because he was concerned by Dicketts' eagerness to proceed to Germany. Owens was of the opinion that the reason the Germans had become suspicious of him was partly the ease with which he had been able to travel to Portugal, given the sate of the war, and also that McCarthy may have given information to the Germans during his visit to Lisbon which had cast doubt on where his true loyalties lay.

With Owens still in Portugal it was difficult to know exactly how much he had revealed to Rantzau, but MI5 was very conscious that the heart of the double-cross operation could be ripped out at any moment. SNOW was the system's central figure and was inextricably linked to every component part, including Dicketts, Williams, McCarthy, SUMMER and TATE. The Germans would also know that Richardson was not a genuine contact at the War Office. The identity of many MI5 officers may have been compromised, including Hinchley-Cooke, Robertson, Burton, Stopford, Marriott and many more. Robertson estimated that if MI5 lost SNOW only three double agents would be left (codenamed TRICYCLE, GIRAFFE and STORK). In effect, there would be very little left of the system and the Germans would surely now be extra careful about any agent working in Britain.

GIRAFFE was Georges Graf, a 22-year-old French soldier who had reached England in September 1940 after being recruited by the Abwehr in Lisbon. While he was considered a reliable channel to the enemy, he was reliant on corresponding with a cover-address in Portugal and therefore could not exchange urgent messages, nor be expected to travel. MI5's other most promising double agent case was TRICYCLE, who had arrived in London under MI6's sponsorship in December 1940 to recruit a network that would include BALLOON and GELATINE. As a Yugoslav lawyer, Dusko Popov was ostensibly employed by his government-in-exile, had the means to travel to meetings with his Abwehr controllers in Lisbon, but his fortunes would be dependent on his cover-story and the vagaries of émigré politics. Accordingly, SNOW's network continued to represent MI5's best window into the Abwehr, and the enemy's only full-time master spy in London.

Eventually Owens and Dicketts flew back to England by plane, and messages from Dicketts sent before his departure revealed that he had been taken to Germany. Initially, MI5's verdict of Owens' behaviour in Portugal was that he had acted with great intelligence, having been informed by the MI6 station in Portugal that it was sorry to see him go as he had been a useful ally. However, it was also remarked that Owens had been enjoying himself and that his position may have gone to his head.

MI5 arranged to have Owens and Dicketts undergo an ostensibly routine customs search upon their return, and Owens, who underwent the first inspection, claimed that he had been to Portugal to buy sardines, a story completely at odds with his original cover-story that he was a manufacturer's agent. He was asked why he did not have a consular endorsement on his passport, and when he could not give a satisfactory answer he was asked to produce all his documents and money. When they were inspected, Owens was told that they were unsatisfactory and that he would need to be searched. At this Owens asked to be allowed to have a word in private, which was when he disclosed that he was in fact working for Major Robertson of MI5, and suggested that he should be telephoned for confirmation. Owens could not understand why he had not been met at the airport, and revealed that CELERY was carrying important papers. It was then explained to Owens by the airport authorities that it was impossible to get in touch with Robertson immediately and so, in view of his curious behaviour, he would have to undergo a thorough search. Thereupon he was strip-searched and found to be carrying £10,000 in banknotes. His pockets contained two fountain pens in leather cases and Owens told the officers that the pens were in fact explosives and very dangerous. A search of his baggage revealed further explosive devices.

When Dicketts was searched he was very nervous and objected, but by the time the officers had completed their work Robertson's men had arrived to placate him. Dicketts claimed astonishment when he heard about the explosives found on Owens, and insisted he had no knowledge of them. He also asked that some information of an operational nature that he had acquired should be passed on to Robertson. He had learned that three 12,000-ton transports with troops would be leaving the Elbe on the morning of 28 March. The troops, he said, would then proceed to the Netherlands. Owens and Dicketts were then taken away to be questioned separately. Much would hang on the results of the interrogation, for this was MI5's opportunity to settle, once and for all, some of the mysteries of SNOW's true loyalties.

Evidently he and Dicketts had survived their prolonged encounter with the Abwehr in a neutral country, but what exactly had happened to them both while in the hands of the Germans over a period of weeks?

Chapter VI

Interrogation

O WENS WAS QUESTIONED on Friday 28 March 1941, and although he was not well at the time he seemed not to resent his treatment at the airport. The interrogation was led by T. A. Robertson in the presence of John Marriott and Miss I. E. Marsden who took down the conversation on a stenotype machine so an accurate record would be retained.

Robertson's interrogation of Owens provides a remarkable insight into the early days of the double-cross operations. Although these would ultimately prove to be among the most successful intelligence operations of all time, at this early stage those running them still had an enormous amount to learn. It is clear from the interrogation that Owens taught MI5 a great deal about how to handle the double-cross agents, many of whom would be just as tricky as Owens himself. What is also clear, and was to provide Robertson and the rest of his team with a good deal of confidence that the double-cross plans would work, was quite how desperate the Abwehr were to obtain intelligence on Britain, to the extent that they were prepared to trust virtually anyone. No one better demonstrated the Abwehr's naivety in their willingness to believe in agents who were ultimately completely unreliable than Owens.

Robertson's tactics were to ask as few questions as possible, and to let Owens tell them what had happened in his own words. As he began to explain,

'The whole thing was most mysterious. I walked right into it. I got into Cintra in the afternoon. We arrived there in the afternoon. Got a taxi into town and checked in at the Metropole Hotel. Some man paid my taxi fare. I don't know who he was.'

'You had no money?' asked Robertson.

'I had ten pounds, but what's the good of that there? Then I contacted the Hotel Duas Nacoes and left a message there and went back to the Metropole. In the evening I got a telephone call from Duarte [the name then was Guarty]

that I had to be outside the hotel at a quarter-past nine. Well the time had changed it's different over there anyhow. I waited an hour you see. Eventually he walked up to me and said "You're Mr Orrington. Will you come with me?" I said yes. So we walked along the street, got into a car. The Doctor was there. "Now" he said, "We've got a very important talk. It had better be done at once. You'd better come with me; we're going to take you opposite the main police station in Lisbon, where you will be well looked after, because the police are in our pay and you needn't worry."'

'Was he pleased to see you?' inquired Robertson.

'Yes, he was definitely pleased to see me,' replied Owens. 'We got there and went up into this place. It was the same place where BISCUIT went – where it is I don't know, because it was dark.'

'It was dark?' challenged Robertson. 'Was that the night after you arrived?'

'Yes, that was the same night. So he sat down, and he said "I've got something rather important to tell you. I want a truthful answer." I said, "Okay, you know me." He said, "We have information that you are in contact with the British Intelligence." I said "That's perfectly true. I've been trying for two and a half months to tell you that. I've sent a lot of stuff over the radio. I sent that SOS (which I didn't) but your operators were so lousy in Hamburg so you didn't get it." He said "How did you manage to get here?" "Well," I said "somebody gave me away in England and they walked in on me two and a half months ago, and they said "We know all about you. We've got two propositions, and if you help us we'll see you are okay – if you don't..." So I said – what else could I do? – I said I'd help them, because I wanted to get in contact with them. That's why I'm here today.'

'"Well" he said, "that's what we know. We know all about it. We've got the story, but we expect you to give the details, and we've outlined a plan of what we want you to do." That plan is this: the transmitter at home is still to be carried on. The messages sent through correct will go through ordinarily. Any fake messages I've got to – I've got in my book what's got to be put down with the messages, and they'll understand it's a fake message.'

'I understand,' said Robertson. 'In general you put down certain words in the message to show it is a fake message.'

'Yes. Now the next thing that's got to be done is I've got to get CELERY or another man over to the Channel Islands with instructions how to contact the military commander, he will then pick up another radio set which will be installed secretly in this country. At the same time the boat, I understand from CELERY that he has instructions to find that and to use it to get agents, explosives and any messages to England, until the radio is installed.

'Now the next thing, which I think is very, very important. I didn't know that CELERY wasn't in Lisbon at the time. I do know that he was in Lisbon a day before we met, and they know he was there. Immediately I met Celery, I said "I suppose you have just arrived." Well, I know now he had arrived the day before and had been out that night.'

'That would be a week or so after you arrived?'

'At least a week. There's no question about that.'

'You left on 14th February. That would be about 24th February approximately?'

'I think so. I think he's got his hotel receipt, and they can check up. As soon as I got hold of him I had a talk, and said "These people know all about it, and it is very very dangerous. I'm in a very dangerous position." I said, "What do you think about it?" He said, "I think it will work alright." I said, "You understand I'm one hundred percent for the Doctor?" and he said, "I'm with you, and with them one hundred percent." Right. Immediately he arrived in the hotel and checked in, I took him up to my room to give him a drink, because he was all in, and had a nasty trip. He hadn't been in the room more than an hour when a telephone call from Duarte came.

'Oh, the previous night the Doctor had waited over and had given up several important appointments in Berlin and Hamburg specially to meet Celery because he said he's an important man and I must meet him.

'After we had been in the room an hour this telephone call came through from Duarte and he said "Your friend's here. He arrived yesterday." Well, he said, "The Doctor decided to stay over to meet him and he's stayed on, as it's necessary to meet him." Well now, was it that evening – yes it was that evening. A meeting was arranged in another apartment in Lisbon with the Doctor and him. They went through all the details there, and he told them that he had been told that when he got back he was going to be given a staff appointment in the RAF and said he could be of tremendous use to them, and that he was to be decorated with the OBE. And God knows what. Then they went through all kinds of details about the different things – I wasn't listening, as I wasn't interested. Arrangements were made for Celery to go to Germany on the Friday.'

'Where did that suggestion come from?' asked Robertson. 'Did it come from you or did Celery put that up himself?'

'I don't know,' replied Owens.

'You didn't say anything to the Doctor about Celery going in?'

'No, in any case he'd have known off the radio messages. You remember that message that was sent.'

'You were all in the same room?'

'Yes.'

'What arrangements were made to go to Germany that evening?'

'I don't know. I know nothing about it, because they were talking together. Anyhow, later Dobel (Duarte) said to me, "You know how Celery is going?" I said, "I haven't the faintest idea." "We're having a special embassy car to pick

him up at 6 o'clock," he said "We've got a German passport for him, and he'll
be Dunkler or something, and we'll take him through to Madrid and he'll fly
from Madrid to Berlin." And he went to Berlin, and he had an apartment at the
Adler Hotel, which I've never had. He went to Hamburg, and he had the best
hotel there, and he was treated like a king. It was remarkable to me. I thought
it damn funny.'

'He told you all this after he came back?'

'Yes.'

It is not clear whether Owens was genuinely jealous of CELERY here or if he
was just trying to emphasise how well CELERY seemed to be getting on with
the Germans. On his return from Germany Dicketts had been accompanied by a man known only as George and he had told Owens how Walter
Dicketts had spent his time in Germany. When Owens had the chance to
speak about Dicketts, he did not take long before moving on to one of his
favourite topics, money.

'I said to this man CELERY,' continued Owens; "'You've had a marvellous time."
He said "Of course I've had a marvellous time. Why not?" I said "By the way,
did you get any money?" "I got £200," he said. "The other man got £450 and
he is to call on me for £5,000 for what he requires."'

'George was a German who was sent back from Hamburg with CELERY to
bring him back?' asked Robertson.

'Yes, they stayed in Madrid as far as I know, two days, then he came to Lisbon.
They had a special car to meet them at Madrid and bring them back. I went
up and I saw your man at the embassy and he told me that they had got information through one of the German agents, that a cable had been sent from
Madeira to this effect: That they wanted to get information regarding a ship
called *Cresado* because one of their best men was on it, who had given them a
lot of information. You see, this was CELERY who was a major in the Air Force.
They added that in the telegram. They told me themselves they know about
CELERY in Germany alright. They knew he was there.'

'Who knew he was there?' asked Robertson.

'The Doctor knew he had been in Germany before. Now when CELERY came
back to Lisbon he said "You're going to get a decoration." I said "What for?"
I said, "I don't need any decoration." He said that was the situation. "You're
going to get a decoration," he said, "and I get a staff appointment." I said, "I
don't want a decoration." Well, he said, "The point is this should be done. I'm
a hundred percent for the Doctor. Are you a hundred percent for the Doctor?"
I said "I am a hundred percent pro-Germany" and so did he. He's an extremely
dangerous man. Very dangerous; he's money mad and he takes dope.'

'Now, when did he come back to Lisbon?' asked Robertson. 'Do you remember that? How long was he away, in fact?'

'He was away about two or three weeks. He left on the Friday at six o'clock in the morning. I know it was Friday morning.'

'That was three or four days after your first meeting?'

'Yes, about three or four days after he arrived. He arrived approximately a week or ten days after me. So it must be the 28th February.'

'And he was in Berlin for a fortnight?'

'Well, Berlin and Hamburg and Stuttgart.'

'Then about the fourteenth of March he returned to Lisbon?' asked Robertson.

'Well, he was away two or three weeks,' replied Owens.

'Now, all this time you were in bed, were you?'

'Part of the time. My temperature was 104 and the doctor said I had to go to hospital. Nobody speaks English in Lisbon. Eventually I got a young lady to look after me, but I still felt like Hell, all the same. But the point is this, what I can't understand. He was supposed to have caught the Lisbon fever and couldn't do this and that. But he was out at night and asked me for 100 escudos and I knew he had a thousand escudos on him. He's had a lot of money for something, what it was for I don't know. He must have got it from other people. He didn't have much when he left. He had only about £10.'

Owens then claimed that Duarte had offered him the opportunity to go up into the mountains outside Madrid in order to recuperate, but Owens was more concerned with what was happening with CELERY and decided not to go.

'When CELERY arrived he said that he had been in company with Doctor Schacht's secretary and he'd been in touch with Goebbels' secretary and had given them dope on improving their propaganda over here, especially over the radio and that he'd had a proposition right from headquarters and that I've got to go with him to see Winston Churchill and get the war settled! He took some papers and got them sealed at the embassy in Lisbon. They wanted to see what the papers were and he wouldn't let them, as he said they were too secret. He said "We must go back immediately, even if it's a case of a special plane."

'He's got particulars about a new secret weapon which will finish the war in two days, if it's used. He has certainly been places in Germany. I'm absolutely positive he's got into places I've never been asked to go and never saw. I have an extraordinarily good standing over there, as you know, but I've never had treatment like that and it's most extraordinary to me, that a man like CELERY who comes straight from the blue has no hesitation at going into Germany. I should never have gone. But there was absolutely no hesitation. The man's a double-crosser and he cannot be relied on. Take it from me, he's working for Germany.'

Owens and Dicketts had plenty of time to discuss what they were going to say to MI5 on their return to Britain but from what Owens was saying about Dicketts they do not appear to have put together a story that showed them both in a particularly good light, or if they did then at this first interrogation Owens was not sticking to it. MI5 had not heard Dicketts' side of the story yet and there is the possibility that Owens was getting his side of the story in first. During the interrogation Owens made it clear that he felt it was important that Dicketts should not know his side of the story. In particular he was keen that Dicketts shouldn't know about the explosives that were discovered on him when he came through customs.

'He must know nothing about that,' continued Owens, 'because it's better he doesn't know anything about it. That came from the other side of the organisation, run in Lisbon by a man called Don Rigo. I had two very long meetings in Estoril in extremely large places, and I gave all the dope to your man in Lisbon and he is checking up on that.'

'I would like to have that dope now, so that we can have your story on it,' said Robertson.

'There's another thing, very, very important. Sunday, the twenty-third of March CELERY said to me, "I'm going to Estoril today. I've got an appointment with Doctor Rosso." Doctor Rosso, as far as I know is one of the German Admirals in the last war, a very important man in the diplomatic service in Lisbon. He said he'd like to see you and I said "Okay. I'll come up with you." And we went up there and had a drink with him and he said "There's lots of things I want to talk over with CELERY and I have some special packages for CELERY here, sealed by the German diplomatic staff, to hand over to him tonight."'

Owens did not seem too keen to explain the explosives he brought back with him but appears to be more concerned to deflect attention onto packages that Dicketts had been given. After several more diversions into episodes concerning an American who was bringing papers into Lisbon via Bermuda, Owens finally returned to Duarte and the subject of the explosives.

'I was supposed to get tablets of a new secret ink, which I haven't got. But he gave me a flashlight which contains time clocks. That is an explosive. You fit a detonator and I've a lot of them in soap. You fit it on and you set this time clock. The detonator explodes and the whole factory goes up. Or you can stick it in a stick of dynamite and destroy reservoirs and so on. He also brought me another set of pen and pencil. They are perfectly harmless. You do certain things with them and – up she goes!'

Whenever possible during the interrogation Owens returned to how well Dicketts seemed to be in with the Germans, and to his belief that he was working for them and not the British. However, within Owens' attack on Dicketts was new information about the structure of the German command system and the position held by Rantzau.

'He showed me nothing except Polish propaganda and anti Winston Churchill propaganda. That's all I know about it, but he's got something extremely important from Goebbels. He told me about the Doctor and he said the Doctor's best friend and the only one he has to look to is Göring. I said "I did not know that, did he tell him that." "Well," he said, "I know it." I said, "I didn't know he was such a big nut." "Yes," he said, "the only man he has to account to is Göring." "Well," I said, "That's nice for me. The only man I'm responsible to is the Doctor."
    'Anyhow I got £5,000 out of them and an extra £5,000 for my loyalty. Actually it's more than that, because I had very heavy expenses in Lisbon, approximately £10,000. CELERY is a most expensive man. He said I had to go out and buy gold watches and bracelets for him and for me and for his wife and for my wife.'
    'And you went out and bought them did you?' asked Robertson.
    'Of course, to keep him in a good frame of mind.'
    'What is your feeling towards him at the moment?'
    'That man is a double-crosser, an extremely dangerous man and what's more, whoever's got the most money he'll work for him. I had a long talk with your man then and asked him what he thought about it and he said "To be perfectly candid, I don't think we'll see that man again" and I said "I think you're right." "Well" he said, "That man's very anxious to get out of the country and he's going to stay where he is." I said, "I've enquired from Duarte for four or five days now for reports from the Doctor regarding CELERY and there's no reply." He said "I'll see about that and if there's any danger we'll get you out at once." But neither of us thought that man would ever come back again, but he's come back and with something important.
    'I said to Duarte: "Don't you think I ought to go back?" and he said: "No, wait here till the time is ready, because there's something going on." And it's definitely what CELERY has got. All I know is what he's told me. It's something that's going to blow the whole works, in his words.'
    'On that point, you think he's playing straight?' asked Robertson.
    'Of course he isn't playing straight, because the first time I met him he was a hundred percent for Germany, and when he came back he was more. He

said "there's not the slightest chance for England." He'd been in shipyards, aerodromes, aeroplane factories and so on and I'm positive no man I sent over myself to them could do that. I couldn't do it myself. Why should a perfect stranger be treated like that? Have a two room suite in Madrid? It doesn't sound right to me.'

Robertson then asked Owens how he could confirm what he was saying, to which Owens replied that George could confirm it, adding that George was coming to London. Robertson then went back over some of the information that Owens had given him, starting with the initial meeting at the Metropole. Owens' answers were consistent, but this time he added some new information about Sam McCarthy whom he suspected of being the Germans' source for the information that Owens was working for MI5.

> 'Duarte said to me "We were always suspicious of BISCUIT and he has written to us two letters in secret ink. The last one in January." Whether it was him I don't know, but somebody has blown the works. Then the Doctor said he had information that I was in contact with the British Intelligence. I don't think he'd known it more than a week or ten days, by the way he spoke. It was evidently something new and I'm sure he didn't know it long. In my opinion, by the way he spoke, not longer than ten days at the outside.'

The problem for MI5 was that it had been let down by one of the double agents, but which one? The organisation was wholly reliant on extracting the truth from SNOW, BISCUIT or CELERY. The stakes were high for both the service and its agents. For MI5, the entire double-cross system was at risk, and if the agents were found guilty of an offence under the Treachery Act they could expect a long period in prison or even execution. For Rantzau and the Germans, the dilemma produced similar consequences. Failure was not tolerated in the Third Reich, but according to Owens the Doctor had taken the news that JOHNNY was now working for the British quite well.

> 'He was very pleased at that attitude and said "We can manage to manipulate that, because we've also had a man at the Army Headquarters. It's very interesting and rather important to know that we've got our own man on the inside, working and they don't know it."
> 'British Headquarters. I don't know whether in France, but I think, from the way he spoke, that it was. It's far too dangerous to ask details about that. Then we talked about how Lily was and I took photographs out and showed them and he said his wife wanted to be remembered to me.'

Owens reported that he and Rantzau then indulged in some general conversation before returning to the subject of fake radio messages.

'How did he put that question to you,' asked Robertson, 'that they knew your messages were fake?'

'He didn't know they were fake. He asked me about the radio messages and I said they were perfectly above board. He said: "When we get the new radio, then you can use your men in South Wales to get the dope for the messages on the new transmitter." I told him that everything that came through was true and I was sure about that, because everything had been checked up.'

'Do you think it is possible he said this to you in order to catch you out?'

'No, not at all,' replied Owens. 'I'm absolutely positive he had direct information and somebody had given it away. It was in the fact that I've known him so long and that there's been no fake messages gone through, that the works haven't gone up.'

Robertson then asked Owens about the second meeting he had with Rantzau. Once again Owens took this as an opportunity to portray Dicketts in a bad light and to show himself as taking the moral high ground.

'Now, this second meeting with the Doctor,' asked Robertson. 'You were building up CELERY and handing certain dope?'

'I had nothing to hand over much because I said I had given it to CELERY. CELERY said to me "I am going to spill it" but I said "I want you to do one thing; that is not to tell these people about the route of the convoys that you've got. For the sake of those poor devils on those boats, don't do it." That's all I told him. He had all the routes but I don't know where he got them. He told me he had them, but I never saw them.'

Another area of interest that had emerged from the interrogation was the use of the Channel Islands as a route through which the Germans could get their agents into Britain. For Rantzau it was an alternative to dropping men in by parachute that was not proving very successful.

'He said "I am very interested in that, because we've lost many men by parachute." I told him about his man who broke his ankle. "Well," he said "We're very dissatisfied with the way these men have gone and we want to open up some kind of contact where they can get across in safety. We can't go on losing men like this." He asked about the infra-red man and I said I thought he must have come down in a canal or the sea.'

'Did he say anything about SUMMER?' asked Robertson.

'Yes he asked me about him and I said "As far as I know, he's beat it. He was very suspicious and I think a lot of enquiries have been made and he got wise in time and beat it." And he said "He's got seaman's papers and I expect we will see him again."

'He wasn't sure about Biscuit because he said "I don't like the man, although he's done good work for us in Lisbon." He said he was very, very surprised he was able to take that radio. And he was getting so drunk here, he said that he shouldn't do that in Lisbon. He made himself ridiculous, throwing away money. Anyhow, I thought, as you had sent him out here that he was a pretty smart fellow, and you could help him over the other side.'

The other agent that Robertson was keen to find out about was Williams' contact Del Pozo, who was also known as the Spaniard, but Owens did not know anything about him so Robertson moved on to Charlie.

'Did he mention Charlie at all?'

'He asked me about him. He said "Do you think Charlie is alright?" I said "I don't know." He said "If you think it's Charlie we've got his family in Germany." They rather cross examined me on who I thought has spilt the beans.'

'But the Doctor must have known who spilt the beans. Why do you think he asked you?'

'I think he wanted to know who I thought was the double-crosser, because he was a little bit afraid about Biscuit. He doesn't like Biscuit definitely. He's finished with Biscuit. Duarte likes him a lot and Duarte's girlfriend likes him a lot too. I met her. She's connected with the International Police in Lisbon and she gives him all the dope through the police.

'It certainly wasn't a leg-pull. He had direct and positive information and I know the Doctor well. He said if I wanted it here's £50 and I could go back. I said "I've all the faith in the world in you, but the information has got out somewhere and from somebody and I feel quite sure it's within the last ten days."'

One piece of information that came out of the interrogation was that the Germans had been experimenting with British gas masks which were left behind at Dunkirk and this was a clue to the nature of the German secret weapon which might have taken the form of a new type of gas. Whilst he was in Portugal the Doctor told Owens that they knew that the British had a radio station at Estoril. Rantzau even showed Owens MI5 messages that had been decoded.

Owens then told Robertson the words that were to be used to indicate that messages were fake. In general these were American slang such as 'This dope is on the level.' Or 'All this stuff is on the up and up.' Or 'This is some line.' Rantzau told Owens not to worry if they said that the information he was giving them was no good as this was only camouflage.

To understand how much of the double-cross system had been compromised Robertson needed to know what names Owens might have mentioned to Rantzau.

'Did he mention any other names, such as Hinchley-Cooke, or Marriott?' asked Robertson.

'No.'

'You didn't volunteer any other names?' pressed Robertson.

'No. Well, I don't know any. I told you I talked to CELERY and he turned over the other side at once. It wasn't just to trap me. He was absolutely genuine and when he went over he went with no hesitation at all. He went over there and when he came back he was one hundred percent full of it. He said: "The game's hopeless." What's more, he said "I'm just going to start things moving and meet Churchill," and he said unless they could get him away, there'd be trouble and he came back and said he had to make arrangements for us to go away and that if necessary they would charter a special plane for us. What he has on him I don't know. All I've seen is the propaganda on Poland and another of those Winston Churchill snaps. Outside of that I don't know; he has told me nothing at all.'

'What happened to the man for Manchester and the people for South Wales?'

'I didn't bring up the question of the people for South Wales and the man for Manchester was sent over. How he came I don't know.'

'You told him he hadn't turned up?'

'The Doctor said "I don't understand. We've sent a lot of men over and nothing's happened. They've gone wrong. There's something wrong somewhere." I said "I don't know. I just hand your instructions on and not only have I tried to find out for myself, but my men too. I know," I said, "about the man who came down near Newbury, who broke his ankle and who shot off his revolver for help." As for the South African he says he thinks the same thing happened, that he came down in a canal and sank because of the radio on him.'

'What are your instructions for collecting information at the moment?'

'Do nothing, as a matter of fact, till I've got the new radio.'

'It's quite clear they're not paying much attention to the radio information.'

'I think they are. They were very pleased with a lot of stuff that went over, which was quite genuine. They were very pleased with it. I said "That's genuine" and they said "Yes, that's very good stuff indeed" and they congratulated me and they said they know that one day the stuff will be doped and they are all the instructions we want you to follow.'

Owens seems to be suggesting that everything could carry on as before. As long as the Germans still trusted him and he included some fake information with the key phrases from time to time then MI5 could continue as before. What MI5 had to work out was whether Owens could still be trusted. This all hinged on whether he was telling the truth about what happened in Lisbon with implications for the double-cross system, for all the information that Owens brought back with him – and for the outcome of the war.

'Have you got any instructions what you're to do in an invasion?'

'The main attack is coming from Gravesend South. They are going to come in after the twenty-first of this month. As far as CELERY knows, the invasion may take place in England. His own personal opinion is that he doesn't think they will attempt an invasion yet.

'I have had no instructions about what to do in the event of an invasion, none at all. I will get them on the radio. CELERY says we've got to go back in a month. I've had quite enough this time without going back in a week or a month. CELERY said "I have it all arranged, that you get a telegram and we get the women out. That will satisfy you won't it." So what he's got I can't tell you. By the way he talks he's been sleeping with Hitler and he's been talking in his sleep.'

Owens claimed to have talked to the MI5 representative in Lisbon and that he had laid a sort of trap for CELERY.

'During the conversation I said "I'll soon find out. If CELERY isn't double-crossing us he will tell the Major when he gets back that I'm one hundred percent for Germany and trying to buy him. If not, if he doesn't say a word about it, I know definitely that he's working for Germany and that's quite true."'

'In fact, if CELERY is working for us, he will faithfully report to us everything that SNOW said to him. If therefore, he conceals anything SNOW had said to him and in particular the fact that SNOW is working for the Germans and one hundred percent for the Doctor, then he himself CELERY must be working one hundred percent for the Germans. That is it?'

'Yes,' agreed Owens.

'What do the Germans think is your personal position now?'

'Quite free now, because I'm working for you.'

'What did they think was your personal position for the two and a half months between the time you were discovered and the time you went to Lisbon?'

'I told him that I couldn't do anything nor go anywhere, because I was watched. That's why I had no information to give them and that CELERY had got it all.'

'Do they think that CELERY had got it all, or that he was watched during that period?'

'They don't think he was watched, I don't think. That was the impression he gave me.'

'They knew that CELERY was living with you?'

'Definitely.'

'But if you were being watched, CELERY must have been watched, if he was living with you.'

'I didn't have that impression at all. Not a bit. He was in Bristol and had all the dope. And I told the Doctor he had all this dope at Bristol and that I couldn't tell him anything about it. That I was unable to leave the place.'

'The doctor knows that CELERY was working for us?'

'Yes, and that he's changed since he arrived in Lisbon. Whether that impression is true or not I don't know. I think there's another answer to the question. About the situation regarding the telegram; how can you account for that? That was sent before CELERY arrived.'

'It doesn't follow that that telegram referred to CELERY.'

'Of course it did. Who else could be on that boat and a major in the RAF? And that cable was sent before he arrived?'

This was Owens' strongest charge against Dicketts but it only made MI5's task more difficult. If Owens was telling the truth and was genuinely working for the British then it offered the possibility of carrying on as they did before. If the Germans trusted Owens then the worst that could happen was a kind of stalemate where both sides would not know whether to trust the information they received, but MI5's role was counter-espionage and as such this was a position which might have been acceptable. For Owens it would mean that he would still receive the money which allowed him to live in the manner to which he had become accustomed. However if Owens was working for Germany and had been all along then he would naturally try to destroy CELERY if he was really working for the British cause. In order to try to unravel what had really gone on in Lisbon and discover the true status of the double-cross system, Robertson set about finding out what Owens thought was the position of the other agents in his circle such as Gwilym Williams and the many fictitious agents that Owens had invented. Robertson knew that if Owens was operating under German control then he should have a logical and pre-rehearsed story.

'Well now,' continued Robertson, 'let's deal with the people who are working for you and what their present position is.'

'All I've got, according to what they know over there, is two men and a woman, outside of Williams. These are two men who worked on sabotage and nothing else.'

'Do you think they know we know about them?'

'No, no, definitely not.'

'Why do you think that?'

'Because I told the Doctor they were working on an entirely different section, only sabotage, no information. They only do sabotage unless anything important turns up.'

'But Williams' name appears in your wireless traffic which we know about.'

'But they're not suspicious of Williams. I don't know why.'

'But if we know all about you, we must know about Williams.'

'They'll probably go through it, when he gets back but at the time he was not suspicious about Williams. In any case, the word Williams in Wales is very common.'

'Quite, but then you say in your wireless traffic "Williams can go" it can be the only Williams they know. You know, they must have known about Williams.'

'Well, he wasn't suspicious about him. Not the slightest.'

'But does the Doctor think that you persuaded us that you are working one hundred percent for us?'

'Well, I told the Doctor, I said, "The situation's this: they walked in on me and told me. I had to work for them one hundred percent or... And I said I wanted to work for them, because I had to get in touch with you again. And that's why I am here now, because I wanted to talk to you."'

'Therefore we should allow you and Williams and the rest complete freedom.'

'Definitely, because you trust me.'

'As, of course, you are still working one hundred percent for the Doctor.'

'Quite, quite.'

'We are not, therefore watching Williams.'

'You are not watching anybody, connected with me, because I'm working one hundred percent for you.'

'And they are all therefore quite free to carry on activity about which we know nothing, simultaneously with activities which we know about?'

'That's what the secret transmitter's for. It's to transmit information gathered during the time that you think we are working one hundred percent for you. And one of my men from South Wales will go over and get it.'

'But we will know about it?'

'How?' asked Owens. 'You'll not be in touch with my men in South Wales. Anyhow, I can get in touch with one of them. They'll then hire a boat, go to the Channel Islands, following the instructions, come back and nobody's any the wiser, because they have been having a holiday.'

Owens had not got on well with Sam McCarthy since the failed North Sea trawler mission and his threats to kill Owens and his family. Before his flight to Lisbon Owens had been warned not to run BISCUIT down because it could backfire on him. As far as he was concerned Owens had of course recruited him in the first place and trusted him enough to use his house as the location for the aborted infra-red document drop. However now that he was back from the mission and he had been exposed as working for MI5 he seemed to believe that these restrictions no longer applied.

'Well now, BISCUIT,' announced Robertson.
'Wash BISCUIT out altogether, because his name is mud with the Doctor. He thinks he is a complete madman.'
'But so far as we are concerned, BISCUIT is an essential part of your organisation. The organisation which we know about. Therefore BISCUIT must go on doing all the things he should be doing.'
'Quite, quite. But as regards the Doctor, he is a wash-out.'
'So BISCUIT's position in your organisation only differs from the other people because the Doctor doesn't like BISCUIT. If the Doctor liked him it would have been alright?'
'Yes.'

The interrogation ended with Owens giving physical descriptions of everyone he had encountered in Lisbon – including the Doctor whom he described as being aged about forty-five or forty-six, and around six foot tall, fairly well-built with broad shoulders, a finely-built man of military bearing. His eyes were blue and he had hair that was lighter than average and was parted on the left. He had a round, full face with a strong chin although Owens added 'not battleship.' He was clean-shaven with a fresh complexion and a slight cleft in his chin. One characteristic Owens noted was that 'he leans back in his chair in an expansive way.' He spoke English well with an American accent, wore horn-rimmed glasses, a belt and a wrist watch. One difference that Owens noticed from his previous meetings with the Doctor was that he no longer seemed to have a gold tooth.

Robertson's conclusion about the interrogation session was that Owens had been very forthcoming but that there were times when he had been holding things back. Robertson considered that Owens' story did not give a coherent version of what had transpired in Lisbon but that this initial statement of events could be used in further interrogation sessions with Owens when they would need to go through his story point by point. During a break in the interrogation Marriott had an unrecorded conversation with Owens and had two points to add to Robertson's assessment. First, he felt that Owens was extremely jealous of the way that Dicketts had been treated during his time in Germany, which Marriott thought coloured everything that Owens said. Secondly, Marriott got the impression that Owens now believed that Britain would win the war and this would obviously have an effect as to which side he wanted to be seen to be supporting. Marriott thought that these factors combined into a psychological soft spot in Owens, character which could be exploited in future interrogation sessions.

Owens had claimed that the reason that Rantzau had become suspicious about him was because it had been too easy for him to gain passage on an aeroplane. Liddell thought that Owens had perfectly good commercial reasons for travelling. Liddell had also received a message from Owens saying that he wanted his wife and child to join him in Lisbon. Liddell recorded in his diary that Owens may have lost his nerve and that the SNOW case 'was bound to come to an end sooner or later.'

The plan was to question Owens again in three days' time but on the same day this was due to happen MI5 received a message that del Pozo the Spanish Falangist had escaped from his penal settlement and was now hiding in the German embassy where he was probably telling all.

***

Robertson's mood was very different at the second interrogation session when he was not going to let Owens avoid his questions by rambling from one topic to the next and in order to achieve this, his approach was much more aggressive. Robertson wanted to discuss the various meetings that Owens had with the Doctor separately and in minute detail because he found some of Owens' story very hard to believe. He assumed that the German Secret Service would be as rigorous as MI5 in their approach and what he had heard about the Doctor from Owens so far displayed nothing of the kind. Initially the interrogation took much the form of the first session but soon things became much more difficult for Owens when Robertson read back Owens' statement concerning the moment when the Doctor confronted him with the fact that he was working for British Intelligence.

'Well' said Owens, 'we sat down and the Doctor said to me, "I've got something very interesting to tell you and I want a truthful reply." I said "Okay, shoot." He

said "I've got information that you are in contact with the British Intelligence."
I said: "That's perfectly true. I've been trying for over two and a half months to
get over to see you about it."

'Didn't it come as rather a shock to you? Did you hesitate when the Doctor
sprang that remark on you?'

'Not at all,' replied Owens.

'... supposing you'd said to him that you were not in touch with the Intelligence?'

'I didn't know what he knew.'

'But you could have bluffed that out, couldn't you?'

'I doubt it. He never makes statements unless they're correct. With me anyhow.'

'But it might have been your old association with us.'

'Well, I didn't know, I didn't have time to think.'

'That would have been the easiest explanation.'

'I might have been able to bluff it out that way, but I didn't know what he knew,
or what he knows even now. I took the easiest way out and to my mind that was
the easiest way out. In any case he knew I came over priority.' Here Owens was
referring to the fact that he was given priority passage on his flight to Lisbon.

Owens then tried to introduce CELERY into his testimony but Robertson
was having none of it, the tension mounting between the two men.

'CELERY doesn't come into this,' insisted Robertson. 'I want to have from you
an absolute truthful account of the whole thing.'

'I didn't understand you Major. Do you think I'm trying to double-cross you?'

'It wouldn't surprise me.'

'Why? What for? Why would I want to double-cross you?'

Having upped the tension Robertson now wanted to use the situation to
let Owens know that he was determined to get to the truth. 'Never mind. I
want an absolutely correct statement.

Having taken a hard line Robertson now softened his approach in order
to emphasise that he needed to get coherent answers. 'You've done some very
good work and I've told you so, but I want an absolutely truthful answer to
every question I ask you. I have put a tremendous amount of trust in you.
You have always been a little mysterious and I want to clear this question up
and this is the time to do it.'

'I'm quite prepared to give all the help I can.'

'You've got to remember that everything you say is being taken down and that everything that CELERY says is being taken down and these two statements are being compared very carefully; whichever of you makes a mistake will be questioned very, very carefully. We're not going to stop at anything to get to the bottom of this.'

'I've told you everything I know.'

'I've been prepared to believe that.'

'It's perfectly true and I'm not fooling you for one second.'

'Now then, I want to go back again to the first meeting. Unless you were absolutely drink sodden at the time, which I very much doubt, you should have a pretty clear memory of what you said and what they said, because a question of that description being shot at you like that which is going to upset the cart, as far as you are concerned and threaten your life and livelihood – it's going to stick in your mind.'

'Not only that. CELERY's life was at stake too.'

'Yes we'll come to that in a minute. I want your side first. When did he give you the code?'

'I think it was the next morning, as far as I remember.'

'Now, you don't mean to tell me that he made up his mind to give you a new code before he got from you an absolutely full story of what happened when we walked in?'

'Quite so. It was after about two or three hours at the meeting the next day.'

'Presumably before you got the code you'd given him the full details of your work?'

'I told him that, definitely.'

'The full details?' pressed Robertson.

'Well, the general details. He had no full details. I told him you walked in on me and I said "What could I do? I had no choice and that was all I could do because I wanted to get in touch with you."'

'That's what you told him? Was he content to accept only that?'

'He said to me: "If I didn't know you as well as I do and worked with you so long, I would never trust you as far as I could see you, but I know that when you tell me things like that, I know you're speaking the truth."'

'This question of the British intelligence walking in on you. You must have gone into that in very great detail. I insist upon having it.'

'Yes, he asked me all about it. I said that you'd walked in on me.'

'What did he say?'

'He said "Who," I said "men from the British intelligence. They went through everything I had."'

'Did he ask how many?'

'No, he didn't.'

'Their names?'

'No. He did but I told him I couldn't remember. He said "Could you give me their height, or something about them?" I said they looked medium English people, thin faces and I think policemen among them. That's all I could tell him.'

'What did you say they did?'

'They went through everything I had.'

At this point Owens started to answer Robertson's questions as if he was answering questions asked by Rantzau.

'Did they remove anything?' demanded Robertson.

'Not that I know of, they went right through the house and furniture and as far as I know, that was all.'

'So they found nothing?'

'No, not as far as I knew. So I told him, anyhow.'

Something had confused Owens, but Robertson continued: 'Did they question you?'

'Who? The Doctor?'

'No, no, the British Intelligence.'

'Oh, definitely, definitely, definitely.'

'How long?'

'About two hours, I told him. They said they were keeping me under observation all the time and they wanted me to work for them. Listen I'm not trying to double-cross you, I could have said nothing to your man in Lisbon. I asked him for advice. I've been perfectly open and above board. You understand that?'

Robertson then moved on to raise the question of Walter Dicketts, code-named CELERY, and this provided an opportunity for Owens to cast doubt on him and learn more about the nature of his relationship with MI5.

'I was most amazed when he said that you met him at Wood Green Station before he left and you had told him that when I get back here I'm going to be shot and you take the numbers of all the money I give him,' said Owens.

'What other details did the Doctor ask about the time the people broke in on you?'

'He asked me how I felt. I said I naturally felt that I didn't want to be in front of a firing-squad and I said the only possible thing was to tell them I would work for them. That's all I could say. He agreed with me. He said: "You've done the right thing."'

'So they must have known that CELERY was one of our people?' challenged Robertson.

'Yes, he asked me about it. I said "Definitely, he was for them, but he's one hundred percent for you. He's double-crossing them."'

'That is rather an important point.'

'I told him that definitely. They seemed to know all these things. Well, as regards myself, they knew I was working for you. I didn't know that they knew about CELERY at all.'

'But it was quite clear from what the Doctor said that he was of the opinion that CELERY was our man?'

'I told him he was your man and I said "He's working one hundred percent for me."'

'You volunteered that information?'

'Yes, I said that and he said "By the way, I'm very interested in CELERY and I shall stay here until he arrives."'

At this point Owens offered up some new information which was the fact that when the Doctor went back to Germany he was supposed to go with him as well as Dicketts.

'Both of you?' asked Robertson.

'Yes, both of us. He told Doebler to make all the arrangements for this.'

'You know, I hate having to drag this out of you.'

'That's quite alright,' replied Owens.

'I'd much rather it came from you, though.'

'But I'd sooner you do that, because it'll bring certain things to my mind, things I can't remember unless you ask me.'

Owens then reminded Robertson that he had doubts about going on the mission because he did not trust BISCUIT who had gone out to Lisbon before him – he didn't know what BISCUIT had said to the Germans. Owens also had his doubts about Dicketts so when the Doctor confronted him with the fact that he was working for the British his first thought turned to his fellow agent.

'The first thing that came into my mind was "Is CELERY here? Has he given the game away?"' recalled Owens.

'But you knew he could not have got there.'

'No I didn't. He said he may be there in ten days. In any case he was there before I expected him. He had time to get there easily.'

'Not easily.'

Owens was trying to float the idea that CELERY had arrived in Lisbon earlier than expected and had got in touch with the Doctor and told him that

Owens was double-crossing him. However Robertson was having difficulty believing the lack of interest that the Doctor seemed to be taking in the moment that MI5 walked in on Owens. If he was in the Doctor's position, Robertson would have wanted to know as much detail as he could about what happened, but the way Owens described the Doctor he did not seem to be acting like one of the heads of German intelligence and as a result the story did not ring true.

> 'This is the point you see,' explained Robertson. 'The Doctor must have known the people you're in touch with. You'll give me that?'
> 'Exactly. He said "Who do you think double-crossed you? CHARLIE or G.W.?" I said "I don't know a lot about it. You should know a lot about it as you know so much." After that he said, "I don't know what you think about that. BISCUIT has helped us a lot over here and he sent us two secret letters."'

It seems that whatever Robertson asked, Owens was determined to turn the attention away from himself onto his suspicions about other agents. Whether he was doing this because he was genuinely trying to find out what had happened or because he was trying to deflect the interrogation away from something that he had got to hide was Robertson's dilemma. Robertson turned his attention to the information that Owens had been sending over in his radio messages, which Owens said the Doctor accepted as having been genuine and very useful. When Robertson quizzed Owens about whether the Doctor had questioned him about how the information contained in the messages was gathered, Owens again gave the impression that the Doctor had not shown much interest in the process.

> 'He doesn't seem to have asked you anything,' observed Robertson.
> 'He took my word for it,' said Owens.
> 'Yes, I quite see that. He's trying to extract a certain amount of intelligence from you.'
> 'No very little; he's not interested in that.'
> 'But it's partly his job. You must admit that. I mean even if it doesn't directly concern him, he would turn it over to somebody else in his department. Therefore he would ask you for descriptions.'
> 'I gave him descriptions, not correct of course. I made them up. And he asked me for names and I said I didn't know any names.'
> 'You've given him my name and description.'
> 'No!' exclaimed Owens.
> 'Well, they've got it.'

'If they've got any description of you he hasn't got it from me. You can take it from me. I give you my word.'

'I don't mind one bit if they've got my description.'

'If he's got a description of you, he's got it from Celery. I never gave it.'

'Now you're satisfied that the first interview has come to an end. Didn't he ask what day we walked in?'

'No he didn't I said approximately two and a half months ago.'

'The Doctor seems to have taken very little interest.'

'No, he took an interest but he said: "We know you so well that we know you're with us."'

'But one thing he would want to know would be just exactly where you stood with us.'

'I told him exactly – that I was working for you one hundred percent, so you thought.'

'Look here. On the first of December we were walking in with guns ready to bump you off, but between the first of December and the fourteenth of February, when you went over there, you'd so got into our confidence and persuaded us that the previous fifteen months of war you had worked unwillingly.'

'I never mentioned anything about the previous months.'

'We must have asked you when you got the wireless set.'

'He asked me about the set that Biscuit brought over. He said "That's peculiar, because that man talks too much and when he was out here drank so much – I think it looks peculiar." I said, "Take it from me, Biscuit has been one hundred percent. He certainly was when I saw him last. Since then, of course, I don't know."'

'He was angry with you in this first meeting?'

'He didn't get particularly angry in the first meeting. He looked very serious, but he was not angry. He made arrangements to meet me the next day.'

Owens explained that at the next meeting they discussed the fact that the Germans had broken the British code but offered no new information. Robertson again found it odd that the Doctor did not ask Owens what he was going to say about his meetings in Lisbon to the British when he got back. Owens obviously was not going to say that he had been discovered so his report back to MI5 as far as the Doctor was concerned was going to be purely operational and would be that he had handed over the usual sort of information about aerodromes. Owens explained that he would say that everything had been given to Celery because since Owens had been discovered he had been accompanied wherever he went.

They then moved on to the third meeting which was described as a sabotage meeting. Owens remembered one piece of information that came up at this meeting that was of interest to Robertson.

'The Doctor took me to one side when we got in and he said: "There's one thing I forgot to ask you this morning. What about your men in South Wales?" I said: "There's nothing to worry about there. They're okay. We can go on with the sabotage in South Wales."'

'These men are not the same as Gwilym Williams?' queried Robertson.

'No, they're entirely different. They're working under me separately from Williams on sabotage. The Doctor's always told me that anybody I employ must not know the other ones. These are my own men in South Wales not the other ones connected with Williams in any way.'

'How did he think you were going to get instructions through to them? You were being watched weren't you?'

'No, no. I am entirely free now and I can get all the dope you like. That's why he was so interested. I have my own men in Wales that you know nothing about.'

'He must think we're pretty good saps, allowing you free. Look at it from the Doctor's point of view. I mean if we catch a red-handed spy, as far as the Doctor is concerned, all your contacts are finished. Did he say that?'

'No. As a matter of fact he still thinks G.W. is one hundred percent.'

'But he can't think we don't know G.W.?'

'The point is, has he been mentioned since two and a half months ago?'

'Yes,' answered Robertson.

'But he still thinks he's one hundred percent. I know nothing about Williams at all, I told him. "The only thing that I know is that he's in contact with del Pozo, and del Pozo is no good." He knew that G.W. was in touch with him, but that he now has absolutely nothing to do with him at all.'

'Did he actually ask you to have nothing to do with G.W.?'

'No. Yes, he told me to turn him over.'

'But you refused. That was one of the reasons why you went over there. Well, we must know about you and your contacts. Then it's not very likely that we would let you loose.'

'Well, you didn't for two and a half months, but now you've let me free.'

'The Germans would never do that, would they? They don't leave a man alone ever.'

'You're telling me,' observed Owens.

'But what I want to say is that the Germans would look on our activities with you here in the light of the way they would treat you.'

'No, the Doctor's entirely different in his outlook he's got an American outlook.'

'I don't think that alters his German outlook, or that of the machine he's working in.'

'The point is this. They've got to get someone off with a new radio, sabotage material and new agents. If he didn't think of that he would never do this. He wouldn't give me ten thousand pounds to come back with.'

This last point was Owens' ace card. Why would the Doctor send him back with explosives and £10,000 unless he still trusted him and wanted him to carry on?

The rest of this interrogation followed the same pattern as the first and so by the end of it, despite his more structured approach, Robertson had learned very little new information. Owens maintained that the Doctor had confronted him with the fact that he knew Owens was now working for the British but was apparently so convinced that Owens was trustworthy that he was happy for him to carry on as before. Owens couldn't produce much to back up this version of events – apart from the fact that he had £10,000 and various devices that could be used in sabotage.

Having assessed Robertson's first two interrogations of Owens, MI5 decided that Marriott should lead another session and this time they would start off by focusing on Owens, accusations regarding Walter Dicketts. Owens had claimed that Dicketts was double-crossing him and MI5, and that he had willingly gone into Germany and while there, had been treated in a way that suggested to Owens that he had been working for the Germans all along. Marriott's first line of questioning was an attempt to try to work out the sequence of events that led to Dicketts being taken to Germany. Owens' strategy at the start of the session was to try and turn the tables on Marriott.

'CELERY told me he had definite instructions to double-cross me and to take notes of all the money I gave him,' explained Owens. 'As regarding yourself he told me he knew about the North Sea trawler episode and that you had told him that I had a gun in front of me for 24 hours and I never turned a hair. That was from you. He told me that you were personally in a bad way with Major Robertson and that several times it looked to him that something he had said had got you into trouble.'

'Did CELERY explain to you the nature of the double-cross which he was supposed to work on you?' asked Marriott.

'Yes, he told me immediately we got there. The same day. The whole thing was wide open to me. "Are you working for the Doctor?" I said. "Of course I

Arthur Owens, as he appeared in a 1948 portrait for his British passport, after he changed his name to White and moved to Ireland. During his career as a double agent he held many passports in various names.

The official birth certificate of Arthur Graham Owens, giving his date of birth as 14 April 1899, in Alltwen near Pontardawe, Glamorgan. Owens remained proud of his Welsh roots and exploited them to his advantage with the Abwehr who believed he headed a network of Welsh nationalist saboteurs.

Arthur Owens, formerly code-named SNOW by MI5. He remained silent about his wartime activities, and his death was recorded soon after the first leaks emerged from the Abwehr's records identifying him as the master spy.

Owens was fond of the high life, and is seen here in a typically jaunty pose with his family and Jaguar roadster.

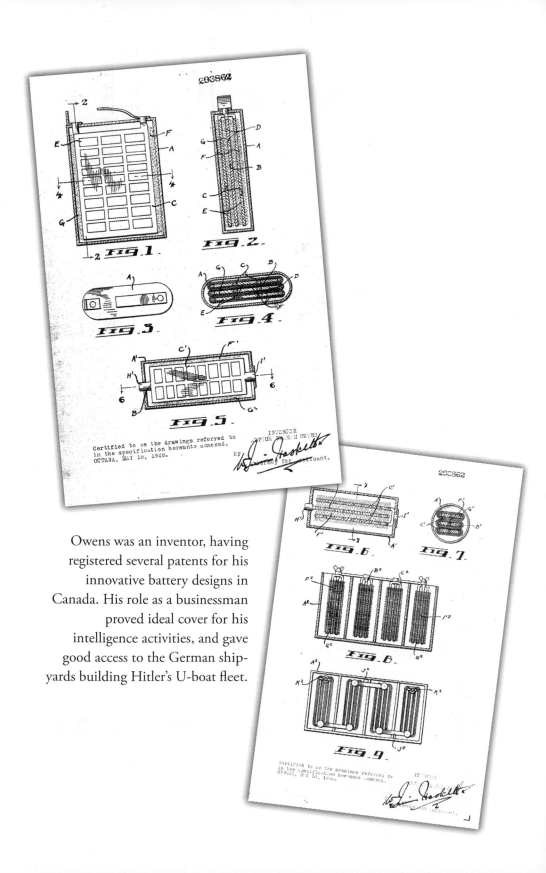

Owens was an inventor, having registered several patents for his innovative battery designs in Canada. His role as a businessman proved ideal cover for his intelligence activities, and gave good access to the German ship-yards building Hitler's U-boat fleet.

Left, Lily Bade, who was SNOW's mysterious mistress with a German background, accompanying him on some of his missons, pictured with their child Jean. Right, Gwilym Williams, in his police constable's uniform in Swansea. Codenamed G.W., Williams was MI5's nominee to run SNOW's spy-ring in Wales, and he accompanied SNOW on a mission to meet the Abwehr, posing as a political extremist.

Having convinced the Abwehr of his sincerity, large sums were passed to his bank account in New York and helped fund MI5's wartime double-cross operations. This transfer in 1940 was typical of many.

SNOW's sub-agent codenamed CHARLIE was a professional photographer who reduced his pictures to microdots so they could be concealed under postage stamps and mailed to the Abwehr's cover-addresses in Germany.

SNOW's wireless transmitter was delivered to him so he could continue to communicate with Germany after hostilities had begun. His transmissions, encrypted in a hand cipher, would allow British cryptographers access to high-level Enigma signals.

Left, the head of MI5's B1 (a) section, Major Tommy Argyll Robertson, known to his subordinates by his initials 'Tar', supervised the Snow case. The architect of the entire double-cross system, he was an inspired counter-intelligence officer. Right, Captain Guy Liddell MC, the Director of MI5's B Division and in overall command of his organisation's counter-espionage operations; he actively supported the high-risk strategy of recruiting the enemy's spies as double agents.

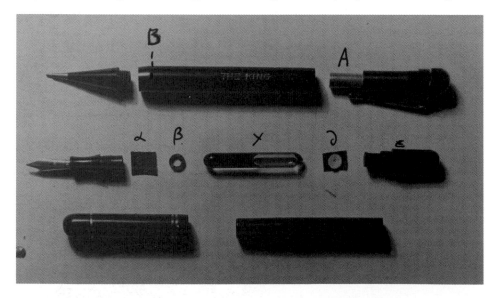

These ingenious concealment devices appeared to be a pencil and pen, but actually consisted of a detonator employing a sulphuric acid empoule and a plunger.

Left, the Hotel Duas Nacoes, largely unchanged in the centre of Lisbon, where SNOW held a wartime rendezvous with his Abwehr contact, Nikolaus Ritter alias Dr Rantzau. Right, the Hotel Metropole in Lisbon where SNOW stayed on his final, fateful mission to Portugal to receive his instructions from the Abwehr.

A Hollywood publicity shot of Patricia Owens who starred in Oscar-winning films but was burdened by the knowledge that her father had been a Nazi spy.

The death certificate
issued in Eire purporting
to record the death on
Christmas Eve 1957 of
Arthur Graham White.

MI5's official file
photograph of B1 (a)'s
legendary wartime double
agent codenamed SNOW.

am working for the Doctor; of course I like the Germans very, very much." He shook hands with me and said "I am with you and the Doctor one hundred percent."'

'Did you tell him that you told the Doctor that he was working for us? pressed Marriott.

'Did I tell him? I didn't tell him at all. When the meeting came up there was a question asked by the Doctor. The first meeting that CELERY had, he brought up British intelligence.'

'When you say "he"?'

'The Doctor,' replied Owens.

'In what way?'

'Regarding the situation I was placed in England and the situation that CELERY was placed. I said he is one hundred percent for me. He turned round to CELERY and said "Is that true?" "One hundred percent. I am with you" he said. If I pull off this okay and go back, I am going to get a staff position. I am going to be made a Lieutenant in the RAF and be of enormous use to you. He said he was promised if he carried out this business successfully and went into Germany and found out all that he could, he was promised a staff job in the RAF and he told that to the Doctor in front of me.'

'How much did CELERY know of your first meeting with the Doctor?'

'He knew nothing at all.'

'He didn't know then that you had told the Doctor that we knew all about you?'

'He knew nothing at all. He asked me after the meeting. He said to me '"Did you tell the Doctor?" I said, "Yes I did." He knew before he went into Germany. He said, "Did you tell the Doctor that you were in touch with the British Intelligence." The Doctor said to me he had information. What could I do? I did not know whether you were. I said yes.'

'You appreciate that this is exceedingly important. CELERY knew before he left Lisbon that the Doctor...'

'That I and he were working for the British Intelligence and that CELERY was working for you. The Doctor knew that, I told him that. I had to be straight and above board with him.'

'What was CELERY's reaction?' asked Marriott.

'Quite okay! "I am ready to go into Germany." I said "This man is working for the British Intelligence. He has given me his word and assured me that he is one hundred percent for you and maybe you can use him." "Well we know a little about that man." Those are his very words to me.'

Owens then repeated the sequence of events that surrounded Dicketts' arrival in Lisbon and how the Doctor had felt it so important that he met

Dicketts that he postponed his return to Germany. Owens added some new facts about Dicketts' arrival in Lisbon which were designed to cast more suspicion on CELERY. 'He was standing by the Office and I said "Good God, if I have ever seen a ghost I have seen one right now." I said, "How did you get ashore?" "I came ashore without the police knowing." That can't be done in Lisbon. Anyhow when he left Lisbon for Germany I looked in his passport and it was stamped by the police.'

Owens was suggesting that CELERY was lying about how he came ashore and that far from doing so in secret he had in fact been let in by the police. However, Marriott was not going to be put off his quest to find out what happened before Dicketts went to Germany and his line of questioning produced cracks in Owens' story.

'Why didn't you tell CELERY as soon as you saw him exactly what you told the Doctor?'
  'I did tell him.'
  'No you didn't,' countered Marriott.
  'I told CELERY the Doctor was wise to everything. He knew exactly what I was doing. No, it is wrong, definitely wrong. I can't have told him.'
  'Then why didn't you tell him? CELERY was a friend of yours.'
  'No, I am sure I didn't tell him. I can't remember anyhow.'
  'It is the most important thing of your trip. Did the Doctor tell you not to tell CELERY?'
  'He didn't say that at all.'
  'The Doctor knew that CELERY was in the British Secret Service?'
  'Yes, I told him. He knew nothing about him except that I said he was one hundred percent for me and that he could be trusted.'
  'I suggest that the Doctor said you should not tell CELERY anything until he had seen him.'
  'I cannot swear to that. I don't remember.'
  'There was no other reason why you should not have told CELERY.'
  'None at all... I don't think I told him.'
  'Until afterwards?' pressed Marriott.
  'I don't think so. Whether I told him before to warn him or not, I don't know. I may have told him.'
  'But you can't be in doubt about things like that.'
  'You don't understand the situation.'
  'I understand too well. There was CELERY who was known as a British Secret Service agent and you allowed him to go to the meeting and did not tell him.'
  'I am sure that I must have warned him. Ask him, he has got a good memory.'

Owens' story appeared to be unravelling and so he then returned to what he perceived as evidence that he has been betrayed. He believed this because Robertson had originally told Dicketts to befriend Arthur Owens in order to find out if he was double-crossing MI5. However, under the pressure of John Marriott's examination Owens decided to reveal what he believed was more evidence that it was he who has been betrayed.

'There is somebody who has double-crossed me. One is the Major, one is CELERY. I have been led to believe certain things in Lisbon from our friend that I don't like at all. I explained a few things to you here. There are other things too which are not very nice.'

'You must tell us,' insisted Marriott. 'It isn't a question whether it is nice or not. What were they?'

'One was that as soon as I got back I would be shot.'

'Why?' demanded Marriott.

'I don't know.'

'Did you ask him why?'

'I didn't ask him why. If I believed him I should never have gone to the embassy. I asked to get back as quickly as possible.'

'If you didn't believe that and you didn't think it is true it doesn't seem to me to be a nasty thing.'

'It is a nasty thing to say don't you think?'

'Certainly so far as he is concerned. In this context you are talking about things which you say are nasty.'

'He said that you were holding Lily and the baby as a hostage for me till I got back. He said that definitely. I come back here and I find that you had made some arrangements to look after her and the baby. I didn't know what to think about that. I was doubtful. Otherwise I would never have asked them to get me back as quickly as possible.'

'All this is most interesting, most helpful and most important,' said Marriott.

'There is something I don't want to talk about.'

'We must know. Did he say those things to you within the first hour of you meeting? Before he met the Doctor?'

'Some before and some after. He told the Doctor I was going to get shot when I got back.'

'Was it this statement by him which persuaded you to tell the Doctor that he was a British Secret agent?'

'He told me that in the first place. The reason why he wanted to get over here so quickly was that he wanted to find out as much as he could about me from the Doctor. Luckily he didn't get through before I did which was a very lucky thing for me. The one thing I was very worried about. Could I contact him and get him in position so that he could not talk before he meets the Doctor. I can't remember. I was in such a terrible position from a terrific shock.

'That man is double-crossing and he is out for the biggest money. In order to get this money he is going to perform some service for the Germans.'

'What service do you think he could perform if he got this position he is going to get?'

Owens explained that Dicketts had information about aerodromes and about convoys. Owens made Dicketts swear that he wouldn't give the position of the convoys to the Germans. Owens then noted that 130 tons of Allied shipping had recently been sunk.

'Most of that information we supplied,' said Marriott.

'I don't think you did. Did you supply the information on aeroplane engines and about Filton?'

'A certain amount. Can you remember any other things that he had?'

'The production at Speke aerodrome, Liverpool. What they are manufacturing there. The manufacture of aeroplane engines. The amount of American stuff coming into Liverpool. Did you supply him with that information?'

'That is by the way,' said Marriott. 'Do you know that he handed that over?'

'He didn't say anything when he came back at all. All I know is that he told me he had some very important stuff. All I have seen is this book on Polish atrocities.'

'You were very surprised that knowing what the Germans knew about him that he went into Germany?'

'He knew and he told the Doctor certain things. After this meeting I was turned down for going to Germany. I don't know why. I was told that it would not be advisable for me to go to Germany.'

'Do you think because the Germans were not sure of you?'

'I cannot think that,' replied Owens. 'They gave me the money and all that. It cannot be that. It turned out that CELERY had to get his photograph taken which he did and in a matter of hours he had a passport. A German passport in the name of Walter Dunkler.

'I bought him a new coat and hat and a new case to go into Germany. I said "You are a very brave man." He said, "I shall be alright. Don't worry about me."'

Owens then said that after Dicketts went to Germany he waited in Lisbon for days without any word. Owens then said that he asked Doebler if he had any news but he had not heard anything. Eventually Owens said that he decided to go to the British embassy in order to find out if they had any thoughts about what might be happening.

'The man at the embassy said "I don't think we will see that man any more. He won't come out of Germany. He will stay there." "Well," I said, "what do you think I should do. I want to get back home. There is something wrong somewhere." Then Doebler said to me "There is something big going to break soon. I want you to stay in Lisbon." Doebler said it was a move into Bulgaria which would take place after the twenty-first of March. They were going to move right through into Greece. I said does that mean there will be an invasion. He said "I don't think there will be an invasion for a month or six weeks. If there is any move in England I will let you know so that you can get back quick." After what I heard at the embassy regarding this cable about his being one of the most important men, I thought, "That man is exactly what I thought he was and he will double-cross me."

'My first impression was that CELERY was there and had given me away. My next impression was that BISCUIT may have given the show away. I don't know what he said when he was there. They told me afterwards they were very surprised that we got the transmitter back safely. After CELERY had talked to me and told me certain things I thought it was you people doing it.'

MI5 pointed out that Owens should have expected Dicketts to profess German sympathies given the nature of their mission. However Owens was saying that even while Dicketts had been living with Owens during the past months he had been running down MI5 and professing his support for Germany.

'There was no need to do it with me,' said Owens.

'Except that if you are going to act a part, you must act it all the time,' replied Marriott.

'Well, why run you down over here?'

Having gone as far as he could down this line of enquiry Marriott returned to the question of whether Dicketts had been told that the Doctor knew that they were working for British Intelligence. 'At your first meeting with the Doctor. Can you remember now whether CELERY knew?'

'He did know at the first meeting,' said Owens.

'Therefore you told him in that hour.'

'I think I must have warned the man. If he knew at the first meeting he could only have known a short while before.'

'When he was with you.'

'I feel sure I must have warned the man.'

'Can you be certain about it.'

'No, I can't say I am certain.'

'If he didn't know at his first meeting with the Doctor it must have been a very interesting one.'

'I was in the room and I was talking to Duarte most of the time. What passed between him and the Doctor I know very little about. What I do know is that I heard in the conversation CELERY tell the Doctor that he had been promised when he got back here a staff appointment and that he could be of valuable service to him.'

'Promised by whom?' asked Marriott.

'You people.'

'Who is you people?'

'British Intelligence.'

'What reason could we have in promising CELERY this job?'

'He said that he had been sent out to get all the dope about the invasion.'

'Any information therefore that he has got about the invasion is bound to be wrong.'

'I told the Major it may be correct. I think it is false.'

'Supposing his information about the invasion is the same as yours?'

'All I do know is that I talked to the Doctor. I said to him, "I am in a very dangerous spot. I am in south-west London and I don't want to be mixed up in this invasion." He said "The mass attack of the invasion is going to come from Gravesend. If you think you ought to go to Wales go. That is all I can advise you at the moment."'

'If you did not tell CELERY before this first meeting that the Doctor knew that he was connected with us what would his object be in saying that the British Intelligence had promised him a staff job unless he knew?'

'Unless the Doctor asked him about me and that?' asked Owens.

'CELERY would not have known what to say unless you had told him.'

'Yes that may be right. I am not quite clear on that.'

'What were the Doctor's opening words to CELERY when he saw him at the first meeting.'

'I said "This is my man CELERY. Here is a man returned from the grave." "Yes" he said, "We have been trying to find him for a long time. We had submarines looking for him. I am very glad he is here. I have put off so many appointments because I knew he was an important man." Then Doebler started to talk to me and we had some drinks. And what the rest of the conversation was I don't know. I definitely heard him tell the Doctor I was going to be shot when we got back to England. He told the Doctor that he was going to get a staff job in the RAF.'

'Would CELERY have used the exact expression Lieutenant?'

'As far as I know. He told me afterwards. What kind of a job is this going to be, £3 or £4 a week. His wife even told Lily that she should get some dresses because they would go to Buckingham Palace for the decoration.'

'What's wrong with that?' asked Marriott.

'How did she know what he was going to do?'

'Kaye knew he was going into Germany.'

Owens now played what he believed to be something of a trump card by introducing the fact that he had told Walter Dicketts that he was double-crossing British Intelligence. However, Marriott did not react in the way that Owens seems to have intended.

'He is alright if he tells you that I was double-crossing you and Robertson and working for the Germans,' said Owens.

'But how does he know that you are double-crossing us?'

'I told him so.'

'No you didn't. He knows you are double-crossing the Germans. When the Germans said to you, you are in touch with the British Intelligence. If you had been double-crossing us you would have said, "You know I am. I have been for eighteen months." Instead of which you said for two and a half months. That was not double-crossing us.'

'I said I was one hundred percent for the Germans.'

'Yes, but he knew that you were one hundred percent as you had told the Germans a lie.'

'There is another point. As far as he knew I was one hundred percent for the Germans. He said are you really one hundred percent for the Germans I would like to know that because I am.'

'He knew you weren't one hundred percent for the Germans if you told them a lie about how you got into touch with us.'

'He doesn't know that unless the Doctor told him.'

'Then you didn't tell him before he saw the Doctor.'

'I can't tell you. I am not quite sure.'

It seems that Marriott was at least as quick at thinking through the various possibilities and implications of the situation as Owens, and then set about trying to disentangle Arthur Owens' version of events. But at the heart of Owens' statement was his uncertainty as to when he actually told Walter Dicketts that the Doctor knew that British intelligence had walked in on him.

'If you did tell him, he knows and he knows that you are not one hundred percent pro-German. Therefore if CELERY does not say to us SNOW is double-crossing us it must be because of the known facts. I.e. that you told the Germans you got into touch with us two and a half months ago and are not one hundred percent for the Germans and are not double-crossing us. How could CELERY come to me and say SNOW is double-crossing us?'

'Because I told him I was one hundred percent for the Germans.'

'If you only told him half the facts.'

'I told him nothing that transpired at the first meeting.'

'Why didn't you tell him?'

'I was suspicious of the man. I was doubtful before I left this country.'

'On mere suspicion you took a tremendous decision not to tell him the most important thing that had happened to you since you arrived in Lisbon. The only thing that mattered.'

'I am not sure.'

'I have simply got to know before I can form any opinion about CELERY.'

'I don't think I told him. I told him later on. I told him everything before he went to Germany. I went and saw the man at the embassy myself, I explained to him he knows.'

'You say that definitely and can't remember whether you told him.'

'I told him after. I am not sure. It was done in such a hurry. I told him definitely afterwards. I don't think I told him before. I have been suspicious of that man for a long time. I didn't want to tell you direct but I hinted to the major direct.'

'This was a matter of your life. You don't safeguard your life by a mere hint. I know that you think you know the Doctor so well that you could get away with anything.'

'That is true. I know this game so well. They can't double-cross me that way. The Doctor is a personal friend of mine. I told that man to say everything that he knew.'

'You do appreciate the importance of the exact moment when you told CELERY?' asked Marriott.

'I understand.'

'Because CELERY, who has got a time, is going to say that you never told him. So in the future now if possible you have got to be certain of the time. I can't help you.'

'No. I don't think it was at the first meeting. After, definitely. There is no question about that.'

'You can't give me any good reason why you didn't tell him beyond the fact that you had no time. It would not have taken a few minutes.'

'I was suspicious of CELERY.'

'He was walking into a trap.'

'I was in a trap. I and nobody else could get him out of it. I got him out. I got myself out.'

'Yes but you were going with a man who did not know the position. You had got yourself out of it by quick thinking. What happened when he went to that meeting? Supposing he carried on the conversation on the footing that you are a British agent. You could not run that risk.'

'The whole thing came on me so suddenly I had to work quickly and work fast. Whether I told CELERY or not before the meeting I told him in the morning.'

'It would seem incredible that you did not tell him the moment you saw him and tell him that the game was up.'

'I may have said that,' acknowledged Owens. 'It is a possibility. I told him to leave everything in my hands. Not to do anything unless I told him.'

'In other words you told him that something had gone haywire, but to leave it to you and you would deal with it.'

'He was in a bad condition when he arrived.'

The interrogation was going round in circles with Owens unable to give a definite time when he had told Dicketts that his cover was blown. MI5 had a similar problem when they tried to work out what had happened during the North Sea trawler mission. One of the reasons that mission went wrong was that Owens had not been told that Sam McCarthy was not a real German agent but was in fact working for MI5. This made it very difficult to unravel whether Owens was telling McCarthy the truth when he said he was pro-German. He might have been telling the truth or he might have been playing his part as a German agent. A similar thing was happening in this case as well – part of MI5's dilemma was that without having a clear and logical version of the order of events they couldn't really know what motives were in play and who was double-crossing whom. Complicating the matter was the fact that Dicketts was on a mission for Robertson who had asked him to try to establish whether Owens was actually working for the Germans. This meant that Dicketts was playing the part of a double-crosser in an attempt to discover Owens' real loyalties. After the North Sea trawler mission they had to give Owens the benefit of the doubt because they wanted the double-cross system to carry on. By 1941 the system was far more developed, with more agents working for them. Their main problem was that Arthur Owens was central to the system and had been in contact with many of the agents MI5 was currently running. If they couldn't trust him then they would have to be sure that bringing his activities to an end wouldn't bring down the whole system.

Owens' inconsistency was becoming a problem for MI5 as it was crucial to know what had really happened in Lisbon in order to understand the viability of the whole double-cross system. However, despite several inter-rogation sessions MI5 still did not know whether Owens had told his fellow agent Dicketts that Rantzau had confronted him with the fact that he was working for British Intelligence. Owens claimed that he had told Dicketts, but was totally unable to say when he did this. MI5 had also failed to discover whether Owens and Dicketts had concocted a story to tell MI5 upon their return to Britain.

It was not just the answers to these questions that concerned MI5; they also knew that the credibility of Owens and Dicketts had an impact on the information about the planned invasion that they had brought back from their mission to Lisbon.

When Dicketts was interrogated he said that as far as he was concerned the Doctor had never confronted Owens with the fact that he was working for British Intelligence, and that Owens, never told him this was the case. This suggests that Owens may not have told Dicketts at all, and Owens' main loyalty may really have been with the Germans. If that was the case why did he come back and feel the need to tell MI5 what the Doctor had said? If Dicketts did not know this had happened, and Owens had wanted to carry on as before, all he had to do was remain silent. He even had the perfect cover of £10,000 and a new code. There was, of course, the possibility that Owens had simply endured enough and wanted to settle down with Lily and their baby. Indeed, Guy Liddell confided to his diary that Owens wanted them to go over to Lisbon to join him, which could mean that he intended taking them to Germany to live.

Robertson thought it unfeasible that the Doctor had not conducted rigorous questioning of Owens regarding what had happened when British Intelligence supposedly walked in on him. In his version of events, Owens gave the impression that the Doctor only spent three and a half hours across two meetings with him, and that during that time he had weighed the situation up, decided that JOHNNY was still a viable German agent, and given him £10,000 and a new code. The only information that the Doctor had to base this decision on was some very poor descriptions of the people who had walked in on Owens. They were a number of men who Owens described only as 'medium English people, thin faces and I think policemen amongst them.' He also said that these men went through his furniture and found the radio transmitter and the code. They had then supposedly taken Owens away and questioned him for a few hours before sending him back to carry on as before, but with someone watching him. Robertson found it very difficult, although not impossible, to believe that the Doctor would have accepted this explanation simply because he trusted Owens.

On the issue of whether Owens told Dicketts what had happened, Robertson was sure that he was lying. But Owens' story was so inconsistent that he could not determine the nature of the lie and its purpose. Robertson believed that there were several possibilities as to why Owens was not telling the truth. First was the possibility that Owens was simply ashamed of the fact that he had let CELERY go on a potentially dangerous trip into Germany while he was unaware that the enemy knew he was working for British Intelligence. The second possibility was that the Doctor had never confronted Owens with the fact that he knew he was working for British Intelligence, and that he had invented the whole story.

Robertson believed Owens to be a clever man; after all he had been living on his wits as a double agent for several years and was quite used to thinking on his feet. Robertson believed that the logical thing to do if Owens was ashamed of not having told agent CELERY that he had been discovered would be to lie and say that he had told him as soon as they had met in Lisbon. However, even though the importance of this had been brought to Owens attention during the interrogation, he was still sticking to the story that he told CELERY after the first meeting with the Doctor and not before.

Robertson knew that Owens had been to see the air attaché at the British embassy after his first meeting with the Doctor. This was before Dicketts had arrived in Lisbon, and he had mentioned nothing about the Doctor confronting him. This led Robertson to the conclusion that it was very possible Owens had made the whole thing up.

During his next interrogation Owens revealed that he and Dicketts had come to an arrangement not to reveal that the Doctor knew that they were working for British Intelligence. Perhaps significantly, Owens had only decided to disclose this at the end of his interrogation and after it had been suggested by Robertson himself. If such an arrangement had been made, Robertson believed that it would have been amongst the first thing, that both men would have said.

Despite the fact that Owens' demeanour under interrogation gave Robertson the impression that he was telling the truth and that Owens himself seemed to believe that he was telling the truth, Robertson concluded that it was highly unlikely that the Doctor knew Owens was working for British Intelligence. He ended his summary of the interrogations, 'I am more than ever convinced that SNOW's is a case not for the Security Service, but for a brain specialist.'

Despite the doubts about the reliability of Owens' testimony, MI5 could not ignore the fact that a Nazi invasion was imminent. As such, plans had to be made for anyone who might have knowledge of the double-cross system including their agents' families. As a result Marriott was told to make his way to Weybridge where he would pick up Lily Bade and her baby daughter Jean, along with Dicketts' wife Kaye. He would then make sure that they, along with Owens' son Robert, were taken to North Wales. All the documents relating to Owens' activities were to be burnt and his wireless transmitter was to be packed up and removed from the house. Marriott had instructions that if it looked likely that Lily might fall into enemy hands then he was to take 'any steps necessary to prevent this from occurring'. If it looked like Robert Owens was going to be captured then Marriott was to assist him in preventing this from happening and was to take with him not less than £10 in cash; petrol coupons for £20; a revolver and two pairs of handcuffs for Lily and Robert Owens. Marriott was instructed to burn these orders once he had learned them by heart.

Such was MI5's concern about Owens that on 4 April 1941 a Harley Street doctor was contacted to assess his physical and mental health. MI5 believed that Owens would agree to Robertson accompanying him in the guise of a friend, but if he did not the doctor agreed to tell MI5 'whether he regarded him as the sort of person whose word could be at all trusted.' It was also mentioned to the physician that, 'if the subsequent treatment of SNOW was a matter of doubt, it would be an advantage to us if the possibility of sending him to a nursing home were not excluded by the medical advice.'

Before meeting the Harley Street doctor there was further evidence of Owens' decline when he claimed to have overheard the barman at his local pub, the Otter, talking about him. The barman was apparently of the opinion that the people living at Homefields where Owens, Dicketts and their MI5 minders were staying, were working for British Intelligence. According to the barman, he also knew that there was a wireless transmitter operating from the house. This had thrown Owens into a state of panic and he claimed that the game was up and the whole operation was now blown. He also asserted that his life was now in danger along with that of his wife and child.

Robertson thought the whole thing a smokescreen, full of Owens' usual embellishments, and Masterman considered it highly unlikely that the Germans would bother sending over anyone to kill Owens, and told him to go home and forget about it.

Up to this point Owens and Dicketts had been kept apart to prevent them discussing what had really happened in Lisbon and the discrepancies in their stories. However, it was decided that one way of bringing the matter to a head would be to force them to recount their differing stories at an interrogation session at which they were both present. Before MI5 brought Owens and Dicketts together there was one more attempt to obtain at a more consistent version from Owens. To achieve this MI5 took a different approach and let Owens tell his story in his own words and write down what he said. The result was a more coherent story which added a few more important details. His description of his first meeting with the Doctor was the same as on previous occasions, with Owens confronted by the Doctor and admitting that he had been walked in on by MI5. Then Owens claimed that the Doctor had asked him about CELERY and Owens had told the Doctor that the reason he had picked him was because he was an Air Force pilot who had fallen out with the authorities and he was very pro-Nazi in his beliefs. Where Owens' story became more logical was in his explanation of why he did not trust Dicketts enough to tell him that the Doctor had confronted him. Owens claimed that when he had first met Dicketts in Lisbon, Dicketts had been in a bad mood because of the terrible boat journey he had been through, and that he had received news about what was going to happen to Owens when he returned. Owens claimed that before he could tell him anything about his meeting with the Doctor, Dicketts had revealed that Robertson had told him that Lily and baby Jean would be held hostage and that Owens was going to be shot when he got back to England. Dicketts had supposedly told Owens that before he left Britain he had been taken to a meeting with Robertson and instructed to find out as much as he could about Owens, and to record the serial numbers of any banknotes that Owens gave him. Dicketts is then supposed to have said 'it looks like a double-cross to me. What do you think?' Owens had replied that he did not think that Robertson would do anything like that, but Dicketts thought that Robertson acted scared. Dicketts claimed that Robertson had told them that there would be no censor in Lisbon and so they could say what they liked – and to tell the Doctor that Robertson would like to see him.

Owens now claimed that he had told Dicketts in the presence of the Doctor that he knew Owens had been approached by MI5, although he added that he was very drunk at this meeting and could not remember everything that had happened. He did, however, recall that the Doctor had asked Dicketts if he was with him, and Dicketts said that he was, and had added 'I shall not sell my country and I am going to do everything in my power to change the system and get rid of certain people who are no use to the country and people who I do not like.' Dicketts is supposed to have told the Doctor that he only received £3 a week, to which the Doctor had replied that he 'was taking a big risk for so little money'.

Owens also remembered that Dicketts had told the Doctor that Owens was going to be shot when he got back to Britain, to which Owens had replied that he thought they were probably trying to fool Dicketts by saying this. Owens claimed that the Doctor had offered him the possibility of going to Germany to work for him, and then being Dicketts' contact in the Channel Islands. Owens claimed to have turned this offer down because it would mean abandoning Lily and the baby. The whole situation regarding Dicketts seems to have worried Owens because he had sent a wire to Lily asking her to get in touch with Robertson to prepare a quick exit from Portugal if he should need one.

In this version of his testimony, Owens claimed that Dicketts had asked him not to mention anything about his trip to Germany to MI5 when they got back and Owens had agreed to this. When Dicketts asked if Owens was going to tell MI5 about the £10,000 he had been given, Owens said 'I shall tell Robby as soon as I get back.'

Owens also appeared to remember more about a conversation he had with someone at the British embassy concerning Dicketts. Owens now claimed that he had been told, 'Between you and me, some of our people on the other side don't like the man and what is more, one of the German Intelligence in Lisbon revealed that a cable had been sent to Madeira asking their people there to trace a man who was on the *Cressado* as this man was a major in the RAF. His name was believed to be Dicketts and that he is one of our best men, and had given valuable information.' Upon hearing this Owens claimed that he nearly had fallen through the floor in surprise. The man at the embassy had then told Owens to watch his step, and that if there was any sign of danger they would get him out at once.

One area in which Owens seemed to have regained considerable recall was the vexed question of what happened when Dicketts had returned to Lisbon from Germany. Owens was now able to recall the conversation and reported that Dicketts had said:

'I have had the most the most remarkable experience of any person. I have never seen such an organisation, I have never seen such a country, I have never seen such people as in Germany. I have got enough stuff to blow the whole works. I have got a free hand, I have been allowed to go everywhere. I have been down the docks in Hamburg, Blohm and Voss. I have got all the dope on shipbuilding, submarine production, aircraft production, the number of aircraft in commission in Germany and approximately the number of men they have. When I was in Berlin I stayed at the Adolph Hotel. I had a meeting with Doctor Schacht's secretary and a meeting with Dr Goebbels' secretary. They were tickled to death with the information I gave them regarding improvements in their propaganda.'

'What is the food situation in Germany?' asked Owens.

'There is any amount of food there. There is nearly twice as much butter there as you get in England,' replied Dicketts.

'There ought to be, pinched from other countries. Were you there for any raids?'

'Yes, there was one, six hours.'

'Where were you?'

'I was in a shelter with some staff officers.'

'Is there much damage in Hamburg?' asked Owens.

'The only place I saw damage was a couple of buildings in St Pauli.'

'Were you in an in air raid shelter for six hours and no damage?'

'No, none. Bombs dropped in the country the opposite side of the river to Blohm and Voss.'

'How many machines went over?'

'About sixty.'

'What is the matter with our people?'

'It is perfectly true, there is no damage and no damage in Berlin.'

'Any instructions for me from the Doctor?'

'Yes, the Doctor gave me £200 and some American money and I am to call on you for as much money as I need.'

Having related this conversation, Owens then recalled that Dicketts had bought 'some dope' which he said was called Veronel and that the bag in which the drugs were contained was from a store in Hamburg. Owens then repeated his accusation that Dicketts said that he and Owens were supposed to go and see Winston Churchill in order to bring the war to an end. This was supposed to earn Owens some sort of decoration and would put them in such an important position that they would be able to take their families to live in Germany.

Owens also claimed that Dicketts had been to the house of a Doctor Rossin who worked for the German diplomatic service in Lisbon and while there had listened to conversations with Roosevelt, Churchill and Hitler which had been secretly recorded in the house.

Whilst certain elements of this statement brought some clarity to Owens' story, there was still the knowledge that he had now been through several interrogation sessions and could fit his story to what he thought would serve his own ends. There were also elements of this statement that seemed to go further than he had previously gone, but whether these new elements were real or not was unclear.

On 5 April 1941 Guy Liddell wrote in his diary about the importance of understanding exactly what had happened in Lisbon:

I attended a meeting of the Wireless Committee in the morning and T. A. Robertson and J. C. Masterman were present. The principal subject of discussion was the case of SNOW and CELERY. Masterman gave a masterly exposition of the case. He put forward the various hypotheses. (1) that SNOW had not given away the whole show to the Germans as he alleged he had, that he had intended this story to enable him to go into retirement with a foot in both camps; (2) that his story was quite true, that Dr Rantzau still thought that he had his uses and could in any case be employed as a paymaster and that eventually his place could be taken by CELERY; (3) that SNOW was a rogue and had been from the start. In this case he would merely have been telling them what they knew already, namely that he was in touch with the British Intelligence but really working for the Germans. Masterman pointed out that the story of CELERY was still obscure. It was not clear whether he had actually gone into Germany or not or whether he was working for us or wholeheartedly for the Germans. A good deal more sifting would have to be done before the position is cleared up.

On 9 April 1941 Owens was interrogated by Dick White, who was then Guy Liddell's personal assistant, and explained that he had been brought in because he had not met Owens before and might be able to form a more objective opinion about what happened in Lisbon. White then proceeded to go through the whole interrogation process again with much the same results. However, after he had gone over the main points he returned to the matter of whether Owens had told Dicketts what had transpired between him and the Doctor at their first meeting in Lisbon.

'You reported to him [Dicketts] the exact words with which the Doctor opened up this matter with you?' asked White. 'The fact that the Doctor knew that you and presumably CELERY also were under British control.'
'Yes,' replied Owens.
'Well, now I think we have come to the point where we must ask him to tell his side of this thing and you do realise how it puts us into this desperately difficult position, you say one thing he says another.'
'Quite.'
'All right, then I think we'll have him in.'

At this point, Walter Dicketts, codenamed CELERY, was brought into the room to join Owens and White.

'I want to make this quite clear,' said White. 'I am sure you are both aware of the seriousness of the position. Therefore I want to hear from you SNOW what you have just told me exactly, the nature of your warning to CELERY in Lisbon.'

'Yes' said Owens. 'Mr Dicketts knew exactly that the Doctor knew I was in touch with the British Intelligence before he left for Germany. That is right isn't it?'

'I had gathered as much but I didn't know,' said Dicketts.

'You didn't know?' asked Owens.

'I had very grave suspicions but I didn't know.'

'You mean to tell me that you didn't know.'

'I'm telling you. I have been told after working out my whole report that you informed me that you had blown the whole project to the Doctor. And had warned me accordingly. You never made any such statement. When did you break it to me?'

'I believe I warned you when I saw you in the room.'

'You believe you did. I don't want to know what your beliefs are, I want to know exactly.'

'Do you remember me telling you in front of the Doctor. I remember this definitely, telling you in front of the Doctor, that the Doctor knew everything about me in connection with the British Secret Service. Don't you remember you sitting there, the Doctor sitting there, me sitting on the bed with Doebler and I said to you, "The Doctor knows everything, you understand." I definitely did.'

'I say that you didn't, and I am also informed that you warned me personally that you had blown the entire party to the Doctor, you tried to assure me that you were the only person who could look after me, to put my whole trust in you and that you would see me back again as you had given your word of honour and you wavered on the last day and were obviously very nervous and you said to me on the pavement when I was getting into the taxi to go to Estoril station, "You are a very brave man, Walter, don't go if you don't want to."'

'To go to Estoril station?' asked Owens.

Unfortunately the record of this conversation cannot tell us whether Owens' last statement was deliberately evasive, flippant or whether he had genuinely misunderstood what Dicketts was saying. Either way, the disagreements between the two men continued with Dicketts suggesting that Owens had been a more active protagonist in the events that occurred in Lisbon than had previously been suggested.

White decided to move the interrogation onto the matter of money.

'Now I'm going to ask a few questions of each of you. When did you tell CELERY that you had received £10,000?'

'The first day I met him,' replied Owens.

'You mean in the first meeting at the hotel. Do you agree with that?'

'No,' said Dicketts.

'I showed him the money,' insisted Owens.

'When do you think he told you?' asked White.

'He told me he had £5,000 then,' said Dicketts.

'I said I had £50,000,' said Owens.

'£50,000?' queried White.

'No, I said that I had American money and here I'd got fifty thousand. That's fifty thousand dollars,' said Owens.

'Well, it was nearly all in English money. You had a small bundle of dollars and...' said Dicketts.

'Large sum of money anyway,' observed Owens.

'£5,000. The other £5,000 comes at a different date,' recalled Dicketts.

'When did you tell CELERY that you had received this £5,000?' asked White.

'I didn't tell him how much I had. I said 50,000,' replied Owens.

Owens' point was that the Germans were not quibbling about money: as far as he was concerned it was a sign of the high esteem in which they held him. For White, the money that Owens was given had further ramifications. 'But this is people who are giving you money at the same time that they know that you are under the control of the British. How did you explain that? It seems curious on the face of it the moment they know you are under British control they give you this large sum of money as a reward.'

'I see your point,' agreed Owens. 'The point is this though, I don't exactly know what I said but I showed him the money anyhow and what I said about it I just don't remember now. Whether I made any explanation or not I can't.'

'Do you remember?' asked White, turning to Dicketts.

'You made no explanation at all. He simply said, "Look what they think of me and how they feed me." And he had it under a bundle of dirty washing locked up first of all in the wardrobe which I thought was very unwise.'

'No, I didn't,' insisted Owens.

'Oh, yes you did. Later you put it in a suitcase. First you had it pushed under a dirty shirt. You said it was the best place to keep it.'

'No, I had it in my case first and I had it in the wardrobe afterwards. It was in my case first. I remember that definitely.'

'... you lifted the shirt up, I can see you doing it now,' insisted Dicketts.

'In my case.'

'In your wardrobe. I said you ought to put it in the safe and you said the safe was too small.'

'Well, look, where it was and how much it was isn't really material because it was such a large sum of money. I must be absolutely clear on this. You must have thought it strange or CELERY must have thought it strange that the moment you declare that the whole thing is known that you are under control of the British you received this large sum of money,' said White.

The disagreement went back-and-forth for some time before White stepped in once more. 'Wait a minute both of you. The points of disagreement here are largely minor ones. May I ask just one question which is personal? May you not have been under the influence of drink at that time and not recollect these minor points?'

'No, definitely not,' insisted Owens.

White then tried to calm things down by offering a summary of what has been agreed and disagreed. He proposed that they both agreed that Owens had said 'Look what they have given me,' and showed a large sum of money. Where they disagreed, was whether Owens had phoned Doebler or Doebler had phoned Owens – which White described as a minor point – and whether there was time for Arthur Owens to discuss why he had been given the money. Dicketts also maintained that he had not been told about the second £5,000 until he got back from Germany. This took the dispute between the two men to a new level.

'I told you that the first time I met you,' said Owens.

'You never mentioned the thing,' said Dicketts.

'By God, I'm certain of that.'

'It was when I came back again that you mentioned the second £5,000.'

'I'm not selling – to Christ you're a liar – to cover yourself as much as you...'

'I've nothing to cover myself on at all,' replied Dicketts.

'You're a bloody liar.'

'Why do you bluff?' demanded Dicketts.

'I'm not bluffing. You know bloody well I'm not bluffing.'

'I know perfectly well that you are bluffing.'

'You know I'm not.'

'Or else giving you the benefit of your mentality, your memory is very short.'

'So you think I'm crazy like you tell me these people think I'm mental?'

'You said to me that you were very simple,' said Dicketts.

The dialogue between the pair can at times appear quite comical, but it is worth remembering that these two men were fighting for their lives. If either one were to be found to have committed treason in time of war, then they could be executed. It would also appear that the tactic of putting these two agents with their distinctly different stories into a room together was only producing a slanging match. However, letting them attack each other in this way had the effect of getting the two men to let down their respective guards.

Dicketts' mission in Lisbon had been two-fold: not only did he have to convince the Doctor that he was a genuine German agent, but he was also telling Owens, during their private moments, that he was a genuine German agent, in order to find out where Owens' loyalties truly lay. MI5's decision to ask him to do this was understandable due to their suspicions about which side Owens was actually on, but it could also have created a good deal of confusion in the mind of Owens as to what side Dicketts was really on.

Dicketts' argument was that he wouldn't have gone into Germany had he known that Owens was a genuine German spy, but he was also saying that Robertson had told him that Owens might be working for the Germans before he left for Lisbon.

'And did you say that you were one hundred percent for the Doctor in every way?' asked White.

'Yes, in every way,' replied Dicketts.

'How did you understand that statement? Did you understand he was a double-crosser?'

'Yes I took it that way naturally.'

'Had you the impression he took it that way?' asked White.

'Yes.'

This clearly was not an ideal position for the two agents to find themselves in. From Owens' account he had experienced the bombshell of the Doctor accusing him of being found out by the British Security Service, and then the man who had been sent out as his ally appeared to have been a genuine German agent who was double-crossing the British. Dicketts, whose first mission this had been, had endured a terrible journey and had arrived with his head full of suspicions, not only about the Doctor, but also about Owens whom he thought might be working for the enemy. He also had instructions to play the role of a genuine German sympathiser, which only complicated an already dangerous situation. MI5's questions to the two men always focused on the belief that one of the two agents was not telling the truth;

they never seem, to consider that their tactics may have been a considerable handicap to the whole mission. Neither did they seem to acknowledge that this tactic may have played a part in making the post-mission analysis incredibly difficult to disentangle.

Having wavered back and forth, Owens seems to have decided that he did tell Dicketts that he had been confronted by Rantzau with the fact that he had been walked in on by MI5. This had little bearing on the hypothesis that MI5 was considering, as it still seemed most likely to them that the Doctor had not in fact confronted Owens in this way.

As a result of the lack of certainty regarding what had really happened in Lisbon, MI5 came up with four possible hypothesis and a course of action for the future of Owens and the double-cross system – if indeed they had one.

Their first hypothesis was that the Doctor never accused Owens of working for British Intelligence and that everything was running as it was before. This would explain the acceptance of CELERY, the £10,000 and the explosives. The only problem with this theory is that it left unexplained why Owens would make this claim. The possibility they considered was that Owens may have thought that things were getting too dangerous and he was finding it difficult to keep up his pretence with both sides. Owens could then take the considerable amount of money he had made over the period he had worked as a spy and retire. It also left open the possibility that at the end of the war he could claim that he had done good service for Britain until his cover was blown. This would also keep his options open in case the Germans won the war because he could then make a similar claim about the services he had performed for them.

The one element of Owens' interrogation which was reasonably consistent was his jealousy of Walter Dicketts and the treatment he had received from the Germans. By revealing that the Doctor had found him out Owens had effectively ended any possibility of Dicketts taking his place.

An alternative variation of this theory was that the Doctor had not accused Owens of working for MI5, but of being lazy. MI5 thought that this might explain Owens' invention of his story about the Doctor and his inability to explain why he had not told Dicketts about this. If Owens was upset by this sort of accusation and then became jealous of the way Dicketts was being treated then this could explain why he said that he couldn't remember whether he had told Dicketts what he claimed had happened. This scenario again brought Dicketts' usefulness to an end but didn't leave Owens open to the accusation of betraying him.

The second hypothesis was that Owens was telling the truth about what the Doctor had said and that he had admitted that this was true. However the Doctor decided that he would gain nothing from bringing his relationship with his most prized asset in Britain to an end. The Doctor would also stand to lose a good deal of prestige with his masters if he had to tell them that he had lost his main agent. This theory relied on the Doctor paying Owens to keep quiet about what had happened in Lisbon. Dicketts was then taken to Germany where he was questioned and it was discovered that he knew nothing about Owens being walked in on. Dicketts could then still be used by the Doctor as an agent and the Doctor's £10,000 would have been well spent in buying a replacement for Johnny. This also meant that agent Celery could still be useful to MI5 in exactly the same way as agent Snow had been up to this point. This assumed that Owens thought Walter Dicketts was unlikely to return from Germany and was therefore convinced that he had joined the Germans when he came out alive.

The third hypothesis assumed that Owens confessed to the Doctor that he was working for MI5 and may even have told Dicketts that the Doctor knew this. The Doctor then gave Celery the option of earning the same sort of money as Owens – which he accepted and went into Germany to train as an Abwehr agent. The Doctor would be doing to MI5 exactly what they were doing to him, with Dicketts turned into a German double agent. Dicketts would then have been told not to tell Johnny that he was working for Germany and the Doctor could run him quite separately from Owens.

The fourth hypothesis was probably the most worrying for MI5 because it proposed that Owens had been working for Germany for a long time and had told them that MI5 thought he was working for them. They even wondered if he could be communicating information to the Doctor by a means of which MI5 was unaware. This would explain why the Doctor only carried out a cursory questioning of Owens after he discovered that he had been exposed by MI5. The Doctor already knew that Owens was pretending to work for MI5 while he was primarily working for Germany. In this version of events Owens was a traitor and had been from the beginning; the only question which remained was where this left Dicketts. The only way to check up on Celery's account of his time in Lisbon and his trip to Germany would be through interrogating him carefully. If his story remained logical and consistent then they would have to believe him that Owens never told him about the Doctor's accusations.

On 10 April 1941 Owens attended a meeting with Robertson and Masterman to hear MI5's decision regarding his future. This decision would have implications for the future of the whole double-cross system and the entire conversation was recorded.

'Will you sit here?' asked Robertson.

'I generally sit here,' replied Owens.

'I will come alongside you, if you like,' offered Robertson.

'Yes.'

'We have come to the conclusion that the only line that we can take with regard to your particular case is that, as far as you are concerned in connection with us, you are no longer of any use to us. We are therefore proposing that you should send a message over tomorrow, saying that you are exceedingly ill and that your nerve has gone and that you are not prepared to go on with the game. Is that alright?'

'Um...' said Owens.

'And also ask for instructions from the other side as to what you are to do with the various equipment that you have got.'

'Yes,' replied Owens.

'Naturally the Doctor must expect that the British Intelligence Service knows exactly what message is being sent over by you.'

'Quite, quite – I follow.'

'Therefore this will give him cause to think and it throws the ball into his hands. Do you follow?'

'Exactly. Quite.'

'Now that is the situation.'

'Can't I do anything to help the country at all?'

'What do you suggest you should do?' asked Robertson.

'I will do anything.'

'I mean, what description...'

'Well, I am not a fool. I have a good education and I have had excellent experience and if my education and my experience is wasted...'

'You have had ample opportunity all these months of doing jobs, haven't you?'

'I have done them, too.'

'I mean apart from the one that you have been doing for us.'

'In what way?'

'Well, I mean it would have been quite simple for you to have kept on a job.'

'Well, I did not want complications at all in that way.'

'I mean, quite frankly, you have been tremendously idle.'

'Oh, there is no doubt about that. I haven't bothered with anything.'

'No. You have done nothing. You have just lived on the fat of the land with an enormous salary – a salary which would make a Cabinet minister's salary look stupid at the present rate of taxation.'

'Quite.'

'Well then, roughly speaking, you will accept that position, will you?'

'Well, if you say so, I have nothing more to say. I should certainly like to do something for the country, all the same and I certainly have got experience and I shall do what I can. Not that I want to be paid for anything.'

'But you see the difficulty; that as they know all about the set and know we are controlling it, there is no more value in it.'

Owens flailed around, but failed to come up with a viable plan of his own that might enable him to carry on working for MI5. But in introducing the other agents he had turned the conversation onto the topic of whether MI5 would be able to carry on with the double-cross system.

'Isn't he rather upset at having lost all the contacts which you are supposed to have had in the shape of Charlie, G.W. and Biscuit?' queried Masterman.

'He doesn't regard those as his men – he regards me as his man, but not them at all. I don't think they mean anything to him at all, not in the slightest. If he lost them all, it would mean nothing to him. He is very cold blooded when it comes down to business.'

'One has to be in this game – very,' added Robertson.

With this ominous thought filling the room, Robertson then moved on to the subject of Tate, proving to be a great success for MI5. It was believed that if the Germans were able to trace that he had been in contact with Owens then he too would be finished. There was also the question of his loyalty to Britain because, according to Owens' testimony, the Doctor considered this agent as a personal friend.

'Might I just have from you again the conversation which occurred between you and the Doctor with regard to the sending of £100 to Tate?'

'Yes' replied Owens. 'He asked me if the £100 had been sent to this Post Office and I said yes as far as I knew it had been sent. And he said, "Well my God," he said "is that man alright?" I said, "I don't know." I said "Why?" "Well," he said, "That's a very good friend of mine and I hope he's alright." And he conveyed to me that he was a very great personal friend of his.'

'Does he regard the whole of our intelligence services as being decadent and incompetent?'

'They haven't got a very good impression of your people.'

'Of our people here. They think we're saps.'

'Yes. Yes,' agreed Owens.

'Yes. But you have no more to tell me about this man TATE at all – about the Doctor's observations about him. Did he give you any indication that he thought that, from his point of view, the man was still alright, or did he think, shall we say, that the man had been taken by us?'

'He didn't know.'

'He didn't know. I see. He hadn't any idea who he was outside of the fact that he was a very great personal friend of the Doctor's.'

'That's all. I feel quite sure that he was a great friend after the way that he spoke about him. He said he was a good friend of his and he didn't want him damned.'

'Quite. And you have no more to say about that.'

'Nothing at all.'

'Well now, I am going on to a second point now. We have been through your statements, very carefully. We have been through CELERY's statements very carefully and we are unanimous in our opinion that you did not tell CELERY that the game was blown before he went into Germany.'

'Well, I did tell him before he went into Germany.'

'Well, that is our opinion and that being the case, you definitely sent a man on a most dangerous mission.'

'That is a lie.'

'You sent him knowingly, I maintain, to put the worst construction on it, to his death probably.'

'I did not. I did nothing of the kind,' insisted Owens.

'Doesn't it seem to you that it was a very treacherous act, to say the least of it, not to tell him before he got to the Doctor?' asked Masterman.

'I am positive that I told him before I went to the Doctor.'

Owens then proceeded to change his story again, at times saying that he was sure that he did tell Dicketts and at times saying that he wasn't sure.

Finally, Robertson slammed the door shut:

'Tomorrow you must say that your nerve and health have gone, that you can't go on any longer and what are you going to do with your explosives and with your sets. Instructions will be given to the operator to send that over and we shall have to consider what becomes of you afterwards. I don't think that we need say any more at this stage, do you?'

'Well...'

'If you wish to make any suggestions of that sort, you had better put them in writing after you have thought it over. Right, that's all.'

'Who can I write to?'

'You know my address.'

'Thank you very much.'

***

It was not of course available to SNOW's interrogators at the time, but later there was to come to light a key source in the SNOW saga. After the German surrender MI5 conducted a lengthy search among captured German intelligence records for information about the double-cross spies, and one item, a report written by Nikolaus Ritter dated 31 July 1941, was found to be a summary of his work with Owens, revealing that when Owens had arrived in Lisbon he had told Ritter that he thought Dicketts was suspect. Ritter had asked why he believed this, and why, if he felt he was not legitimate, Owens had brought him to Lisbon. Owens claimed that he had only recently become suspicious due to having overheard Dicketts say that he was working in the interests of the British. Owens pointed out that to end the mission at this point would have caused suspicion about his own position, but Ritter had been unconvinced and had suggested that if a British agent had been in touch with him, then he must have been put up to this by the British Security Service. Ritter believed that if this was the case then the only reason that the British had not arrested Owens at once was to allow him to incriminate himself further during the Lisbon mission. Dicketts' role would be that of a witness who could pass on what he learned to MI5 upon his return. Ritter was also well aware of the implications for the future of Owens' network of sub-agents and all the agents with whom he was in contact.

Ritter claimed in his report that he had told Owens that because he knew so much about him and his organisation, he would have to consider whether he could let him return to England at all, informing him that it was entirely within his power to liquidate his case instantly. Owens was frightened by this threat and revealed that he had met Dicketts ten weeks previously in a public house where he had confided the details of his RAF career and the criminal record which had prevented him from regaining his commission. Supposedly, this had made Dicketts angry towards the authorities and Owens accordingly had cultivated him as a potential agent. However, when Owens finally asked Dicketts if he was interested in working for Germany, he had accepted so readily that Owens' suspicions had been aroused. Owens had then made some enquiries about Dicketts and had discovered that he had been asked by the British Security Service to hang around in bars and report any suspicious individuals to the authorities. As payment for carrying out this work, Dicketts was to receive thirty shillings a week which he was also unhappy about.

Ritter's report stated that this revelation had put Owens in a serious predicament because if he broke off contact with Dicketts he knew Dicketts would be likely to report this suspicious behaviour to MI5, so he had decided to go ahead with the mission to Lisbon despite the dangers. Owens had gambled that if Dicketts wanted to win back his commission he would come along in an effort to build up a cast-iron case against Owens. He also let Dicketts see that he had a lot of money from a source which Dicketts would be encouraged to speculate about. Owens had told Ritter that Dicketts was 'an extremely grasping man' who was genuinely impressed by tales of German efficiency and strength. Knowing all this, Owens believed that, despite his connection to the British Security Service, there was a good chance that Dicketts could be persuaded to work for Germany.

According to Ritter, Owens had claimed not to have included any of this in his messages to Hamburg because the issue was too complex to insert into his short, nightly transmissions. He also claimed that he had once sent an SOS, but had received no response from Hamburg.

Owens had conveyed this tale in a disjointed and confused manner, but from his long acquaintance with Owens, Ritter said that he was inclined to believe that 'he was telling the truth so far as he knew it.'

Unable to be sure whether Owens' assessment of Dicketts was accurate, Ritter decided to postpone his planned return to Germany and meet him, but he was concerned that maybe the *Cressado* had been sunk by a U-boat and he would never learn the truth about his main asset in Britain.

According to Ritter, Dicketts had arrived in Lisbon on 21 February 1941 and, having met him, Ritter quickly agreed with Owens that he looked like a crook who would probably do anything for money. Owens had been present at the first meeting between the two men but had been under instructions from Ritter not to mention anything of their previous conversation as Ritter had wanted to hear what Dicketts had to say before reaching any conclusion. Despite his first impression, Ritter thought that the only way he could be certain about Dicketts was to take him back to Germany for a full interrogation. This, he thought, would also impress, or frighten, Dicketts into working for the Abwehr, and he reckoned it would be much easier to dispose of him on German soil than in Lisbon, should the need arise. To keep the two men apart, Ritter had told Owens that he could not accompany Dicketts on his trip to Germany.

Ritter had calculated that if Dicketts was incorruptible then Owens was already lost, but even in those circumstances he would gain a conduit through which he could convey false information to the British. This could only be achieved by keeping Dicketts in the dark about what Ritter had learned from Owens. If Dicketts thought he had genuinely fooled the Germans into accepting him, then they could use him in a similar way to MI5's use of Owens. Somewhat surprisingly however, this was a trade-off which Ritter was not willing to make. Ritter's reason was that Owens had not only been his main source of information and control in Britain – but he had also come to like the little Welshman.

Ritter acknowledged that the interrogation of Dicketts in Germany would have to be carefully planned to avoid him realising that Ritter knew he was working for MI5. The Germans were more than happy that fear, combined with the temptation of money, should be employed to persuade Dicketts to reveal his true position and come over to the German side. According to Ritter, the subsequent interrogation, conducted in Hamburg, confirmed Owens' version of events, and Ritter bribed Dicketts to switch his loyalty and keep quiet about Owens. Dicketts was to be given some money but was then to become dependent on Owens for any further instalments. This procedure was designed to ensure that it was in Dicketts' interest that Owens was at liberty and available to make the payments. Ritter considered that this situation need only last for a few weeks, by which time it would be too late for Dicketts to credibly denounce Owens, and this expedient would ensure the Abwehr would benefit, whatever the truth was. Either Owens continued to operate as before, or a channel had been acquired to pass false information to the British, through an agent who had no idea that his cover had been blown.

In his conclusion, Ritter mentioned radio transmissions made by an agent he referred to as LEOHARDT. Ritter's report revealed that he had devised a test to see if the British had known about Owens' messages as early as 14 February 1941. Ritter had decided that the next agent he would send to England would contact LEOHARDT, and if it became clear that LEOHARDT had fallen into enemy hands, the agent was to return to Germany at once. This plan, he thought, would place the British in a dilemma. They could either let LEOHARDT go, or they would never hear from him again. Either way, the Abwehr would know the true situation. What Ritter did not know was that his agent LEOHARDT had already been turned by the British, and would work for MI5 under the codename TATE.

When Ritter later heard that Owens had fallen seriously ill, he took this as an ominous sign. He then learned that the man he had sent over to contact LEOHARDT had failed to do so. While Ritter was evaluating these developments, he received news that Dicketts had arrived in Lisbon again. This time he was alone, so arrangements were made for him to be taken to Hamburg where he was questioned again.

Ritter confided that what he could not understand about Dicketts was why the British had employed someone so obviously untrustworthy, but the very fact that Dicketts had returned alone suggested that he was much more important than Ritter had previously thought. He speculated that in all probability Owens was blown and in jail, but he knew how clever Owens could be, and assumed that the British would encounter the same problem that he had when they tried to interrogate him. Although Ritter was worried about Owens' network, he reasoned that as the British were not sending messages over Owens' wireless, then Owens had not yet confessed and therefore his other agents were still undetected. At that time G.W. was reporting regularly through the Spanish channel and his material did not seem to be under MI5's control. Nevertheless, Ritter decided that G.W.'s messages should not be trusted unless they could be verified by another source. In early July the Lisbon Abstelle informed Ritter that an opportunity had arisen to plant a double agent in Britain, and had requested information that could be given to the British to establish the agent's bona fides. In response, Ritter had offered a photograph of Dicketts and an authentic version of what had happened to him, omitting any mention of Owens. This, Ritter had calculated, would make the British suspicious of Dicketts and draw suspicion away from Owens.

Chapter VII

Dartmoor

OWENS' CONDUCT WHILE under Robertson's interrogation served to confirm MI5's growing concern about his unreliability and his vagueness on vital issues. Combined with his failure to carry out the tasks allocated to him in Lisbon and his careless talk, MI5 came to the conclusion that he could not be allowed to continue his double agent role. Accordingly, Owens was instructed to tell the Doctor that 'he is becoming very ill, that his health is really broken and his nerve has gone. He cannot continue any longer and must throw up the sponge.'

Owens was then to ask what he was supposed to do with the explosives and his wireless transmitter. If the Germans tried to persuade him to carry on or to find a replacement then they would know that he probably still had their trust. MI5 would also be able to watch Owens' reaction to the termination of his role as a British agent which, it was hoped, would reveal to what extent he was involved with the German intelligence services. If Owens simply accepted this decision without saying anything, then the plan was to tell him that MI5 believed CELERY's version of events and that he was a traitor. The reason for doing this was that MI5 hoped it might elicit a further response from Owens and that he would then be likely to make further accusations against CELERY, revealing more information about what really happened.

MI5 had to decide what to do with TATE, whom they suspected might be compromised if the Germans thought that he had been in contact with Owens. It was concluded that TATE should make an urgent request for money as he had run out, claiming that he was having trouble travelling and collecting information. This was, of course, another way for MI5 to gauge the Doctor's reaction and assess whether the Lisbon affair had wider implications for their organisation as a whole. As far as CELERY was concerned, it was determined that he should write a letter to Lisbon stating that he was trying to secure passage for a return trip to Lisbon, as had been requested by the Doctor, but that it was proving ever more difficult to obtain a seat on the plane and he could not be sure that he would get one. He was to ask for further instructions while he waited.

Another way that MI5 had tried to get behind Arthur Owens' mask was to send him to a physician. Whilst he was in Lisbon he had claimed to be ill but MI5 suspected that his incapacity may have been due to drink. After his return from Portugal, Owens had been sent by MI5 to a reliable Harley Street specialist for a full medical examination. This took place on 18 April and the X-rays revealed no evidence of the duodenal ulcer which Owens often claimed plagued him and, although it was noted that it was possible any scars might have healed, the consultant was doubtful that Owens had ever had an ulcer. However, he also noted that while Owens had high blood pressure, he found him to be in reasonable health and thought it unlikely that he been drinking to the extent that was often reported. Owens' physical characteristics seemed to be as contradictory as his personality.

The doctor's investigation into Owens' health had given him contact with his local doctor in Surrey who revealed the rather disturbing news that Owens was probably suffering from a venereal disease. As far as his character was concerned, the doctor believed Owens to be a 'consummate liar' who could not be trusted and would probably try to deceive MI5 if he felt it would benefit him.

As there was a Detention Order outstanding on Owens, there was no need to apply for a new one and MI5 requested the local police in Addlestone to execute it. A place was made ready for him at Stafford prison and the governor briefed to expect him. It was when he was admitted to Stafford that an administrative error was made, assigning Arthur Graham Owens with the middle name George. This error has been widely repeated ever since.

Stafford was one of the secure facilities where full-blown enemy agents were detained for the duration of hostilities, and the governor was told that his prisoner had done some work for the Security Service, but that MI5 had become unhappy with his recent activities and he was to be considered untrustworthy. MI5 asked that all of Owens' correspondence be intercepted and sent to MI5. Any requests for visits were also to be passed on to the Security Service, and MI5 asked that they should be informed about any-thing of interest he might have to say. Owens was to be treated like any other prisoner with the proviso that if he wanted to speak to MI5 an officer would make the journey to Stafford, but only if there was good reason to do so.

MI5 sent the final signal to Dr Rantzau in JOHNNY's name, disclosing that he had become ill and had lost his nerve, and this message was monitored by Radio Security Service intercept operators as it passed through the German system from the Abstelle in Hamburg to the Abwehr's headquarters in Berlin. The resulting ISOS text, decrypted from the original, revealed the German reaction to the news about 3504, as JOHNNY was referred to in internal communications: 'For Major Ritter. For information. Received today following message from 3504:- Impossible to carry on. Will call you eleven thirty to see if any further instructions. If not I am going...' Then, on 24 April, the Abwehr signalled: 'Cont. To pack up all gear. Regards our answer, agree. Standing by even days. Best wishes. Regards.' And the correspondence continued on 1 June: 'Question 3504 thoroughly concerning sudden illness: something is wrong here. Signed RITTER.'

Whilst Owens was languishing in Stafford, MI5 began to learn more about Walter Dicketts from a diary that mentioned the *Cressado,* the ship on which Dicketts had travelled to Lisbon. A German agent in Lisbon had expressed in her diary concern about a source who was believed to be reliable. The source had at one time served in the RAF and was described as 'a valuable medium for planting false information on the British.' This message could mean that either the Germans still believed in Dicketts or, more worryingly, that he had been turned by the Germans at some point and was in fact feeding the British bogus information.

On 1 August 1941, MI5 received an unexpected telephone call from Owens' son Robert, then aged twenty-two, who expressed a desire to talk to an MI5 officer. Accordingly, he was interviewed at the Piccadilly Hotel by J. C. Masterman. The following day he sent a further letter:

Dear Sir,
   I have information regarding the means which enable me to gain entrance and exit into occupied and enemy countries.
   Therefore I hereby offer my services to the state.
   If you will arrange for me to see you as soon as possible, we will be able to fully discuss the details of my proposal.
   I remain, yours faithfully, Robert Owens.

Several days later MI5 asked Robert to come to the War Office where he was interviewed by Robertson and Masterman. At this meeting Robert explained that while he had been eating at the Mars Italian restaurant in Frith Street, Soho, a regular haunt of his, a man had sat opposite him and said 'You are Robert Owens'. He revealed that he knew a great deal about Robert and that he had followed Robert from his fiancée's house. The man said that things were going very badly for Britain, the U-boats had inflicted terrible losses on the country's shipping, and that Britain would lose the war. Finally, the man allegedly asked Robert if he would 'join up with them', and when Robert refused, the man turned nasty. Robert was trailed to another restaurant and asked to reconsider this offer, but ended the encounter, stating: 'I'm fed up with the whole thing.' From this incident Robert concluded that the man must be from the German Secret Service, but only later realised that through this man he might be able to gain entry into occupied territory, and that he could therefore be of some use to MI5.

Robertson and Masterman found Robert to be vague and even evasive in his account of what had supposedly occurred, and when they questioned him about his family he told them that he had stopped sending his mother Jessie money because she pestered him, and that he had not seen his father since his last visit to Stafford several months ago. Robert admitted that he had no way of contacting the man again, and that he might be making a great deal out of nothing. However, he felt sure that this approach had been an attempt to recruit him to the German Secret Service. Robert even offered to go to Lisbon, France or Germany and bring back information for MI5.

However, Robertson and Masterman put it to him that the whole episode was in fact just an attempt to help his father, and that he seemed willing to take any risk to try to ensure this. When it was suggested that the man might not have been a German agent, but a criminal trying to entangle him in some illegal activity, Robert became angry and claimed that he had worked for the Germans before, and that this might be the reason they had approached him. Robert then confessed that before the war he had mapped some of the aerodromes surrounding London for the Germans. Naturally, this admission raised the suspicions of the two MI5 officers who pushed him to tell them what he had done with these plans. Robert's refusal only made things worse for him and it was also pointed out that he was not helping his father's cause. Robert finally admitted that he had sent them to the Auerbach Battery Company, which he had known was a cover for the headquarters of the Abwehr in Hamburg. Robert explained that his father had known nothing about this at the time, and had become very angry when Robert eventually told him what he had done. When asked about his father's loyalties, Robert confessed that he thought his father 'would swing over to Germany at the beginning of the war, though he now considered him to be entirely pro-British.'

The MI5 officers informed Robert that they would have to write a report about what had happened, which would then be sent to a higher authority, and that he could expect to have to make a further statement under oath. Robert was told that if he had any further information he should reveal it now, rather than wait until the next time he was interviewed, but he said that he had nothing to add to what he had already told them. The gravity of his situation was pointed out to Robert, who may not have realised that execution by hanging was the penalty for a conviction under the Treachery Act, the criminal statute covering espionage that had been hastily passed in the summer of 1940. He was advised to write down the details of all his contacts with the Germans, and to send a copy to Robertson. He was also told that if the stranger contacted him again, he should try to keep in contact with him and to inform MI5. Robert ended the interview by remonstrating with the pair that he was taking great risks in order to help his father, and that his efforts were not being welcomed by MI5. The officers responded by pointing out the seriousness of what had happened and the position in which he had now placed himself.

MI5 knew that Robert Owens was aware of some of his father's activities because he had accompanied his mother Jessie to Scotland Yard in August 1939 when she had denounced her husband as a spy. Jessie had probably done this because she discovered that he was having an affair with Lily and had even taken her to Germany. However, one of the reasons she had given to the police was that Arthur had attempted to recruit Robert and some of his friends as German agents. The motive behind Robert's approach to MI5 may have been an attempt to help his father, but what he had not foreseen was the can of worms he had opened regarding his previous contacts with the Germans.

Robert's encounter with Robertson and Masterman prompted MI5 to review their records and to conclude that he knew enough about his father's recent work to enable him to communicate with the German Secret Service, and that he was 'consequentially potentially very dangerous'. Accordingly, the Home Secretary signed a Detention Order for Robert, and it was served on him immediately. At eight o'clock in the morning of 27 August 1941, Superintendent Curry of the Surrey County Constabulary arrested him and he remarked, 'This does not surprise me, I was expecting it.' Robertson then went to visit Lily, who expressed anxiety about how long Robert would be held, and asked what he had been up to. Robert was taken to Brixton prison where he decided that there would be no point in making an appeal.

On 13 April 1941 Robertson and Masterman made their way to Stafford to interview Johan Dirk Boon, one of Owens' fellow prisoners. Boon had spent a good deal of time with Owens and had told him that he expected an invasion of Britain after the campaign in the East had been won. Owens had also shown an interest in new types of aircraft but the main reason for approaching the authorities was that Owens had confided in him, as he was a Dutch fascist and, as far as Boon was concerned, Owens was 'the most important German spy in England'. Allegedly, Owens had admitted to Boon that the authorities thought they had plenty of evidence against him but had been unable to take any action because Owens 'knew too much for the important people'. Boon claimed that Owens was planning to escape, and had asked Boon to go along with him. Their plan was to break out and then make their way to the German legation in Dublin, and Owens had apparently promised that he would arrange for a submarine to take Boon back to Holland.

The news that Owens was plotting to escape from prison, and that his plan was quite well-advanced, must have come as a terrible shock to the MI5 officers indoctrinated into the SNOW case at their St James's Street headquarters in London. If he succeeded in extracting himself from the premises, which were in the city centre, few would have doubted that such a resourceful individual might be able, even under wartime conditions, to make his way to Northern Ireland. He could then have stepped over the completely unregulated border into the republic and established contact with the legation where the minister, Dr Edouard Hempel, retained an illicit transmitter and was in frequent communication with Berlin. Even though his encrypted traffic, enciphered on what he had been assured was an unbreakable one-time pad system, was read on a regular basis by RSS cryptanalysts who designated the channel PANDORA, the very thought that SNOW might betray his extensive knowledge of the double-cross system was hard to contemplate. At potential risk was not just TATE, who remained active with his wireless link to Hamburg, but other spies who had turned.

According to Boon, Owens had been talking to one of the warders, and had uncovered some gripes about pay and conditions. This discontented officer was now supposed to be in his pay and had even taken a letter out of the prison to Lily. The warder had given Owens a small saw on the basis that he should give it back the following day. Boon had taken the saw and broken it, returning all of the broken saw apart from a very small piece of the blade which he kept hidden. Boon claimed that he suspected Owens was a traitor who would desert him as soon as they had escaped. Boon told the MI5 officers that the reason Owens wanted to escape was that in the event of invasion the prisoners in Stafford would be shot. Owens had also used soap to take an impression of one of the guard's keys, and was planning to make a copy.

Having given his account, Boon was sent back to his cell where he retrieved a cardboard replica of the key that would be used to make the copy, and the small portion of the saw blade that he had kept. Boon was told to make note of any further developments and to report them to the governor.

By October 1941, MI5's John Gwyer had completed a comprehensive review of the SNOW case to decide how best to proceed with the double-cross system. Gwyer concluded that Owens, for all his faults, had provided 'an immense amount of detail, which subsequent cross-checking has shown to be true'. He therefore recommended that, as in Owens' case, it was invaluable to place someone close to the German command, even if this person could not be trusted. The value of such an agent lay in their delivery of accurate background knowledge which more than offset the problems caused by the agent not being completely trustworthy. So long as the agent was not given any truly sensitive information, then he would not be able to cause too much damage. MI5 reasoned that even if the agent was double-crossing his case officers, he would deliver information which could be checked because he would not lie about information believed to be unimportant. In time this trivial information would be integrated with other items, building up a picture of the way the German Secret Service operated. Gwyer believed that sending over a spy who might be double-crossing MI5 was more advantageous than handling a more dependable type of man because the spy would be more likely to want to make contact with senior German Secret Service personnel. On his return the spy would unconsciously reveal the sort of information that MI5 wanted. The big surprise of Gwyer's review was that MI5 might still be able to exploit Owens, and Gwyer ended his report by observing, 'I believe that on this view it might even be worthwhile sending SNOW back again to Lisbon since he would almost certainly get an interview with the Doctor which is a thing that a much more reliable man might perhaps fail to secure.'

Gwyer had made a very logical and potent point; however, MI5 still considered it a step too far to release Owens, but neither did it want to lose the man who had been its most important asset in the genesis of the double-cross system. MI5 realised that Owens' transmitter still offered an opportunity to stay in touch with Rantzau, either by supervising Owens closely or by having someone mimic his Morse style. There were, of course, problems with this proposal because if such a scheme was to succeed the Germans would have to be fooled into believing that JOHNNY had recovered from his mysterious illness and was back in business. MI5 would need to be prepared to give the appropriate answers to the questions the Germans would be bound to ask about what had happened when SNOW and CELERY had returned to Britain. Further, this meant that MI5 would need to establish precisely what Owens had said to the Doctor while he was in Lisbon. If Owens had revealed that his radio communications had been blown, then it followed that other agents they were running, such as TATE, were also compromised.

MI5 decided to proceed on the basis that Owens' motive was jealousy of Dicketts: his intention had been to undermine Dicketts, and the way he had accomplished this had been by revealing to the Doctor that Dicketts had been working for the British. MI5 also had to decide which code to use and what to do about the new codewords which Owens had brought back, to let the Germans know when the messages he was sending contained fake information. These technical difficulties meant that MI5 deferred reactivating the SNOW case until there was a chance to interrogate Owens one more time.

However, MI5 did not want SNOW to know that he was being considered for reactivation and, having weighed up the pros and cons of the matter, it was decided that Owens should be interrogated by John Gwyer under the pretence that he was an expert on the German Secret Services who wanted to talk to him about certain German officers he might have met. This tactic proved to have the benefit of putting Owens at ease with Gwyer, because he was not presented as someone who was there to judge Owens. However, there were also serious disadvantages to the tactic because it meant that Gwyer could not interview Owens in detail without raising Owens' suspicions about his true motives.

Always concerned that Owens should not pass on any sensitive information that he had picked up while working as a double agent, MI5 wanted to keep Owens' whereabouts as secret as possible, but in November 1942 he was accidentally included in a group of prisoners from Stafford prison that was transferred to Dartmoor. Most of them were detained under Section 12(5)(A) of the Aliens Act, but among them was Owens who had been held under Regulation 18(b). There was some doubt about the legality of whether someone held under this rule could be kept in a convict prison like Dartmoor, and after some discussion it was decided that the move was after all legal, and Owens need not to be returned to Stafford. MI5 was not concerned by the unintentional transfer of Owens, although he would be the only British subject at Dartmoor. MI5 felt that the conditions there were probably better than at Stafford, and the governor could be made aware of his responsibilities concerning a prisoner like Owens. The Home Office report on the move stated that the slip 'seems to indicate some slackness but as he has been transferred to Dartmoor he may as well stay there'.

Owens did not share MI5's attitude about the benefits of Dartmoor and made several applications for a transfer. By January 1943 his whereabouts had become known to Robert, also still an 18(b) detainee held at House 1, Peveril Internment Camp M, near Peel on the Isle of Man. Robert seems to have understood the legal complexities of his father's move to a prison like Dartmoor and asked the permission of the Commander of Camp M to write to the Home Secretary, Herbert Morrison.

> My father, Arthur Owens has been interned in Dartmoor Prison since last September and can you tell me under which defence regulation he is detained.
>   If he is detained under Def.Reg.18B I wish to make a formal application to be transferred to Dartmoor Prison with him for the rest of my internment.
>   Thanking you in anticipation of a rapid and concise reply.
>   I remain, yours faithfully Robert Owens

On considering Robert's request, Major W. H. Coles of the Home Office advised against such a move, noting that the cases of father and son overlapped and it would therefore be undesirable for them to be 'thrown unnecessarily into each other's company in present circumstances.' The principal concern was that if young Robert was to find himself in the company of other inmates he would be bound to pick up information of a potentially sensitive nature. In the eyes of the authorities, this would make Robert even more of a danger than he had been before, and therefore the likelihood of his release would be severely reduced. Accordingly, the Home Office responded that 'in the circumstances we can only advise, really as much in the boy's interest as anything else, that he should be told that his application has been considered but cannot be acceded to.'

On 26 June 1943 Robertson made the long trip to Dartmoor to interview Owens who, far from pleading for his release, expressed a keen desire to stop leaks from internment camps which, he had learned, had become a problem. Actually, Owens was seeking a transfer from Dartmoor to an internment camp, and the one he had in mind was on the Isle of Man where his son Robert happened to be. Robertson, however, had other matters he wanted to discuss, and raised the topic of German secret weapons. MI5 had picked up talk of rocket guns and wondered whether Owens had come across any information on this subject. Owens told Robertson that the Doctor had once mentioned a huge gun which could fire a shell up to 120 miles, but this was not a rocket gun.

During their discussion, Owens revealed that one of his fellow prisoners was Jurgen Borreson, a Dane who had been captured in Greenland where he had supposedly been on a hunting trip, but had actually been setting up a meteorological station in the Arctic. Owens explained that Borreson had been working for German Intelligence across Europe and in Norway and Finland before his capture. Apparently he had friends in high places and had told Owens that he knew the names of many British and German agents. Robertson found Owens' account of Borreson's activities the usual garbled mess, but knew Owens well and thought that through his close contact with the enemy agents kept at Dartmoor he might just pick up a piece of information that could prove useful.

Robertson's visit seems to have given Owens a new lease of life and a sense of duty, and he took on the new role he had given himself as a stool-pigeon with considerable enthusiasm. Thereafter Owens wrote regular letters to Robertson using only the initial 'T' whenever he thought that he had picked up a useful piece of information. Having gained Borreson's confidence, Owens was able to gather information such as the secret code on his passport which had allowed him to move freely across borders, and the deployment of tanks at Dieppe. Owens reported that Borreson had been particularly active in Finland and Owens was able to let MI5 have useful information about Finnish counter-intelligence and claimed that Borreson had told him about a secret agreement that existed between the German intelligence service and Finnish counter-espionage before the first Russo-Finnish War. Boresson's mission had been to gather intelligence about the Russian military situation and to recruit agents willing to go into Russia itself and conduct espionage operations. Owens supplied MI5 with the names of agents working in the command centre at Stettin and an agent who was currently working as a consul in the United States. Equally important for MI5 was the assertion that Borreson had information about German rocket experiments in Heligoland. Owens reported that Borreson became more talkative after receiving letters from home and advised MI5 to let him have as many letters as possible.

Thus Owens delivered extremely useful information about Borreson, and his report of rocket experiments in Heligoland attracted particular attention. Borreson was not very technically-minded and did not give a very clear account of the information he had picked up from a Dr Erdman who knew a good deal about the experiments, but technical matters were of course Owens' forte, and he believed that he had 'arrived at a fairly accurate and important picture of what had been done.'

Owens described the rockets as being in excess of six feet in height and said they were fired from a long tube. When the rocket reached a certain altitude a section of it was ejected, fins were extended and the rocket ignited its exhaust. Owens believed that what he was describing was Germany's most important secret and, potentially, an incredibly powerful weapon. He promised to try and find out as much as he could about these rockets at a time when the Allies were increasingly preoccupied with identifying the secret weapons that Hitler had referred to in several public speeches. A Whitehall committee, codenamed Crossbow, had been empanelled under a Cabinet minister, Duncan Sandys, to investigate all reports of Nazi rockets, and Owens' contribution became part of the intelligence jigsaw-puzzle being addressed by intelligence analysts in London.

In August 1943 Owens wrote to Robertson to tell him that a combination of letters received by Borreson and bad news from Denmark, along with Owens' own cautious efforts, had led the detainee to crack and reverse his Nazi views. As a result, Borreson was now willing to expose the inner workings of the German Secret Services in Stettin and Hamburg, and to disclose the names of agents in Denmark, Norway, Sweden and Russia. Owens finished his letter with his usual self-deprecating style:

> It has given me great pleasure in bringing this situation about for you without mentioning how important this information will be in helping the war effort, as of course you will now see how important this man was and what a large amount of knowledge he has of the German espionage service.

I leave the next move in your capable hands and await your further instructions. Very sincerely, T.

In early January 1944 Robertson put into motion the train of events that would eventually lead to the release of Owens and his son. Owens' recent contributions from Dartmoor were interpreted as a sign that he was no longer a serious threat to the security of the country and, having had time to review the case, Robertson was now of the opinion that Owens probably had not told Dr Rantzau that he had been under British control when he was in Lisbon. MI5 had learned that Dr Rantzau had been sacked from the Abwehr following the collapse of his main asset in Britain, and had been prevented from taking up a prestigious job in Brazil. Instead, when JOHNNY had fallen silent, Rantzau had been despatched to North Africa.

The Home Office agreed with Robertson's assessment of both Arthur and Robert Owens, and decided that they should both be released from detention. Imposing restrictions on the two was considered, but MI5 felt this would not be necessary and recommended that, given the good work that Owens had done recently, both men should be helped to find jobs. It was believed that Robert probably was not suitable for military service because his knowledge might compromise operations if he fell into enemy hands, so arrangements were made to exclude him from the call-up.

The final snag that delayed their release was the imminence of the D-Day landings, for there were those who considered that the prospect of the pair being at large and uncontrolled at a time of such importance was highly undesirable. It was thought to be risky to release one without the other and, as they had both been in detention for quite some time, it was felt that it would not do too much harm for them to remain in custody for a few months longer.

The conduit to the enemy provided by double agents, of course, was the principal method of conveying strategic deception to the enemy, and several were employed in support of Fortitude, a sophisticated campaign designed to mislead the Germans into the belief that the invasion was likely to occur in the Pas-de-Calais region. BRUTUS, TATE, BRONX and, most importantly, GARBO were all engaged in a coordinated effort to persuade the enemy that the Allies would take the shortest route across the Channel, and once the landings had begun in Normandy the objective was to characterise the operation as a diversionary feint in preparation for the major assault further north. Having SNOW on the loose at such a sensitive moment was considered inadvisable. The irony of the situation would probably have been lost on Arthur Owens, the man who was responsible for the genesis of the double-cross system, because he had little idea of how MI5's system had developed in his absence.

While still in prison, anxiously awaiting news of his release, Owens learned of the German rockets falling on London and recalled some information which he felt might be useful. He offered a report about the enemy weapons and was interviewed on the subject on 23 July 1944.

Between the time that he had first mentioned the rockets and the time he was interviewed, Owens had remembered an incident from his visit to Hamburg before the war. The Doctor had been visited by four scientists and had to go away with three of them urgently, to witness some important tests of a new invention. The fourth scientist had stayed in Hamburg with Owens and this gave him the chance to question the scientist about the tests. The scientist informed Owens that the new invention was a concentration of lethal acid vapour. The vapour was highly corrosive and could melt away the flesh of the sheep on which it was tested and could also disintegrate metal. Owens had realised that if the Germans could find a way of combining this vapour with the rocket then they would have at their disposal a weapon which could change the course of the war.

When challenged, Owens explained that he had never thought to mention this exchange with the German scientist before because he had thought that the idea was too fantastic, but now he was worried that there might be some truth in what he had heard.

Owens was finally released from Dartmoor on 31 August 1944 and escorted to London by John Marriott. As he had nowhere to live and no job, MI5 offered assistance until he could establish himself. His identity card and ration book had been taken from him on his admission to Stafford prison and the authorities at Dartmoor seemed to know nothing about their whereabouts. On receiving the few possessions he did have, Marriott observed that Owens had £2.10s and therefore decided not to help him out financially. The two men did not have much to say to each other on the trip back to London and Owens' first concern was his son, but Marriott said nothing as he did not know when he was to be released. When Owens asked about the whereabouts of Lily and their daughter Jean, Marriott told him that he had no idea where they were.

Robertson had hoped that Owens would settle back into a normal civilian life and find himself a job. However, as 1944 turned into 1945 the feeling was that he was not really trying to find employment and was happy to live off the state. Owens was nearly fifty years old and had not actually held down a proper job for years, and Robertson realised that this probably made him unemployable 'except in the one job of which he has any recent experience, namely as an agent and for this he is for a variety of reasons no longer suitable.' Accordingly, Robertson decided that if Owens was to fend for himself it was only right that he should be paid a lump sum. Robertson calculated that total expenditure on the SNOW case amounted to less than £4,000, and that while it was unknown precisely how much Owens had kept for himself, he definitely had passed on £13,850. This meant that alongside the considerable intelligence benefits and the genesis of the double-cross system itself, Owens had made a very substantial profit for MI5. In these circumstances Robertson recommended a payment of £500 as a goodwill gesture and that Owens should be told that he was now on his own. It was also pointed out to him that he should not reveal the nature of his war work and that he should not consider writing his memoirs or he might find himself falling foul of the Official Secrets Act which he would now be required to sign.

Evidently Owens had not expected the money and expressed his gratitude, saying that he had been treated fairly and generously. On his MI5 receipt Owens wrote: 'I have received this day a cheque for £500. I have no claim of any kind against those paying me this money.' After receiving his final payment and his warning from MI5 about the Official Secrets Act, Owens began a new life in the Norwood area of London, falling back on his skills as a chemist and inventor. On 14 May 1945 Owens applied for a patent for a quick-drying adhesive that could be used in the production of lampshades or hats. This innovation was an improvement on stitching and offered the ability to bond fabrics almost invisibly. He took on premises in Hoddesdon in order to pursue this business and the company had some initial success and even supplied lampshades for the royal yacht.

Chapter VIII

Debrief

Soon after the German surrender, British counter-intelligence person-nel began screening captured Abwehr staff officers. Those thought to have information about spies in Britain were detained either at Bad Nenn-dorf, or taken to Camp 020 at Ham Common for detailed interrogation. One such officer was Nikolaus Ritter who, during his time in charge of the Abwehr in Hamburg, had used the alias Dr Rantzau. He was questioned first by MI5's John Vesey, and then by John Gwyer. MI5's objective was to learn from Ritter all he knew about JOHNNY, without disclosing that actually Owens had been under British control. Ritter's version of the case, offered at the end of May 1946, was astounding because, according to Gwyer, Ritter claimed that after the Lisbon mission in March 1941 he had realised Owens was under British control.

In 1941 the double-cross system was teetering on the edge of destruction and all the benefits gained later could have been lost. A collapse would have been due to the same man who had been responsible for the system's genesis: Arthur Owens. Due to his central role in the early days of the system Owens was intimately linked to the most important agents that MI5 relied on as the backbone of the organisation. Owens was also essential to Ritter's network in Britain but by the end of 1941 he knew that JOHNNY had been compro-mised, yet he did nothing about it. His reasons were complex and involve his own personality, his political position and the historical circumstances in which he found himself.

The Allied security agencies had accumulated a considerable dossier on Ritter, which involved great successes and spectacular failures. His most notable success came when one of his spies in America acquired the design for the top secret Norden bomb-sight. His biggest failure was the FBI's infil-tration of his spy-ring in America which had many parallels with Britain's double-cross system. This FBI operation culminated in the arrest of thirty-

three of his spies in America. However, little was known about Ritter after
he left the Abwehr and was posted to the frontline. He served in Libya with
the Afrika Korps as an intelligence officer on Erwin Rommel's staff, and
then commanded a battalion in Sicily, and upon his return to Germany was
placed in charge of the air defences of Hanover, a post from which he was
dismissed after the last Allied saturation bombing. Apparently, just before
the air-raid, Ritter had misread the radar returns and had stood down the
city's anti-aircraft batteries.

When questioned about Owens, Ritter acknowledged having run him
under the alias Johnny O'Brien after he had volunteered his services to the
German embassy in Brussels in 1936. Thereafter Owens had been handled
by Hans Dierks, and had only come under his direct supervision in March
1937. Known as JOHNNY or 'Der Kleiner', he was given the number 3504
and was described as: 5'6'; very slender and wiry; between thirty and forty
years of age; thin face, short nose, thin lips, light eyes, pale complexion,
thick dark brown hair parted on the left. Clean-shaven. Spoke uneducated
English with a Welsh accent. Very highly strung and jumpy. Heavy cigarette
smoker. Drinks beer. Very partial to women. Dresses plainly.

When questioned by John Vesey, Ritter denied any knowledge of the
agent destined for Manchester, or the South African or the source of the
infra-red information, insisting that he had not arranged those operations.
He said that even before their encounter in Lisbon he had lost faith in
JOHNNY because of the North Sea incident, and he had found the ease with
which Owens was able to travel to Portugal suspicious. According to Vesey,
Ritter had been informed of his transfer away from the Abwehr before he
travelled to Lisbon, and therefore had rather lost interest in Owens and was
only really interested in his legacy, and ensuring that any bad news about
the case would only emerge long after his departure from the organisation.

Ritter confirmed to Vesey that Owens had suspected that Ritter knew he
was working for the British. Ritter also stated that he thought Dicketts was
a British agent who was trying to penetrate Owens' network. Under interrogation in Hamburg, Dicketts had admitted that he was a British agent and
had offered his services to Germany. Ritter had accepted in order to save the
case from complete collapse, rather than because of any belief in Dicketts.
He also asserted that he had only given Owens between £300 and £400 in
cash, and expressed surprise when informed that Owens had been carrying
£10,000 when he returned to Britain. Ritter speculated that this money may
have come from the Abstelle in Lisbon without his knowledge.

Vesey's report documented that Ritter had supervised JOHNNY's training in wireless procedures, code systems, microphotography, meteorological observation, aircraft recognition, and airfield description, while Hauptman Rudolf of the Abwehr's *Kriegsorganisation Spanien* had taught him sabotage. Before the war JOHNNY had been paid £20 a month, plus bonuses of £10 to £20 for good work, as well as his expenses. After the war had started he received larger bonuses of £200 twice in Belgium, the sum of £200 twice in Lisbon, and a last payment of £800 in Lisbon. Apparently the Abwehr had intended to drop money near Bristol, a plan that had been abandoned when JOHNNY had said he could come to Lisbon. His letters to Hellmut Timm, the director of SOCONAF in Antwerp, sometimes contained messages written in invisible ink, and during the war Ritter said that Owens had sometimes received letters through an Abwehr cover address unknown to MI5.

And as for the vexed question of Owens' true motivation and loyalty, according to Ritter, Owens had told him that 'he was a true Welshman and as such had no sympathy with the English'. The origin of his beef with England was also tied in to his grudge against the government, blaming them for the loss of a large private yacht which he had inherited from his father. Allegedly the authorities, had refused him a large sum of money for an invention which had been put to military use in the First World War.

Epilogue

UPON HIS RELEASE from prison Owens had abandoned Jessie, and Lily had disappeared, but before long he had taken up with Hilda White, a woman who lived in Dollis Hill and worked for the Post Office, perhaps at the top secret Post Office Research Station nearby. The couple set up home together in Great Amwell in Hertfordshire where they rented a house for £5 a week, and he adopted Hilda's surname White. He would later explain that Hilda had been married to Frank White, a builder from Crystal Palace, but this relationship had ended and her husband would not give her a divorce. Although they may not have married, Arthur formalised his change of name by deed poll on 2 October 1946, and their son Graham was born on 15 November 1946 in Streatham.

Nothing, of course, was known of SNOW's extraordinary career as a double agent until a *John Bull* scoop, which had been based on the wartime diaries of Colonel Erwin Lahousen, a senior Abwehr officer who had revealed the existence of JOHNNY, a master spy in London. These diaries, made public after Lahousen's death in 1955, then became the basis of a book, *Hitler's Spies and Saboteurs* by Gunter Peis and Charles Wighton, published in 1958.

A well-known newspaperman based in Munich, Peis spent years cultivating Abwehr retirees; combined with Wighton's research in England, and clues gleaned from Lahousen's dairies, they produced a book which lifted the veil of secrecy surrounding SNOW, speculating that he might have been recruited by one of four German agents who had been active in Wales before the war. The first of these was Heinrich Kuenemann, the managing director of an engineering firm, who had worked for Reinhard Heydrich's Sicherheitsdienst and had lived in Marlborough Road, Cardiff. He had fled just before the war. The second was Professor Friedrich Schoberth, a visiting lecturer at Cardiff University. There was also Franz Richter, the manager of an enamel company who had also left the country, and Dr Walter Reinhard, described as a spy in North Wales, who had been expelled in 1939.

Peis and Wighton asserted that, whoever had recruited him, Owens was soon in touch with Reinhold and Co. of Gerhoffstrasse, Hamburg, which was the cover-name for Nikolaus Ritter's import-export company. As a test, JOHNNY had been paid to report on the Woolwich Arsenal, a site the Germans already knew about.

According to Peis and Wighton, JOHNNY was to prove himself an exceptional agent and the Doctor had soon come to rely on him as his master spy in England. JOHNNY even became close friends with Ritter and his wife, and frequently visited their home where JOHNNY would sing Welsh songs to entertain them.

In recounting Ritter's memory of his first encounter with CELERY, the meeting in Lisbon that had caused MI5 so much concern, the book supported Owens' claim that he had been confronted by Ritter with his suspicion that he was working for the British Security Service. As we know, MI5 had decided to put an end to Owens' career as a double agent on the basis that this had *not* happened.

Some years after the publication of Ritter's memoirs, and his death, his son-in-law, Colonel Manfred Blume, claimed that Ritter had deliberately misled his post-war MI5 interrogator, John Gwyer, because of the consequences for him if his time with the Abwehr was deemed to be a success. He was already in detention and feared that the British might prosecute him as a war criminal. 'This was not the time to reveal the truth nor his achievements', Blume stated.

Blume's defence of his father-in-law leaves open the extent to which Ritter duped Gwyer, and because his memoirs omit any reference to a British deception scheme, it is hard to assess where the truth lies. Certainly Ritter must have learned eventually that Caroli and Schmidt, codenamed SUMMER and TATE respectively, had survived the war by becoming double agents for MI5. However, he must have also guessed that if Owens had been playing a double game from the outset then CHARLIE, BISCUIT and G.W. must also have been working under MI5's control. If G.W. was compromised, then it followed that all his contacts at the Spanish embassy must have been contaminated too, and the overall picture, from Ritter's perspective, must have been bleak indeed, and might explain his motives for keeping the secret of the British double-agent programme from his superiors.

There are other possibilities for Ritter's behaviour. Prior to the Lisbon mission Ritter had just been given a new appointment and there is always the possibility that his mind may not have been entirely focused on his old department. Arthur Owens had been Ritter's main agent in Britain for many years and had been introduced to his wife. Mrs Ritter had even given him baby clothes to take to Lisbon for Owens to take back to Lily. To distrust Owens was to distrust his own judgement so it is not impossible that Ritter let his feelings cloud his analysis of JOHNNY.

If Ritter were acting in fear of what might happen to him if the collapse of his system became known, then this speaks to the success of the British operation. The double-cross system did not emerge fully formed; it evolved gradually in response to the feedback that MI5 got from agents like Arthur Owens. MI5 simply outwitted the Abwehr. The success of the system may have had something to do with a flawed German system in which officers feared failure more than they valued success, but this would not in itself have guaranteed the triumph of the double-cross system. Rather, this was due to a superior structure – and the development of that structure would not have been possible without SNOW.

* * *

Owens' older son, Robert, was released from prison after D-Day, married in Norwood on 21 October 1944 and worked as an engineer in the Baglan Bay steel works in South Wales. Also an inventor, he would develop a device that acted as an automatic tourniquet for use in medical operations. After his death in 1981 his possessions included correspondence dated 23 June 1972 from Prime Minister Edward Heath's private office at 10 Downing Street, apparently written in response to earlier correspondence in which Robert had attempted to restore his father's reputation:

> The Prime Minister has asked me to thank you for your further letter of 21 May.
> Mr Heath fully understands the motives which prompted you to write to him again; and sympathises with the concern which you feel about some of the publications in question. Nevertheless, as I said in my letter of 17 May, the government are bound to try to ensure, wherever possible, that all who took part in, or have knowledge of, sensitive wartime operations maintain the maximum of reticence and discretion about them. Even when some details of the operations in question become known in circumstances over which we have no control, the damage can be aggravated if this knowledge is confirmed or amplified; and the Prime Minister hopes that you will continue to maintain the same discretion which you have so signally observed hitherto.

> Yours sincerely A. J. C. Simcock

Evidently Robert had initiated the correspondence after Ladislas Farago's *The Game of Foxes* had been released in the United States in 1971, containing an account of the double-cross system with many references to SNOW. Robert's sister Patricia, then living in America, had sent a copy to Robert who had been horrified by the accusations laid against his father and had annotated the relevant passages. On one page he had noted that Sam McCarthy, the double agent codenamed BISCUIT, had been arrested in East Grinstead in 1951 and charged with embezzlement.

* * *

Patricia Owens took the first step on the path to fulfilling her dream of becoming an actress when, aged fourteen, she was admitted to the Central School of Dramatic Arts in London. She won her first acting role after working for several months as a prompter, scene shifter, furniture and sign painter. She met Eric L'Epine Smith, a casting director from Warner Brothers Studio at Teddington, who suggested a screen test. As her relations with her mother were poor she took a test as Trilby to another actor's Svengali, and was offered a year's contract by Gainsborough Studios.

In 1943 she made her first film, *Miss London Ltd,* directed by Val Guest and starring the British comedian Arthur Askey. Thereafter she was often asked to play Americans because of the Canadian accent she had acquired.

The film for which Patricia is best remembered is the 1958 science fiction classic and cult film *The Fly* in which she plays the wife of a scientist who invents a matter transmitter, but things go wrong when he gets entangled with a fly as he tries out his machine. The film also stars Vincent Price as the scientist's brother, but it is Owens' depiction of inner turmoil thar is the emotional epicentre of the film, as she struggles to come to terms with the horror of her husband's dilemma and the terrible fate that awaits him.

In the 1970s her mind turned once again to her father, from whom she had been estranged for so many years, and she returned to England with her son to find his grave but, despite her best efforts, she could find no record of him. She never spoke about her father, and her son Adam only started to hear about his grandfather's secret career when he was twelve. His recollection is that Patricia completely denied the interpretation of Owens' activities contained in Ladislas Farago's *The Game of Foxes.*

Patricia Owens developed cancer and died in Lancaster, California aged seventy-five on 31 August 2000. Her son Adam believes that the stress of keeping the family secret took a toll and holds the opinion that Arthur Owens made her feel that it was her responsibility to keep his secrets. She was made to believe that if she told anyone about her father's situation it could lead to his death. Adam says: 'So here's a girl who loved her father so much that she took his secrets to her grave.'

* * *

Each member of Arthur Owens' family lived with a mystery in their lives, each of them knew a part of the story but none of them had the full picture. The only person who knew the full story was Owens himself, but even he paid a price in his later years for having taken the gamble of entering the perilous world of espionage.

The reason that none of his family could find Arthur Owens was because after the war Owens used the considerable skills he had learned during his period as a double agent to disappear.

Owens' first post-war money-making scheme was a fuel additive developed with his son Robert which they called Wenite, a combination of the names Owens and White. It failed to catch on, and Owens fell on hard times.

In March 1948 Arthur White – as he then was – asked his son Robert if he could borrow £5 and without any explanation suddenly moved his new family to the Republic of Ireland.

After a few days in Rosslare, they found lodgings in Kilrane where Owens worked as a self-employed chemist, making soap which he sold in Wexford. Later the family moved to Wexford permanently and rented a property in Barrack Street before Owens found a shop on Commercial Quay. Here Arthur found a use for the skills he picked up during the war and established a business repairing radios and selling batteries. As a sideline he bought beef dripping and Sloane Liniment which he mixed together and sold under the name Zing Salve.

During his time in Wexford Arthur used to attend Sinn Fein meetings. Even though the speeches were often in Gaelic, which Arthur did not understand, he would always clap enthusiastically when they were over.

On 9 September 1948 Arthur White received a letter from Jorgen Borreson who had been in Dartmoor with him. The letter appears to be in response to earlier correspondence which might have predated the move to Ireland and this may go some way towards explaining the haste with which he left England. It is not impossible that he was concerned that his wartime activities might one day catch up with him in the form of a bullet. After all, Owens had made enemies on both sides and he knew that in time they might come to learn how he had endangered their lives. In the letter Borreson sends his regards and explains that he had been moving around since the end of the war because it had become impossible for him to live in Denmark. The reason for this was that Borreson had been arrested on his return to Denmark and accused of being a spy. He had employed a good lawyer and evaded any punishment. He was however re-interned until 1947. His letter then goes on to say:

> I am in contact with most of our fellow prisoners, not only those in Germany but in the Argentine, England, France, Spain... we had an organisation for bringing escaped Scandinavians to Spain.

He identified his current alias as 'Jorgen Heidinger' and remarked 'I was glad to have your news, thus seeing that nobody has cut your throat.' Borreson ended the letter with: 'I suppose you are having a good time in Ireland. Perhaps you are writing your memoirs. Now let me hear how you are getting along.'

Arthur Owens did not talk much about his wartime experiences but before she died, Hilda told her son Graham that his father was the Arthur Owens who was the subject of a newspaper article, 'Hitler's Spies in Britain' written by Gunter Peis and Charles Wighton.

Hilda also took Graham to see *The Fly* starring Patricia Owens, whom Hilda revealed was his sister.

To Graham, his father was a rather ordinary, pleasant, gentle man who only ever walloped him once with a newspaper when he had been irritating. One of Arthur's hobbies was photography and he enjoyed developing his own pictures, but drinking appears to have been his main pastime. In Wexford, they lived only a few doors away from the local pub, The Keyhole, and Arthur was a regular there. His friends would frequently have to help him back at night because he was unable to walk but he was never reported to be violent when he had had too much to drink; he just became very talkative.

Graham White's recollection of his father's behaviour when he was drunk do not match many of the stories that circulated about his life as a spy. Graham does not remember Arthur singing the Welsh folk songs that Dr Rantzau described. Neither is there any evidence that Arthur Owens, the arch Welsh Nationalist, could speak Welsh.

Despite the apparent normality of Arthur's home life, there was evidence of the past that Arthur Owens could not help but carry with him wherever he tried to hide. On one occasion, when his son was playing soldiers with a friend, the two boys made flags and one had a swastika on it. When Arthur saw it he flew into a panic and said 'are you trying to get me arrested?'

MI5 believed that Arthur Owens' pretended to have a stomach ulcer but his son Graham remembers him being crippled by stomach pains, for which he took bread soda. In November 1957 Arthur Owens was taken ill with breathing difficulties and on Christmas Eve he was taken to hospital but died before he got there from myocarditis or cardiac asthma. He was buried a few days later in an unmarked grave, plot 57 section O of St Ibar's cemetery, Crosstown, just outside Wexford.

After Arthur's death Hilda was visited unexpectedly by a man from Dublin claiming to repesent the Royal British Legion. The man gave his name as Considine and claimed to be checking whether Hilda qualified for a war pension. Apparently, having discussed her husband's war record, he decided she was not entitled to a pension and left. What he didn't explain was how he knew that the late Arthur White had been Arthur Owens the spy. Owens died only two months after the first release of his wartime exploits into the public arena in *John Bull* magazine. Given his penchant for taking advantage of coincidences, the Security Services could not be blamed for making sure that the reports of his death were accurate.

After over fifty years lying in an unmarked grave Arthur Owens' family have finally decided what to put on his headstone:

Arthur Graham White (Owens)
Born 23 April 1899, Pontardawe, Wales.
Died 24 December 1957, Wexford.
(Also known as "Snow" and "Johnny")

Conclusion

By the end of hostilities MI5 had acquired great skill in the handling of temperamental double agents, the manipulation of their enemy handlers and the development of imaginative ploys designed to mislead the Axis, but in the early days inexperienced case officers made fundamental mistakes and consistently over-estimated their adversary's competence and resources. Slips were all too frequent as SNOW was allowed considerable latitude to strengthen his links with his mysterious, American-accented spymaster, Dr Rantzau, his beautiful secretary, and the members of his largely imaginary network of spies and saboteurs. Without the benefit of reading Rantzau's mind, or at least his daily reports to Berlin, MI5 sought to build a double-cross system on a foundation based on the dubious, shifting loyalties of a single duplicitous, philandering Welshman who was boastful and brave, reckless and calculating, ruthless and occasionally weak, mercenary but patriotic. A mass of contradictions, Owens was sometimes nervous and highly-strung, while at other times he operated with supreme coolness in an environment where any slip-up could lead to him being executed for treason by either side. Far from being shy about his clandestine activities, he was often loquacious and appeared never to hesitate in compromising others, including his fellow agents and on occasions even his own family.

Although Owens was the key player in the SNOW drama, he had an impact on the successful prosecution of the war that he himself could never have imagined. For it was Owens' communications with his German controllers that would be responsible for the first British breakthrough in the German Enigma cipher.

ISK and ISOS, as components of the signals intelligence source later known generically as ULTRA, would provide MI5 with the most detailed order-of-battle for its adversary, and by the end of the war there was scarcely an Abwehr officer or agent unknown to Allied counter-intelligence analysts, who compiled huge card indices of their internal communications, handbooks detailing the structure of each *Abstelle*, and a series of constantly updated *Who's Who* of those on the enemy's payroll. However, before this invaluable source came on stream, MI5 had just three methods of learning about the professionals just the other side of the Channel who were master-minding espionage operations in Britain. That knowledge consisted of the very meagre information gleaned before the war, admissions and confessions made by captured spies who might not be wholly reliable, and SNOW himself, the only agent who had maintained consistent contact with the Abwehr, and could shuttle back and forth between neutral Antwerp, Brussels and Lisbon to attend *trefs* with his German controllers.

SNOW's case is unique and significant. It was not just the first of its kind, it also led to the development of a sophisticated, coordinated structure for controlling the enemy's intelligence service. And it contained a constantly changing, variable dynamic: the determination of a born deceiver to survive, and thrive, in a world of espionage in a war that was claiming lives by the million. Who was SNOW really working for? How did he dupe his German controllers? To what extent did he implicate his wife, mistress and children? Was he a mere mercenary and opportunist? Did he ever win the trust of his sceptical British case officers?

Ever since Sir John Masterman released his *Double Cross System of the War of 1939–45* in 1972 there has been much speculation, especially among historians, about the scale of the coup pulled off by the Allied intelligence agencies. Did the Abwehr not suspect that so many of its agents were operat-ing under enemy control? Was Ritter anxious to save his own neck and so kept silent about any doubts he harboured concerning JOHNNY? Was the Abwehr in the hands of anti-Nazis who cared little for the Reich's ultimate victory? Certainly it is true that any German case officer admitting to hostile penetration would have been rewarded for his candour by a transfer from an attractive billet in a sunny neutral country to a combat role on the Eastern front. In those circumstances it might be thought that there was little incen-tive to test the integrity of individual agents or challenge their performance or motives.

On the other hand, the Allied counter-intelligence specialists found them-selves with a great advantage once they had gained access to their adversary's most secret communications, and they exploited that edge with consummate skill, always ensuring that their messages were devoid of internal contradic-tions, and arranging external corroboration where practical. A report of a concentration of armour in a particular location would be supported by dummy tanks and tell-tale tracks, all available to be photographed by a Luftwaffe aerial reconnaissance flight, and this imagery would be validated by the appropriate, conveniently intercepted wireless traffic. This was a brilliantly coordinated campaign, usually providing the evidence that the Wehrmacht's analysts were predisposed to believe. The deception schemers went to considerable lengths to ensure that the overall impression conveyed was both practical and likely, and invariably conformed with conventional military doctrine. In other words, the genius of the planners was to offer an entirely plausible solution to a logical problem. The Abwehr knew what to look for, and were not surprised when their analysts found it.

From the Allied perspective, the ability to tap into the Abwehr's private thoughts, by monitoring its Enigma channels, enabled British and American counter-intelligence experts to anticipate awkward questions and stay one step ahead of their opponents. As the original agent of this system, Arthur Owens' story exposes the first stumbling steps along the way to this highly tuned organisation.

Towards the end of SNOW's personal file an anonymous MI5 officer entered this opinion:

> As a man, SNOW's principal characteristic is vanity, combined with an inherent untruthfulness. He has a perpetual itch to inform other people of his importance and when he does so (which is usually when he is rather drunk) has no regard for truth or discretion. He is probably not completely aware on these occasions that what he is saying is a lie or a gross exaggeration and a similar doubt seems to have pervaded his motives in acting as an agent. At times in his complicated career he has, most likely, genuinely seen himself as a patriot doing dangerous and valuable work for his country; at other times, not less genuinely, as a daring spy, clever enough to outwit the British Intelligence.
>
> It has often been reported to us that SNOW drinks heavily – as much as a bottle of whisky a day or more; but curiously, when he was medically examined earlier this year, his condition was said not to be consistent with his drinking on anything like this scale. It is probably true to say that he drinks fitfully, and makes use of the habit (as of almost every other known protective) to extricate himself from difficulties or an unpleasant situation. He is certainly lazy when he can afford to be and is usually in some financial difficulty, even when he has a certain amount of money to spend.

This summary was written at a point when the double-cross system had been established and Arthur Owens was no longer needed. Arthur Owens' role in the birth of the double-cross system has often been overlooked; this is partly because he changed his name and disappeared after the war. The vacuum created by his absence was quickly filled by myths and speculations. However, despite the opinion of the anonymous MI5 officer, the one thing that is clear from an examination of Arthur Owens' career as a double agent is that people on both sides of the Security Services seem to have liked him and this was obviously one of his main assets. He was an enigma, an immoral adventurer, someone who wasn't scared to try new things and someone who wasn't overly concerned about the risks involved in being a spy until things started to go wrong. However even when it became clear that he had been behaving in an apparently duplicitous manner, facts would almost inevitably emerge that created doubt in the minds of his accusers. No matter how serious the situation was with regard to the fate of the nation, be it Britain or Germany, Arthur Owens always seemed to have been primarily concerned with whatever advantage he might accrue personally. So if we are tempted to try to answer the question 'which side was Arthur Owens really on?', the only answer that can be given, when we take all the available evidence into consideration, is that Arthur Owens appears to have been a very keen supporter of his own side.

Chronology

1899   Arthur Graham Owens born in South Wales
1919   Owens marries Jessie Ferrett
1920   Owens and Jessie move to Swansea. Robert is born
1921   The Owens family emigrates to Canada
1926   Patricia is born in Canada
1928   Arthur registers patents in Ottawa
1934   The Owens family returns to London
1936   Arthur approaches the German embassy in Brussels and corresponds with Post-box 629, Hamburg
1937   Arthur holds a meeting with SIS
1938   Arthur attends a meeting at the Admiralty, and another at Scotland Yard.
1939   Arthur travels to Ostend. Jessie denounces Arthur to Scotland Yard. Arthur is detained at Wandsworth. Lily and Arthur visit Hamburg 11–24 August. G.W. and Arthur visit Brussels and Antwerp 19-23 October. Arthur visits Antwerp in December
1940   Arthur visits Antwerp in April. North Sea rendezvous fails in May. BISCUIT travels to Lisbon in July. Arrival of SUMMER and TATE. Birth of Jean Louise Owens
1941   Arthur and CELERY visit Lisbon in March. Robert detained with Arthur
1942   Arthur interrogated in prison by John Gwyer
1943   Arthur detained at Stafford prison
1944   Arthur and Robert released from Dartmoor
1945   Arthur and Hilda White live at Great Amwell, Hertfordshire
1946   Arthur changes his surname to White. Graham is born
1947   Jorgen Borreson released from internment
1948   Arthur, Hilda and Graham move to Wexford
1957   Arthur dies in Wexford, Ireland

Appendix I

Finding SNOW

TRACING THE HISTORY of any family is difficult enough but when a master spy uses all his experience to go missing the difficulties increase greatly. Finding Arthur Owens was then made more difficult by the inaccuracies and myths that grew up around him and the secrecy that surrounded the records of his career as a double agent.

The files of MI5 refer only to agent SNOW. They tell us that he was Welsh, 'an underfed Cardiff type' and that he was 42 years old. The search for SNOW narrowed to an 'Arthur George Owens' from South Wales, possibly Cardiff. (The 'George' eventually turned out to be a clerical error dating from his internment.)

The MI5 archive revealed that Owens had a wife, a son and a daughter. The son is referred to as SNOW JUNIOR in the later files and some of his early letters mention SNOW's children Bob and Pat.

There were several Arthur George Owens born in 1899 and several born in the year before and the year after, but further research revealed that none of them fitted the rest of the information in the files. The only other Arthur Owens who looked promising was born in Graig Road, Alltwen, Cilybe-byill, near Pontardawe in Glamorgan, but his middle name was Graham not George. The Registrar of Marriages revealed that he had met and married a Jessie Irene Ferrett from Bristol in 1919 and the certificate gave Owens' occupation as a manufacturing chemist. An examination of the births in the years following showed that Jessie gave birth to a son, Graham Robert Owens, on 25 September 1921. However nothing could be discovered about him from the record of births, deaths and marriages that took this line of enquiry any further. There was no mention of a daughter called Pat and Robert's birth certificate gave the information that by now Arthur Graham Owens was running a confectionery company in Lime Kiln Road, the Mumbles,

Swansea. However the fact that this man had a son with the middle name Robert made him worthy of a little more investigation.

The next step was to look at the ships' lists from the period because it was known from the MI5 files that Arthur Owens had lived in Canada and in those days the only way to get there was by ship. The lists were examined from the time of his birth up until the early 1930s when it was known that Owens was back in Britain. From this enquiry it was discovered that on 21 October 1921 an Arthur Owens along with his wife and son had travelled to Canada. The wife's name was Jessie and their one-year-old son was called Robert. They sailed on board the *Sythia* from Liverpool bound for Halifax. Tracing people in Canada is very difficult. Unless you are a close relative then it is impossible to get hold of any certificates that might reveal the information needed to confirm the identity of an individual. This meant that it was not possible to find any birth of a Pat Owens and the only Pat Owens with a Canadian background who came to light was a famous Hollywood film actress so this was dismissed as being nothing more than a coincidence.

The only Canadian records that could be of use and that are available to the public are the patent records. The hope was that a patent for dry cell battery accumulators could be found in the name of Arthur Owens. A search was carried out and patents numbers 293862, 294047 and 303677 were discovered to be concerned with improvements to the accumulators used in dry cell batteries and the use of those batteries in torches. Each of these patents was taken out by the same man, and his name was Arthur Graham Owens.

Arthur Graham Owens seemed to fit the description. He was born in Wales in 1899, he had a wife and a son who was known as Robert despite his first name being Graham. This Arthur Graham Owens had travelled to Canada and had patented inventions for battery accumulators. It seemed likely that this was the man who went on to make contact with the German Secret Services and then act as double agent SNOW for MI5.

Further evidence in his favour came to light when a return to the ships' lists showed that in 1934 Arthur Owens, aged thirty-four, and his son Robert, now thirteen, were on board the *Pennland* heading for Southampton. Arthur Owens' profession was recorded as research engineer. However there was no mention of Jessie or a daughter called Pat on this ship. The proposed address of Arthur and Robert was Grosvenor House, Park Lane, London. From the MI5 files it was evident that on his return to the UK Arthur Owens the spy was living with his wife Jessie and son Robert, but that he also had a daughter named Pat.

A further search of the ships lists showed that on 21 February 1934 Jessie Owens, aged thirty-four, and her daughter Patricia, aged eight, were on board the Cunard liner *Berengaria* sailing for Southampton with a proposed address of 112 Stratford Road, Plaistow, London.

An examination of the ship's lists tied in with the names, ages and addresses of the redacted MI5 files. There was even one letter in the files which slipped through the process of removing agent SNOW's identity and confirmed that his real name was Arthur Owens.

During the course of this research many other people looking for Arthur Owens had come to light. Most of them were looking for Arthur George Owens but there was one who made the claim that a lot of the material about Arthur Owens was wrong and that he could correct it himself. This sort of claim is not unusual to anyone familiar with some of the wilder corners of the internet but what made this stand out was that the claimant stated that his Arthur Owens had the middle name Graham. An exchange of emails led to Graham Lee White, who confirmed that he had been told by his mother Hilda that his father, whom he knew as Arthur White, was in fact the double agent Arthur Graham Owens. The internet claimant turned out to be Paul White, the son of Graham and Norma White who now lived in County Wexford, Ireland.

Graham filled in many of the blanks in SNOW's post-war life, including how Arthur had changed his name to White; how he had taken out patents in Canada; that his first wife was called Jessie and that they had a son named Robert. Most surprising was the news that his daughter from his first marriage, Patricia Owens, was the Canadian actress who went on to have a successful Hollywood career. Graham also provided the details of Arthur's life after he moved to Ireland and revealed his letter from a wartime acquaintance that mentioned spying; the *John Bull* article which first mentioned SNOW as a German spy and the fact that Arthur Owens had died in 1957.

The main written source of information about Patricia Owens was an interview she did with a journalist called Tom Weaver, which he included in his book *Monsters, Mutants and Heavenly Creatures*. Her son Adam Nathanson supplied the details of Patricia's life and how she had struggled with her father's past. Adam knew nothing about the existence of Arthur's post-war son Graham, now living in Ireland, but he did have contact details for his aunt, Jenny Owens. Jenny Owens was the wife of Arthur's eldest son Robert. Jenny was able to uncover some of the story surrounding Arthur's mistress, the mysterious Lily, and the child they had together. Jenny found a locked black box which Robert had left after his death which contained pictures of Lily. On the back of one of these photographs was the name Lily Bade. The register of births revealed that the child of Lily Sophia Bade and Arthur Graham Owens born in 1940 was called Jean Louise. Further information about Lily Bade came from her daughter Jean Louise Pascoe (née Deadman, née Owens).

Jenny also still had the copy of Ladislas Farago's *The Game of Foxes* that Patricia had sent to Robert from America.

Appendix II

Abwehr Cover Addresses

P. Straaten-Kol & Co, Post-box 160 Amsterdam. Source of money orders paid to Snow

Mrs B. Toft, 43b Oslogaden Oslo, Norway. International post-box

Rothebaum Chausses, 14 Hamburg. Home address for Nikolaus Ritter

George Campbell, Edgar Rose Str. 5, Hamburg. Campbell was one of Ritter's aliases

L. Sanders, Post-box 629 Hamburg. Sanders had answered *Times* advertisement by army officers looking for jobs

Dr Krause, Mittelweg 117a Hamburg. Only used once – letter returned as undeliverable

Dr Richter, Mittelweg 117a Hamburg

Dr Wilhelm Wentzel, Jungfernsteig 48, Hamburg 36. In September 1938 Snow stopped writing to Dr Richter and started writing to Wentzel

Mrs Wentzel, 51 Kloster Allee, Hamburg

Mrs A. Nohl, Wandsbeker Chausee, 30.11 Hamburg

Walter Auerbach Wandbek, Kampstrasse 45, Hamburg

Frau Heise, Sallstrasse 27, Hanover

Eddy Lagrange, 185 Saraphate Street, Amsterdam. Emergency address, never used.

Mrs L. de Ridder, Avenue Helene 22, Antwerp. Address given to G.W. from which he would receive stamps

Louis de Mercader, 57 rue Bosquet, Osborne Residence, Brussels. Supplied to G.W.

Appendix III

SNOW's Wireless Cipher

BASED ON THE word CONGRATULATIONS, each letter was assigned a number which, in this case was, 3,9,7,4,11,1,13,15,6,2,14,5,10,8,12. The numbers were determined by where the letters come in the alphabet.

A grid was then drawn, comprising of fifteen squares wide (the fifteen letters of CONGRATULATIONS) and twelve squares deep. Blank spaces were then placed in the grid. The first was placed arbitrarily, in this case on the fifth square of the top row. The next blank was placed six squares later, then the next seven squares later and so on. The grid was then turned upside down and the same procedure followed. The message was then written in the grid but not on the blanks which would later be filled in with random letters. The letters of the message were written downwards starting in the row that coincides with the date of the month. If the date was higher than the fifteen columns then fifteen was subtracted from the date and that column was used. The resulting string of letters was then broken up into blocks of five letters and transmitted. As this was intended to be a daily code the date and time of each message was also transmitted. Again this was done by assigning numbers to the word CONGRATULATIONS but this time recurring numbers were not used. This time C was 1 O was 2, etcetera, with I and S both being given the number 0. Therefore a time of 21.21 would be sent as OCOC. The date was sent in the same way, which was then followed by the number of letters in the message.

A Note on the Sources

THE MAIN SOURCES used in this work are the records of the British Security Service (MI5) held by the National Archives at Kew in London. The KV2 series are personal files (PF series) and cover a period from 1913 to 1979. The documents that cover the SNOW case are the first in a subseries within KV2 titled Double Agent Operations, they are KV2/444–453. There are also documents that cover Gwilym Williams, KV2/468; CHARLIE KV2/454; and Celery KV2/674. There are also files on SUMMER KV2/60 and TATE KV2/61 and 62.

In a subseries of KV2 entitled German Intelligence Officers are files on Nikolaus Ritter KV2/85-88 and Erwin Lahousen KV2/173.

The source of much of the information about Arthur Owens' later life comes from interviews carried out in Ireland with his son Graham White, his wife Norma and their son Paul. Graham also has a recorded interview with his mother Hilda who married Arthur shortly after his release from internment. Graham also provided many photographs of his father in later life and a copy of the original *John Bull* magazine about JOHNNY, written by Charles Wighton and Gunter Peis and published on 26 October 1957. This article later became the basis of their book *Hitler's Spies and Saboteurs* which was published in January 1958. These are the first works to mention JOHNNY and they are based on the diaries of Erwin Lahousen who was of course the victim of false information provided to the Germans by JOHNNY under the guidance of MI5.

A valuable source of the German point of view is Nikolaus Ritter's *Deckname Dr. Rantzau: Die Aufzeichnungen des Nikolaus Ritter, Offizier im Geheimen Nachrichtendienst* published in 1972. Ritter's autobiography offers a picture of his understanding of the Abwehr's relationship with the German agent they codenamed JOHNNY.

J. C. Masterman's *The Double Cross System of the war of 1939–1945* gives an overview of the whole system and how it developed during the period that Arthur Owens was active. This was the first work to reveal the activities of the double-cross system and the extent to which MI5 had outwitted the Abwehr and was in fact running the system of German agents in Great Britain.

Both volumes of *The Guy Liddell Diaries* are an invaluable source of the day-to-day events and thoughts of someone at the heart of the double-cross system. Being diaries dictated each evening, they were not subject to revision in the same way that a resumé of the MI5 files might be, and as such reveal the ad hoc way that the double-cross system developed in the early years of the war.

Ladislas Farago's *The Game of Foxes* gives a colourful version of the events surrounding the double-cross system and paints a gaudy picture of agent SNOW. His book is responsible for many of the myths surrounding Arthur Owens. Farago seems to have picked up on some of the details from German sources and filled them out in his own flamboyant style. For all this, his work is one of the first attempts to make sense of the double-cross system and it must be remembered that it was written before any files were released into the public domain by the British government.

Further information about Owens' later life came from his eldest son Robert's wife Jenny Owens. It was she who provided access to Robert's copy of Farago's book with the notes that he had made in the margins. Jenny Owens also made available a copy of Robert's letter to Edward Heath and the photographs of Lily Bade and her baby.

For a Hollywood film star, information about Patricia Owens is very hard to come by so it was necessary to turn to several sources. The most direct source is her son Adam Nathanson who also provided family photographs of her. His story of how she coped with the family secret is both remarkable and touching. Tom Weaver's interview with Patricia Owens which appears in his book *Monsters, Mutants and Heavenly Creatures* is the only account of her life in Patricia's own words of any substantial length. Diane Kachmar and David Goudsward's *The Fly at Fifty* is the closest thing to a biography of Patricia, and Diane also provided access to contemporary newspaper reports about Patricia during her time as a Hollywood film actress.

Further information about Lily Bade came from her daughter Jean Louise Pascoe (née Deadman, née Owens).

Information about Gwilym Williams came from the Personnel Files of the Swansea Constabulary D/D Con/S9/5107 which are held at the West Gal- morgan Archive and from his great-nephew Ceri Price who has researched the family history.

Bibliography

Andrew, Christopher, *Secret Service*, (London: Heinemann, 1985)

Andrew, Christopher *The Defence of the Realm*, (London: Penguin, 2009)

Batey, Mavis, *Dilly: The Man Who Broke Enigma*, (London: Dialogue, 2010)

Bower, Tom, *The Perfect English Spy*, (London: Heinemann, 1995)

Chapman, Eddie, *The Real Eddie Chapman Story*, (London: Library 33, 1956)

Crowdy, Terry, *Deceiving Hitler*, (Oxford: Osprey, 2008)

Curry, Jack, *The Security Service 1909-1945: The Official History*, (London: PRO, 1999)

Farago, Ladislas, *Game of the Foxes*, (New York: McKay & Co., 1972)

Garby-Czerniawski, Roman, *The Big Network*, (George Ronald, 1961)

Haufler, Hervie, *The Spies Who Never Were*, (New American Library, 2006)

Hesketh, Roger, *Fortitude: The D-Day Deception Campaign*, (London: St Ermin's Press, 1999)

Hinsley, Sir Harry, *British Intelligence in the Second World War: Security and Counter-Intelligence*, (London: HMSO, 1990)

Holt, Thadeus, *The Deceivers*, (London: Simon & Schuster, 2004)

Kachmar, Diane and David Goudsward, *The Fly at Fifty*, (BearManor Media, 2009)

Kahn, David, *Hitler's Spies*, (New York: Macmillan, 1968)

Kross, Peter, *The Encyclopedia of World War II Spies*, (Fort Lee, NJ: Barricade Books, 2001)

Liddell, Guy, *The Guy Liddell Diaries*, (London: Routledge, 2005)

Macintyre, Ben, *Agent Zigzag*, (London: Bloomsbury, 2010)

Masterman, J. C., *The Double Cross System of the War of 1939-45*, (Boston, Mass: Yale University Press, 1972)

Miller, Russell, *Codename TRICYCLE*, (London: Pimlico, 2005)

Moe, John, *John Moe, Double Agent*, (London: Mainstream, 1986)

Mosley, Leonard, *The Druid: the Nazi Spy who Double-Crossed the Double-Cross System*, (New York: Atheneum, 1981)

Owen, Frank, *The Eddie Chapman Story*, (New York: Julian Messner, 1954)

Peis, Gunter, *The Mirror of Deception*, (London: Weidenfeld & Nicolson, 1976)

Pincher, Chapman, *Traitors*, (London: Sidgwick & Jackson, 1987)

Polmar, Norman and Thomas Allen, *Spy Book*, (New York: Random House, 2004)

Popov, Dusko, *Spy Counter Spy*, (London: Weidenfeld & Nicolson, 1974)

Pujol, Juan with Nigel West, *Garbo*, (London: Weidenfeld and Nicolson, 1985)

Ritter, Nikolaus, *Deckname Dr. Rantzau*, (Hoffmann and Campe, 1972)

Sergueiev, Lily, *Secret Service Rendered*, (London: William Kimber, 1968)

Simkins, Anthony, *British Intelligence in the Second World War*, (London: HMSO, 1990)

Stephens, Robin, *Camp 020: MI5 and the Nazi Spies*, (London: PRO, 2000)

Waller, John H. *The Unseen War in Europe*, (London: I. B. Tauris, 1996)

Weaver, Tom, *Monsters, Mutants and Heavenly Creatures*, (Midnight Marquee Press, 1996)

West, Nigel, *MI5: British Security Service Operations 1909-45*, (London: Bodley Head, 1981)

West, Nigel, *Counterfeit Spies*, (London: St Ermin's Press, 1998)

West, Nigel, *Seven Spies Who Changed The World*, (London: Secker & Warburg, 1991)

Wighton, Charles and Gunter Peis, *Hitler's Spies and Saboteurs*, (New York: Henry Holt & Co., 1958)

Index

Espionage Classics

The Bletchley Park Codebreakers
Edited by Michael Smith
and Ralph Erskine
502pp paperback £9.99
9781849540780

The Kremlin's Geordie Spy
The man they swapped
for Gary Powers
Vin Arthey
352pp paperback £9.99
9781906447144

The Emperor's Codes
Bletchley Park's role in
breaking Japan's secret cyphers
Michael Smith
352pp paperback £9.99
9781906447120

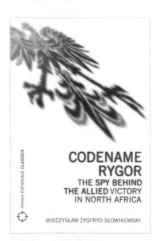

Codename Rygor
The spy behind the Allied
victory in North Africa
Mieczyslaw Slowikowski
352pp paperback £9.99
9781906447083

www.bitebackpublishing.com